The Sacrament
of the Future

The Sacrament of the Future

An Evaluation of Karl Rahner's Concept of the Sacraments and the End of Time

George Vass, SJ

GRACEWING

First published in 2005

Gracewing
2 Southern Avenue
Leominster
Herefordshire HR6 0QF

All rights reserved. No part of this publication may be reproduced, stored in a retrieval system, or transmitted in any form, or by any means, electronic, mechanical, photocopying, recording or otherwise, without the written permission of the publisher.

© George Vass 2005

The right of George Vass to be identified as the author of this work has been asserted in accordance with the Copyright, Designs and Patents Act, 1988.

ISBN 0 85244 619 5

Typesetting by
Action Publishing Technology Ltd, Gloucester, GL1 5SR

Contents

Introduction	vii
Acknowledgements	x
Abbreviations	xi
Chapter 1: The Sacramental Life of the Church	1
1.1 Church: the Basic Sacrament	1
1.2 What is a Sacrament?	6
1.2.1 Rahner's own Approach	7
(A) *A Copernican Revolution?*	7
(B) *The Church and her 'Self-Realization'*	13
(C) *Word and Sacrament*	15
1.2.2 Permanent Features	25
(A) *'Ex opere operato'*	26
(B) *'Ex genere signi'*	29
(C) *'A Christo Jesu instituta'*	34
1.3 The Sevenfold Gift	41
(A) *The Lord's Supper*	43
(B) *The Sacrament of Ordination*	53
(C) *Initiation in the Spirit: Baptism and Confirmation*	62
(D) *You are Forgiven: the Sacrament of Penance*	69
(Including the sacrament of the sick and indulgences)	79
(E) *Marriage: the Mystery of Human Love*	85

vi *The Sacrament of the Future*

Chapter 2: Comments and Questions:
The Ecclesiology of the Sacraments   93
    2.1 The Sacraments and the Doctrine of the Church   94
        (A) *The Church as the Primordial Sacrament*   94
        (B) *The Sacraments and the Self-Realization of the Church*   97
        (C) *The 'Deification' of the Church through her Sacraments?*   99
    2.2 The 'Sacramentalization' of the World and the Sacraments   101
        (A) *From 'Sacralization' to the Sacraments*   102
        (B) *'Sacramentalism' and Sacramental Existence*   106
        (C) *The Sacraments and the 'Self' of the Church*   108
    2.3 The Church is a Sacramental Event   113
        (A) *The 'Ontology' of the Symbol*   114
        (B) *Symbols and 'Performatives'*   119
        (C) *Sacramental Grace: Promise and/or Reality?*   121

Chapter 3: The Eternal Future   127
    3.1 Eschatology and 'Eschatological'   128
    3.2 Time and Eternity   136
    3.3 The Absolute Future   154
    3.4 The Last Things   177
        (A) *Individual and Collective Eschatology*   177
        (B) *The 'Definitive Validity' of the Individual*   183
        (C) *Church and Parousia: a Collective Eschatology*   204

Epilogue: Sacramental and Eternal Presence   235
End Notes   244

Introduction

The current state of the Roman Catholic Church seems to require some revision of sacramental theology. Both the practice of the faithful and the theology of the sacraments raise questions that need a contemporary answer.

There are two trends discernible in the way in which sacraments engage the attention of theologians and the devotion of the faithful. One is a rigid adherence to traditional teaching and practice, both of which are perceived as central to a spiritual life. Another is to relegate sacraments to secondary manifestations of our Christian faith in God's salvific will. The first trend regards sacraments as the unique and exclusive means of salvation; the second holds that they are no more than possible, though authentic, expressions of an interior, personal devotion. Hence there is a clear difference with regard to the necessity of sacraments: absolute for some, conditional only for others. Both trends indeed can become heretical if they are over-exaggerated; one leads to an exclusive ghetto 'Church' outside of which there is no salvation, the other to a 'Church' incapable of forming true ecclesial community.

The clearest example of this difference of emphasis is the recent debate about intercommunion. The more absolute position holds that intercommunion between Catholics and other Christian denominations is inadmissible under any circumstances until complete doctrinal unity is achieved.[1] Another position makes room for intercommunion on the grounds that, doctrinal differences notwithstanding, such intercommunion fosters a common understanding of the Eucharist. The practice of penance and the necessity of infant baptism could indicate a similar split. Such differences of Christian understanding can be disastrous for religious practice, and demand some resolution.

A lifelong study of Karl Rahner's theology has inspired the present volume. In sacramental theology, which is basic to the theology of the Church, he addresses these difficulties and attempts their resolution. This is why I had intended the discussion of his account of the sacramental system in general and the seven of the Roman tradition. Technical difficulties, however, prevented this volume being published as the conclusion of a five-volume work containing the presentation and analysis of his entire theological thought. It will sometimes be necessary, therefore, to refer to my *Understanding Karl Rahner*[2] and I shall follow the method which I used in those volumes: a systematic presentation of his views gleaned from many and diverse contributions to the subject; followed by either a separate chapter or an ad hoc comment in reflection on his teaching. This exercise will lead to a critical assessment of Rahner's eschatology through which I shall suggest that the fuller understanding of the sacramental life of the Church may best be expressed. It is also my belief that the divergent contemporary trends mentioned above may well find their systematic resolution in the concept of eschatology.

Although my presentation of Rahner's thought is doctrinal in content, the title of this volume also signals some detailed discussion of his approach to Christian life. The consideration of the sacraments shows how they are and can be integrated into a genuine Christian spirituality. As Rahner wrote in one of his early works on the Church and sacraments: 'It is possible to present a theology of Christian life in terms of the "actual frequentation" of the sacraments'.

Rahner's thought is admittedly tortuous, a necessary consequence of his careful originality; it tries to bridge the gap between an antiquated scholastic and contemporary language. Many of the quotations[3] from his works have been paraphrased from current English translations in search of clarity. Nevertheless it became necessary for me to frequently quote his own words, even if his background imposes the use of technical terminology. You will find philosophical terms: scholastic ones such as *forma* and *materia* and the different kinds of causality, and more recent ones: *a-priori* and *a-posteriori, categorial* and *transcendental, supernatural, existential, fundamental option*, and so on; theological concepts like *mystagogy, eschatology, opus operatum* or *operantis, res et sacramentum,* and so on. The meaning of these will be clarified in their own context. Furthermore, you will be asked to follow my own reflections on Rahner's thought and weigh them up according to their merits. In doing this we shall pursue the same purpose: the deeper penetration into the mystery of God. The resultant understanding of faith may be slight as compared with what we shall know at the end of time. For now it is all we have in anticipation of the vision of God.

Acknowledgements

Before introducing the reader to the subject of this book I express my sincere gratitude to my friend Fr W. Hewett SJ, who encouraged me to revise my manuscript – which was intended to be the closing volume of presentation and critical analysis of Karl Rahner's whole systematic theology – and submit it to Gracewing for publication. My thanks are also due to Jo Whale, their long-suffering Publishing Manager.

Living away from an English-speaking environment my use of its idiom was obviously impaired and I had to rely massively on the generous help of Fr Peter Hackett SJ, who not only corrected the mistakes and some of the oddities of my text, but also proved to be a most inspiring partner in developing my own contributions on the difficult topics of the sacraments and eschatology. Even if his own theological viewpoints were not always the same as my own, I am sure that his original style influenced my writing. For Fr Hackett's collaboration I shall forever be indebted.

Last but not least I should mention with thankfulness the late Alison Wilson BD, a student of mine at Heythrop College, without whom I could not have published five previous volumes of my Rahner studies which lead up to the present book. Her sudden death this summer leaves a gap in the life of those who admired not only her scholarship, but also her genuinely saintly life. May she rest in peace.

Abbreviations

Rahner's articles and other publications frequently quoted or referred to in the text take the form of single key words: for example: 'Questions', '*Kirche61*', and so on. The following is a list of these key words for the complete volume. In the endnotes I give the number of the first page of an article in both the English translation and the German original, and further numbers (in brackets) refer to the corresponding German text; for example: *Kirche61*p. 39(=36). Articles referred to several times without a key word are listed in alphabetical sequence.

For references to other works by Rahner himself or works in collaboration with other authors, I have adopted standard acronymic abbreviations: for example DS, SM, ZKT, where usually no corresponding German (or English) translation is indicated. References to literature consulted are quoted in full in the endnotes.

Rahner's Theological Investigations, one of my main sources is referred to as TI 1 (volume: Arabic), and the corresponding German *Schriften zur Theologie* ST (volume: Roman numerals). Other less frequently used articles of Rahner and other authors are quoted in full in the endnotes.

Active Role	'Consideration of the Active Role of the Person in the Sacramental Event', TI 14, pp. 161ff = ST X, pp. 405ff.
Assumption	'The Interpretation of the Dogma of Assumption', TI 1, pp. 215ff = ST I, pp. 239ff.
Baptism	'Baptism and the Renewal of Baptism', TI 23, pp.195ff = ST XVI, pp. 406ff.

Celebration	*Die vielen Messen und das eine Opfer*, Freiburg in Breisgau, 1960; partial translation: 'Multiplication of Masses', in *'Orate Fratres'* 24(1950) pp. 553ff; in the series *Quaestiones Disputatae*, 'The Celebration of the Eucharist', London, 1968.
Consummation	'Immanent and Transcendent Consummation of the World', TI 10, pp. 273ff = ST VIII, pp. 593ff.
DS	H. Denzinger, *Enchiridion Symbolorum* (ed.) A Schönmetzer/ K. Rahner, Freiburg in Breisgau, 1962^{32}.
Dying	'Christian Dying', TI 18, pp. 226ff = ST XIII, pp. 269ff.
Eternity	'Eternity from Time', TI 19, pp. 169ff = ST XIV, pp. 422ff.
	'Faith and Sacrament', TI 23, pp. 181ff = ST XVI, pp 384ff.
Foundations	*Foundations of Christian Faith: an Introduction to the Idea of Christianity*, London, 1978.
Future	'The Quest of the Future', TI 12, pp. 181ff = ST IX, pp. 519ff.
Handbook	*Handbuch der Pastoraltheologie*, vols I–II: *Praktische Theologie der Kirche in ihrer Gegenwart*, Freiburg in Breisgau, 1964.
Hermeneutics	'Hermeneutics of Eschatological Assertions', TI 4, pp. 323ff=ST IV, pp. 401ff.
Hope	'On the Theology of Hope', TI 10, pp. 242ff = ST VIII, pp. 561ff.
Ideas	'Ideas for the Theology of Death', TI 13, pp. 169ff = ST X, pp. 181ff.
Indulgence	'A Brief Theological Study on Indulgence', TI 10, pp.150ff = ST VIII, 472ff.
Jüngel/Rahner	E. Jüngel and K. Rahner, *Was ist ein Sakrament? Vorstösse zur Verständigung*, Freiburg in Breisgau, 1971.
Kirche55	'Kirche 55: Kirche und Sakramente', in *Geist und Leben* 28(1955), 434ff.
Kirche61	*The Church and Sacraments*, W. J. O'Hara

	(London, 1963): a translation of *Kirche und Sakrament*, Freiburg in Breisgau, 1961, which was published in six further editions.
LTK	*Lexikon für Theologie und Kirche*, 10 volumes (eds) J. Hofer and K. Rahner, Freiburg in Breisgau, 1957^2–1968.
Marriage	'Marriage as a Sacrament', TI 10, pp. 199ff = STI, pp. 519ff.
'Methodology'	'Reflections on Methodology in Theology', TI 11, pp. 68ff = ST IX, pp. 79ff.
'Mystery'	'The Concept of the Mystery in Catholic Theology', TI 4, pp. 36ff = ST IV, pp. 51ff.
MS	*Mysterium Salutis*, 5 volumes (eds) J. Feiner and M. Löhrer *et al.*, Einsiedeln, 1974–76.
New Image	'The New Image of the Church', TI 10, pp. 3ff = ST VIII, pp. 329ff.
Presence	'The Presence of Christ in the Sacrament of the Lord's Supper', TI 4, 287ff. = ST IV, pp. 35ff.
Priesthood	'The Point of Departure in Theology for Determining the Nature of the Priestly Office', TI 12, pp. 311ff = ST IX, pp. 366ff.
Purgatory	'Purgatory', TI 19, pp. 181ff = ST XIV, pp. 435ff.
Questions	'Questions on the Theology of the Sacraments', TI 23, pp. 189ff = ST XVI, 191ff.
Reconciliation	'Penance as an Additional Act of Reconciliation with the Church', TI 10, pp.125ff = ST VIII, pp. 447ff.
Revolution	'A Copernican Revolution', (A secular view of the sacraments) two articles published in *The Tablet*, 6 March 1971, pp. 236ff; 13 March 1971, pp. 267ff.
Risen body	'The Resurrection of the Body', TI 2, pp. 203ff = ST II, pp. 211ff.
Sevenfold	*Die siebenfältige* (sevenfold) *Gabe*, Munich, 1974; the English edition, 'Meditation on the Sacraments', New York, 1977.

Summa	Thomas von Aquin, *Summa Theologiae*, (I–III + Supplementum; Q: Quaestio 1f; a: articulus 1f;)
Tanner	*Decrees of the Ecumenical Councils*, vols. I–II, (ed.) N. P. Tanner, London and Georgetown, Washington DC (1990).
Time	'Theological Observations on the Concept of Time', TI 11, pp. 288ff = ST IX, pp. 302ff.
Truth	'Forgotten Truths concerning the Sacrament of Penance', TI 2, pp.135ff = ST II, pp. 143ff.
Utopia	'Marxist Utopia and the Christian Future of Man', TI 6, pp. 59ff = ST VI, pp. 77ff.
Vass	*Understanding Karl Rahner*, vols 1–5, Sheed and Ward, London, 1985–2001; vol. 1: *A Theologian in Search of a Philosophy*; vol. 2: *The Mystery of Man and the Foundations of a Theological System*; vol. 3: *A Pattern of Doctrines (1) God and Christ*; vol. 4: *A Pattern of Doctrines (2) The Atonement and Mankind's Salvation*; vol. 5: *A Pattern of Doctrines (3) A Man of the Church*.
Word	'The Word and the Eucharist', TI 4, pp. 253ff = ST IV, pp. 313ff.
Worship	'On the Theology of Worship', TI 19, pp. 19ff = ST X, pp. 405ff.
ZKT	*Zeitschrift für katholische Theologie*, published by the Theological Faculty of the University of Innsbruck.

Articles frequently quoted

'An Investigation on the Incomprehensibility of God in St Thomas Aquinas', TI 16, /244ff./ = ST XII, pp. 306ff.

'Following the Crucified', TI 18, pp. 157ff = ST XIII, pp. 188ff.

'Foundation of Belief', TI 16, pp.17ff = ST XII, pp. 17ff.

'Fragmentary Aspects of a Theological Evaluation of the Concept of Future', TI 10, pp. 235ff = ST VIII, pp. 555ff.

'Guilt – Responsibility – Punishment within the View of Catholic Theology', TI 6, pp. 197ff = ST VI, pp. 238ff.

'Guilt and its Remission: the Borderland between Theology and Psychiatry', TI 2, pp. 265ff = ST II, pp. 279ff.
'Ideology and Christianity', TI 6, pp. 43ff = ST VI, pp. 59ff.
'Jesus' Resurrection', TI 17, pp. 16ff = ST XII, pp. 344ff.
'Justified and Sinner at the Same Time', TI 6, pp. 218ff = ST VI, pp. 262ff
'On the Spirituality of the Easter Faith', TI 17, pp. 8ff = ST XII, pp. 335ff.
'Personal and Sacramental Piety', TI 2, pp. 109ff = ST II, pp. 115ff.
'Remarks on the Importance of the History of Jesus for Catholic Dogmatic', TI 13, pp. 201ff = ST X, pp. 215ff.
'Sin as Loss of Grace in Early Church Literature', TI 15, pp. 24ff = ST XI, pp. 48ff.
'The "Intermediary" State', TI 17, pp. 114ff = ST XII, pp. 455ff.
'The Inexhaustible Transcendence of God and the Concern for the Future', TI 20, pp. 173ff = ST, pp. 405ff.
'The Life of the Dead', TI 4, pp. 347ff = ST IV, pp. 429ff.
'The position of Christology between Exegesis and Dogmatic', TI 11, pp. 185ff = ST IX, pp. 197ff.
'The Renewal of Priestly Ordination', TI 3, pp.171ff = ST III, pp. 203ff.
'Theological Problems Entailed in the Idea of the "New Earth"', TI 10, pp. 260ff = ST VIII, pp. 580ff.
'Unity – Love – Mystery', TI 8, pp. 244ff = ST VII, pp. 504ff.

Chapter 1

The Sacramental Life of the Church

Karl Rahner's sacramental theology is implicit in his ecclesiology. From the very beginning, almost, of his theological activity he accepted and frequently used his confrère, O. Semmelroth's thesis expounding the Church as a sacrament.[1] When Vatican II adopted this same approach, it became part of the common language of the Church;[2] we can better understand the Church through the idea of sacrament, and, indeed we can come to a better understanding of the sacraments through the idea of the Church. This close alliance must be the starting point of our investigation.

1.1 Church: the Basic Sacrament

Two main themes characterize Rahner's writing about the Church as sacrament. In *Kirche61*, he explains the way in which Church and sacraments are related. That there is a relationship is common doctrine: it has always been held that sacraments are a means of divine grace and that the administration of them has been entrusted to the Church by Jesus Christ. This dispensing-function, however, tells us nothing about the Church herself. The Church and the sacrament(s) remain parallel theological concepts. Rahner wants to put them into a true correlation through which neither can be understood except in terms of the other: the very structure of the Church is sacramental; each single sacrament is an encounter with the Church.

In *Kirche55* this 'correlation' is characterized as *Christological;* the doctrine of the Incarnation directs

Rahner's thought. This early work, written before Vatican II, substitutes the term 'people of God' for the generic term 'Church': 'through the coming of the Logos in the flesh one single mankind, the people of God, has been consecrated in its humanity'.[3] This 'people of God' is not merely a religious institution, but has a particular status in the history of salvation: the Church is Christ's permanent presence (*Bleiben*) charged with the task of fulfilling the Master's mission throughout history. This train of thought further develops into the idea of the Church as Christ's continued eschatological presence within redeemed mankind, an expression of God's triumphant and irrevocable will to save everyone through grace.[4] The historical and social reality which is the Church, therefore, is the manifest sign and symbol of redeeming grace, now definitive for and available to all. The conclusion is self-evident: the Church is herself the basic or proto-sacrament of our salvation both in the present and eschatological order.

Rahner's reasoning of course presupposes his understanding of the nature of incarnation and redemption. These I discussed in detail in volumes 2 and 3 of my work on Rahner's theology,[5] and showed that his adopted stance lay somewhere between a western notion more often presented in terms of satisfaction wrought by the Cross, and that of the Greek Fathers who had favoured a so-called 'physical' theory of redemption: the incarnation of the Son of God itself permanently changes the nature of sinful humankind. Rahner is indeed nearer to the Greek understanding. The germ of his theory, though not fully developed, is certainly present in *Kirche55*.

For Rahner the incarnation means that God has offered mercy (*Erbarmen*) to the whole of mankind: in his concern for mankind he decides that its destiny, which was still in the balance before Christ's coming, is now definitively one in Christ. Jesus the Christ is the ultimate Word of grace mysteriously woven into the very structure of this world. The incarnate Christ is both the irreversible appearance of God's Word and the embodiment of the proper response to it on our behalf, that is, the ground of grace is offered to every human person. The Incarnate Word is therefore the sign of the offer of grace, a sign which is not just a possibility, but an opportunity, a real likelihood, a real probability available for all. Rahner has still to be fully explicit, but he will affirm that the Church is the continuation of this sign: the Christ is *Ur-sakrament,* and the Church is *Grundsakrament.* In summary: 'the Church is "the ... presence of Christ's grace throughout the known history of one single mankind."'[6]

The early article *Kirche55,* however, was Rahner's summary attempt to work out the nature of each single sacrament; the notion of Church as a sacrament was just a quasi-unifying premise. It was written in fact for the spirituality periodical *Geist und Leben,* as a prop to ecclesial and sacramental piety, but it confirmed the author in a position that he never abandoned.

When he returned to it he did so in a slightly different context and with a slightly different emphasis. His introduction to *Kirche61* in the series *Quaestiones Disputatae,*[7] employs the idea of Church as a sacrament and though it often quotes *Kirche55* verbatim, the altered background to his theological thought is evident. His more developed treatment of the concept, people of God, is now in contrast with the organized Church; he explicitly talks of mankind's supernatural destiny for which the incarnate Christ is both the effective salvific symbol, and the continual offer of redemptive grace. Rahner's *Kirche61* presupposes an insight into his idea of the 'supernatural existential' and of man's divinisation through grace.[8]

How ought we to understand Rahner's concept of *offer?* Since an offer presupposes the freedom to accept or reject, the overwhelming offer of grace needs to be reconciled with human freedom. Rahner explains that the drama that is redemption does not face our freedom with an equal choice; rather 'God himself has taken part, acted and furnished the dénouement he himself desires: salvation and eternal life'.[9] Rahner shares the view of Thomas Aquinas:

> God by his *efficacious grace* 'can' decide the *free* consent of man to his salvation, not by abolishing free consent but by constituting it.[10]

Problematic as this statement is, it is taken over by Rahner who expands it by means of the biblical insight that God's promise of this grace through the merit of Christ's Cross affects the whole of history, and more particularly its supernatural consummation:

> grace, viewed in relationship to the totality of the history of the world and mankind, is a grace which brings about the acceptance of what it offers, for, of course, all is grace, the possibility and its realisation, the capacity and the acceptance itself, God's word and man's response.[11]

This grace gained through Christ is also an eschatological promise to each individual as a member of the people of God. It has become an irreversible promise in as much as Jesus the Christ is the *Urwort* (the definitive ground) of our history. Since the Church is the continuance of this *Urwort*, 'the original sacramental word of definitive grace', she enjoys her own sacramental structure, one which in consequence affects each individual. The sign she utters takes effect in the individual who accepts the Church's sacramental word. The single sacraments are grounded on (though not deduced from) the premise of Church as sacrament – a matter for further consideration.

A further development in the concept of the Church as sacrament appears in 1966.[12] It builds on the ideas present in the publications of 1955 and 1961, but with an additional emphasis: the sacramentality of the Church is now discussed in view of the necessity of the Church and her sacraments for human salvation. Doubtless, the decree *Gaudium et Spes* (on the Church in the World), has influenced Rahner. For by this time Rahner is coming to the idea of 'an anonymous Christianity', a concept which may seem to militate against the absolute necessity of the Church and her sacraments.

The idea of salvation presents us with a dialectical tension between the old adage of *extra ecclesiam nulla salus* (there is no salvation outside the Church) and its universal availability. Rahner resolves this tension by supposing that the possibility of salvation, the grace of redemption, is not restricted within the confines of the visible Church. Men and women can be justified outside of this social unit. If, however, the Church is the comprehensible social phenomenon and the sign of this grace, she is the sacrament of salvation, not only for those social units in which the word of God is preached and the sacraments (baptism and Eucharist) administered, but also for the whole world. The conclusion is that wherever this grace does take effect it is

> already visibly signified as an element in the saving history realized in this world by virtue of the fact that the Church has the power to be the basic sacrament[13]

Rahner's reasoning could be summed up: the justification by grace of someone outside the Church should not be regarded as an exceptional event, since the Church *is* the sacrament of salvation not just for her own members, but *for the whole world*. There is of course this pre-supposition: that justifying grace has the same sacramental structure as the Church; it is a symbolic event, as is the incarnation.[14] We have then, according to the mind of Rahner, an experience (*Erlebnis*) of the Church as sacrament, which is 'even there where she is not'; evangelizing, as it were, an unevangelized world. The Church is not experienced as one of several competing *Weltanschauungen*, nor yet as an aggregate of clever theological statements, but as the spearhead (or *vanguard* as Rahner puts it) for the evangelization of those who, without knowing it, share the one grace of justification. As *the* sacramental sign she leads us beyond tangible, visible, and sociologically definable confines into the existence of an anonymous Christianity. Those who are within, 'at home', are aware, but for the outsider

> Christianity has not yet come to its full maturity as an objective entity and therefore has not yet realized its own nature in the explicit awareness and reflective objectivity ... of the visible Church herself as providing an organized structure definable in sociological terms.[15]

With this quotation we return to the idea of the anonymous Christian which has now become a slogan in contemporary theology.[16] We can recapture indeed the excitement of the author in launching this new concept. His first essay on the subject appeared in 1962/3 and there had been no need then to define what explicit Christianity added to its anonymous counterpart. 'New Image' confines the difference to the believer becoming aware of the truth hidden from the non-believer. Rahner indeed becomes quite poetical as he speaks about awareness of engracement that comes through faith:

> he can now regard himself and professed Christians, the Church, as the vanguard of those who are journeying along the passage of history towards salvation ... and eternity. For him the Church is, in a certain sense, the uniformed section of the army of God.[17]

In summary: Rahner wanted the theology of the Church in the world to provide a common denominator to each single sacrament. This common denominator was the Church as the primordial sacrament to which the seven sacraments of the Church are related.

1.2. What is a Sacrament?

It is correct to suppose that Rahner had worked out the final details of his approach to the sacraments by the middle of the 1970s. Although he may have changed his method of access to the definition of the sacraments, his basic ideas about sacramental theology remained on the whole consistent. In 1974, Rahner published a series of meditations on the sacraments, to which I shall refer as *Sevenfold*.[18] In it he combined a general introduction with an attempt to describe each sacrament. His purpose at that time was not to determine a definition apt for modern circumstances, but rather to give an existential description of what it means to *receive* each of the seven. Although Rahner's own ideas provide the background, he does not, however, abandon the permanent elements so well known to most Catholics. His 'meditative' description nevertheless conceals the tension that exists between the traditional and more recent ways of thought.

The traditional approach is concerned with men and women living as Christians in a profane world. They search for a proper relationship with God who imparts the mysterious quality we call grace. God gives it freely, but in certain circumstances upon the condition that the recipient is willing to perform certain rites as proposed and defined by the Church. 'The events in which this grace is imparted are the sacraments, the sacred signs performed by the Church';[19] so runs the traditional view.

There are, however, three aspects of traditional view which Rahner's own approach will improve. According to this view, God repeatedly imparts sacramental grace but not always and everywhere.[20] Furthermore, this sacramental grace is imparted exclusively by means of the ritual sign. Lastly, this sacramental grace is beyond experience: it is known only through belief in the teaching of the Church or by 'indoctrination'.

Rahner will address each of these in turn. He considers that there is another way of understanding grace and the sacramental event through which it is received. His purpose is to show how his own approach throws new light upon the nature of the sacraments and how this new light enables an explanation of the sacraments more suited to contemporary experience. *Sevenfold* undertook this task meditatively; there are also other, more theological, writings by means of which he argues his own individual access to the theology of the sacraments.

1.2.1. Rahner's own Approach

To start with Rahner's own ideas; he will emphasize three main points:

- Sacramental practice is not imposed, as it were, as tradition seems to suggest, but arises naturally from our secular experience of life.
- Sacramental grace is not a direct intervention of God, but the self-realization of the Church.
- Awareness of the sacramental event is a function of the Word of God in as much as it is communicated through the symbolic action of the Church.

(A) *A Copernican Revolution?*

Rahner visited Great Britain early in 1971. *The Tablet* published one of his lectures under the main title *A*

8 *The Sacrament of the Future*

Copernican Revolution[21] in two parts. The beginning of the first part, 'Secular Life and the Sacraments', gives Rahner's own version of this 'revolution': speaking of the sacraments we are accustomed to think of

> an intellectual and spiritual movement from the sacramental event towards its effect 'in the world'; instead what we have now is a spiritual movement of the world towards the sacrament.

Most of *Revolution* had been published the year before in *Geist und Leben*,[22] and that too was in part republished in *Sevenfold*. A further summing-up appeared in 1979 containing the qualification that his earlier expressions, 'revolution' or 'turning point' was over-exaggerated:[23] it is, rather a *transitus* from one conceptual model to another. Whether it were by 'revolution' or 'transitus', Rahner has certainly changed the traditional approach.

Rahner's main criticism is that the old model does not correspond to our contemporary mind, and may well appear as an 'empty ritualism'. It seems to be an escape 'from the rigour of real life into an ideological world of unreality'. Furthermore, the obligation to receive the sacraments may result 'in establishing just one more moral norm'. Such norms imposing 'good works' 'whose worth (allegedly) increases by repetition' command little respect these days. Rahner contends that the 'reception of the sacraments was meant to overcome' precisely such moralizing and sacralizing tendencies.[24]

He opts for some 'desacralization' while acknowledging elsewhere its questionability. What then is acceptable in this anti-sacral tendency? Both in *Revolution* and 'Active Role' Rahner argues in favour of a contemporary concept of freedom; there are two levels of freedom: one, the 'authentic basic drive of our existence'; the other, the choice of various conceptual alternatives through which we try to express or reflect on this basic drive. Rahner, as elsewhere, is making a distinction here between existential freedom and freedom of choice; the first is the primary concept 'because freedom itself exists at a deeper level than the ideas we may use to express it'. The reception of the sacraments operates at the existential level, because in the absence of a radical commitment the sacrament must appear as something inauthentic, even dishonest.[25]

Such severe criticism of past theology is modified in Rahner's later essay, *Worship*. Eight years after *Revolution*, he distinguishes two conceptual models (*zwei Vorstellungsschemata*) of grace (and therefore of the sacraments) co-existing in the Church. They are not contradictory. The first model[26] understands the sacraments as:

> events in a particular time and space ... through which grace comes into a world otherwise deprived thereof. It is easy to understand the causality of the sacraments: they produce something not otherwise available.[27]

The prototype is infant baptism in which grace is 'produced purely as the effect of the sacrament'. The second model depends upon a view of grace that rejects the notion of grace as a moment of intrusion into the secular world and replaces it by grace as a 'spiritual movement of the world towards the sacrament' (the teaching of *Revolution*).

Rahner explains this new model by using (or anticipating) most of the insights of his later theology: grace is present wherever and whenever the struggle of human living and dying takes place (unless of course, this grace is not rejected through mortal sin). This world of ours is filled with grace; the world is maintained and is constantly in the care of God's self-communication; the inner reality of the world is continually and ceaselessly possessed and permeated by God's grace. Grace is therefore the *'entelechy'*, that is, the inner dynamism of this (secular) world; it proceeds from the innermost heart and centre of the world; it constitutes the meaning and the holiness of the secular dimension and, as such, can be experienced by everyone even in the trivialities of everyday living; grace is therefore the 'radicality' of human transcendence to the Mystery of God and by this the world is 'divinized' and mankind is enabled to connect with the 'immediacy' of this Mystery.[28]

Jesus Christ, the origin of grace, is, of course, ever present in the 'engraced' world; there is nevertheless a 'particular point in time and space' in which the world receives the full and irrevocable manifestation of this truth in Jesus of Nazareth. To accept him as this truth is to believe that

> in the human life of Jesus of Nazareth ... the salvation of one's own life has been granted ... definitively. If someone believes that in Jesus, and nowhere else, the final, definitive and never to be surpassed Word of God has been pledged and accepted ... he can also believe that he has, through the grace of Jesus, already said *yes* to God (the basic purpose of man's existence). He is saved.[29]

This Christological statement brings Rahner nearer to a new and 'revolutionary' interpretation of the sacraments.

The second part of *The Tablet* article, 'The Mass and the World', offers a straightforward description: the sacraments

> are to be seen as the manifestation of the holiness of secular existence, as the expression of the salvation that penetrates man's existence and his world.[30]

Rahner's *Revolution* illustrates this explanation by means of the concept of worship or liturgy implied in the Eucharist. Following (as I believe) Teilhard de Chardin's 'Hymn of the Universe',[31] the whole history of salvation is defined as the 'liturgy of the world'. While *Revolution* expounds this by impressive rhetoric, *Worship* applies characteristic Rahnerian principles to the liturgy of the world. They presuppose his teaching on the supernatural: if human nature is to be the theatre in which 'liturgy' is enacted, that same nature only exists because God wants to give himself in the love that is grace: 'Nature is because grace has to be'.[32]

Rahner's soteriological insights are also at play in countering the traditional view according to which sacraments are intermittent irruptions of grace into a totally secular world: the history of salvation is the 'deification' of the world brought about by God's free initiative and man's free acceptance: (The 'history of the ever present deification of the world by God's self-communication'). From which the idea of the sacraments follows:

> The sacraments are not properly to be understood as successive individual incursions of God into a secular world, but as 'outbursts' (*Ausbrüche*) ... of the innermost, ever-present free endowment of himself to the world in history.[33]

Rahner's anthropological approach is also at work, for grace is accepted whenever man freely accepts himself and his 'deification' along with that acceptance. Such freedom does not of itself define the sacraments, for wherever it happens it constitutes a sacral dimension of the world. Sacraments are to be understood rather as 'particular individual events ... within that *sacral* sphere', a sphere, however, in which the presence of effective grace becomes apparent, finding explicit expression in the ecclesial community.

Rahner's interpretation of symbol is also an influence when he concludes:

> the liturgy of the Church is the symbolic presentation of the liturgy of the world [whose significance] consists in presenting that liturgy in space and time and within the context of real society. It gives mankind a clear image of the performance of this liturgy and of salvation history.[34]

The history of Jesus the Christ is of course the actual acme of the 'liturgy of the world'.

The experience of this 'cosmic worship' is at once ubiquitous and, in this sense, transcendental. Although it is identical with the routines of ordinary life, it is a condition *sine qua non* for its exact expression in the sacral order. Rahner then returns to his idea of the 'mysticism of everyday life'[35] in which the celebration of the sacraments is a kind of *mystagogy*, through which the world is 'divinized' and mankind is enabled to make immediate contact with God's mystery:

> worship is the explicit celebration of the divine depth of ordinary life [so that in consequence] its open representation of everyday occurrences can be subject of free, decisive acceptance.[36]

This new approach developed more explicitly in *Worship* had been applied already to the Eucharist in *Revolution*. A man at Mass (the language is near poetry) is 'profoundly aware of the

12 *The Sacrament of the Future*

drama into which his life is constantly drawn; the divine tragedy and the divine comedy [that is] the drama of the world.' The rhetorical vein continues when Rahner states that the Mass does not renew the sacrifice of the Cross in as much as it is already mysteriously present in the world. A man at Mass allows

> the yearning of his heart to reach expression and be accepted ... He offers up the world under the form of bread and wine ... He knows that he is proclaiming the death of the Lord in as much as this unique death is always there at the innermost centre of the world ... He knows that he proclaims the Coming of the Lord at Mass because that Coming is already coming about in all that drives the world towards its final end.[37]

Rahner describes here what happens in cult and ritual activities which would indeed be worthless unless they were supported by the experience of God and grace, for 'as long as this experience is really lacking, then the sacraments are bound to appear as no more than a form of ritual magic'.[38] Consequently it is true then for all sacraments that 'they declare forth what is otherwise hidden in the darkness of the world and the depth of conscience'.[39]

In *Sevenfold* Rahner uses more elegant language to express this insight; he refers to moral actions as the embodiments or signs, of man's ultimate relationship to God. These signs (which need not be religious) are themselves ambiguous in as much as they can be a real acceptance of God's self-communication or not. They can lose their ambiguity however when they are interpreted in terms of inter-personality, that is, as communication to others within a social situation. If Jesus Christ's salvific action is a clear '*yes*' to God and as such manifested to the world, then he is the primordial sacrament of salvation. The Church, in announcing his history, is the basic sacrament. So

> When the Church pledges herself with total commitment as the basic sacrament of salvation in human situations that are crucial for an individual group, and does this so that commitment is manifest in history; and when man in turn accepts that

pledge and acts on it as a sign of acceptance of interior grace: we have the essence of the sacraments of the Church.[40]

This complex statement is for Rahner an adequate answer to the question, 'What is a sacrament?'.

(B) *The Church and her 'Self-Realization'*

The first manifestation of the action of Jesus Christ is therefore the Church with her sacramental nature. She, in her turn, needs herself to realize her own divinely founded selfhood, if she is not to be an empty sign. Such a sign must actively express, 'actualize', itself in such a way that it may be recognized and accepted for what it is, otherwise the Church would cease to exist. If she 'as a society renounced once for all her self-realisation [her functioning as a visible sign], she would have renounced the very ground of her existence'.[41]

> This is indeed Rahner's scholastic mind at work according to which the 'givenness' (*Vorhandensein*) of an object is (in technical language) *actus primus* ('first act or state'). When it is 'actualized' by functions proper to its nature it reaches the stage of *actus secundus* ('second act or state') in which the scholastic thinker regards the object as truly *existent*. Hence:
>
>> The Church exists ... in the highest degree of the actual fulfilment of her nature, by teaching, bearing witness to Christ's truth, by carrying the Cross of Jesus Christ throughout the ages, by loving God in her members, and by making ritually present ... her particular saving grace. The sacraments are thus the actualizations [self-realizations] of the Church.[42]
>
> The Church then functions in *actu secundo*, that is exists in her 'self-realizations' (*Vollzüge*).

It is however far from easy to interpret the real meaning of Rahner's position. Were it solely about the connection between sacramental activity and the Church as functionary, the meaning would be patent: the Church is the agent and the dispensation of the sacraments is one of her 'actualizations'; this would add only an accidental modification to her definable essential quality. But Rahner wants also to emphasize that the Church is more than just an *actus primus* in its narrow sense. The Church, on the contrary, has an active dynamic character and when she *realizes* herself in *some* activities (*actus secundus*), she expresses her very essence. The administration of the sacraments is one of these activities. In technical terms, Rahner's notion of the Church is not essential, but functional.

Take for instance the *Handbook,* the second volume of which contains a distinction accepted by all contributors.[43] The Church is in origin *Heilsfrucht:* she is the result of the effect of Christ's redemptive grace. The Church as an institution and a society within history is *Heilsanstalt.* Fulfilling her task of bringing salvation to the individual believer makes the Church a *Heilsmittel*: she is indeed a means of salvation in as much as she witnesses Christ, preaches the word, teaches the faithful and fashions the policies of the society of believers. She cannot, however, actualize her own nature unless she so touches individual believers that she initiates the process towards their final salvation; she is also *Heilsprozess.* It is not, however, just the free self-communicating God within the Church, nor the Church herself as the mediator of salvation that makes the Church's function possible; the free acceptance of the individual believer is also required. The active self-realization of the Church as *Heilsmittel* comes about through initiating *and* participating in the *Heilsprozess of* the believers. The administration of the sacraments is one of the Church's activities in which she realizes, 'actualizes' her own nature:

> When and where the Church acts in accord with her fundamental nature as the primordial sacrament of salvation by enabling someone freely to accept the salvation proffered, we have properly a sacrament.[44]

In other words, the sacraments are *Grundvollzüge*, primary and fundamental activities of the Church – the emphasis is on the words 'primary and 'fundamental' *(Grund-).* Not all activities of the Church, however, meet this primary (*Grund-*) qualification: some because the activity does not represent the fundamental nature of the Church as the outward sign of God's triumphal, eschatological presence, others because they do not engage the individual in a decisive free acceptance of that presence. There is a difference between sacraments proper and 'sacramentals' (*sacramentalia),* that is, the further extra sacramental rites in aid of individual holiness. The treatment of the seven individual sacraments will unpack them in more detail.

In a footnote Rahner explains the characteristic trait of a true sacrament: its administration and reception gives a person a share in 'the spirit of the Church'. This position seems also to depend on the traditional analysis of the sacrament into: *sacramentum tantum, sacramentum et res, res sacramenti,* as the three moments of the sacramental action.The sacramental sign in itself is the promise of grace which, when it is conferred, puts the recipient in a relationship with the Church, which in turn leads to the free acceptance of God's grace (*res sacramenti*). For Rahner, the middle stage (*sacramentum et res*) is the relationship with the Church.[45] The sacraments are not something which the Church possesses and gives to the individual, but something which belongs to, or rather, constitutes the very existence of the Church:

> The sacraments are basic self-realizations of the Church in as much as they are both administered and received ... Sacramental activity is a unity of the giving and receiving of this *Grundvollzug* of the Church (even though giver and receiver have different functions).[46]

The reception of the sacraments, therefore, is a true manifestation of the evolving Church. It is the total sacramental action, including their reception, that builds up and develops the Church: *'Die Sakramente "erbauen" die Kirche, indem sie aktiv empfangen werden'.* Those, therefore, who only receive the sacraments *are also the Church*, not only those who (with the status of clerics) administer them.

(C) *Word and Sacrament*

Roman Catholic theology came late to regarding the word of God as of equal importance to the sacraments and regarding the sacraments as part of that word. For a long time the Church of the Word and Church of the Sacraments were in opposition and controversy: the one claiming salvation that comes about solely through listening to the word in faith; the other teaching that salvation is wrought through the grace conferred by the sacraments. This opposition came to an end with Vatican II. The constitution on *Divine Revelation* sketches a theology of the Word presenting it as an event effectively communicating God's creative and salvific presence; the constitution on *Sacred Liturgy* states that this presence of God is to be found, not only in the Church and the sacrifice of the Mass, but also in the word of God:

> He (Christ) is present in the sacraments ... he is present in the word, since He Himself speaks when the Holy Scriptures are read in the Church.[47]

Some years before the Council indeed Rahner had already addressed the similarity and dissimilarity between word and sacrament. His long essay *Word*[48] was repeated in summary and published along with E. Jüngel's attempt to define an evangelical theology of the sacraments.[49] This slim volume of ecumenical dialogue has a common theme: Roman Catholics and Reformed Churches both assign to the Church the essential task of preaching the word of God and administering the sacraments. It will be seen that the agreement of the two authors does not however extend to the precise meaning of the concepts employed.

In both *Word* and in *Jüngel/Rahner*, Rahner is at pains to explain why Catholics have neglected a theology of the Word and to attempt a sketch of it. The lack of a developed Catholic theology of the Word is easily attributed to the Council of Trent's preoccupation with doctrinal definitions directed against those Protestant opinions regarded as heretical. The attempt to relate word and sacrament became the subject of controversy between the two denominations. In post-Tridentine systematic theology a treatise on the theology of the Word was no more than an incidental interest within the treatises on divine Revelation, and as such was treated either as a doctrinal, even a dogmatic statement defining a truth to be believed, or as verbal information *about* something to be communicated. The Word was regarded as a means of *teaching* and not as a word in which, as Rahner puts it, 'reality itself draws nigh and announces itself and constitutes itself present'.[50] Some Catholic circles have never understood the Word as a soteriological reality, as a 'force' contributing to salvation, unless as an element of a sacramental action. The sacraments were regarded as something entirely different from the word; they conveyed no message, but grace to those who received them.

In response to this 'defective' theology Rahner proposes six theses the basis of which has already been stated: the word of God is an essential characteristic of the Church, and entrusted to her preaching. Without the word of God the Church could not exist, for that word conditions the very possibility of her existence. So far we have doctrine common to Catholic and Reformed churches alike. While the next stage also conforms to Protestant convictions that 'the word of God in the Church is an interor moment of God's salvific activity',[51] Rahner develops this statement by bringing his complex philosophical and theological arsenal into play, and advances the classical reformed stance which sees the *salvific word* as a divine utterance to be heard and answered in an act of faith. For Rahner the word is itself God's action in grace that 'renews man interiorly by making him participate in the divine nature' and creates the capacity for righteous action (of course, with the help of grace). 'Man's act (of faith, hope and love) is (also) an intrinsic moment of the whole process' of salvation. This process entails on our part the *acceptance* of God's gift of justification as well as that of enlightenment and inspiration. These last two gifts are inner words illuminating and inspiring a person already 'divinised' and on the way to eternal salvation. Even though they be not clear utterances, they are *'inner words of grace'*.

Rahner now asserts that this 'inner grace' has two characteristics: it is 'transcendental' in the sense that it is bestowed by God on each and every creature in the world; and requires its proper expression in human terms (or in Rahner's terminology: in the 'categorial' sphere[52]). Should this kind of expression be lacking salvation would be just some 'secret depth' within the soul. This tangible ('categorial') expression is quite normal[53] in as much as the human person is a social being:

> Knowledge about a person's grace cannot adequately proceed only from an inner experience of grace; it must also come from without, from (though not exclusively) the world, the community and that history of salvation which is the historical transmission of an event of social nature.[54]

This communication through (and throughout) history, the preaching of the Church is therefore an inner moment of God's salvific activity. Further, the external word elucidates the inner experience: 'it makes it the subject of conscious belief and compels the decision' of faith (the awareness of acceptance of the inner word of grace); it transposes faith and grace into a function of the historical community. Inner and outer realities unite as 'the mutually complementary moments of the one word of God'.

Having stated what is to him obvious Rahner proposes his thesis concerning the word of God; it is (*mutatis mutandis*) identical with the traditional definition of the sacrament. The word of God is:

> the salutary word which effects what it affirms. It is a salvific event therefore which ... brings about what it signifies. It renders the grace of God present.[55]

Though this is not yet Rahner's fully developed teaching, it lays the foundation for the explicit statement of it: 'the full realization of the word of God is the sacrament'. The Catholic concept of sacraments thus becomes a particular case of the full theology of the word, a special event (*Wortereignis*) which differs from other words uttered by the Church. This last statement in *Word* brings us nearer to the teaching of his essay in *Jünge/Rahner: Was ist ein Sakrament?* The sentence quoted however comes from a marathon sentence of about 180 words in which he summarizes his long essay, *Word* (1960).[56] In *Jüngel/Rahner* (1971) he does not propose all his tortuous arguments in support of the basic proposition that word and sacrament can be brought together without asserting *full* identity between them. To emphasize both the difference *and* identity he uses the notion of *exhibitive word* taken, I believe, from linguistic philosophy, which then survives in his later theology. Since however Rahner's own background together with that of much of his audience is scholastic, he must show that the word of God in this context is not a set of doctrinal statements neither is it an intellectual description of religious truth, but

> a revelatory, operative word in which and through which alone the matter designated is present ... [This word] is given presence by its utterance, and exists precisely by its capacity to be heard.[57]

This truth should, of course, be evident from the scriptures of the Old and New Testaments. Creation and liberation by God, the kerygma of salvation, come about through that word through which 'the arrival of the thing proclaimed itself takes place'. It is indeed the way by which we come to faith: we can hear and accept the proclamation of the word in faith if, and only if, the word itself confers God's gift of grace enabling our acceptance. The reality communicated by word causes its reception to be 'lovingly believed'.

> Thus the Word of God, imperative in its preaching, is the very substance of what is preached, and creates the possibility of the acceptance of the reality itself which is preached.[58]

The truth of this ought to be self-evident: Rahner approaches the sacraments not from the angle of sacred signs instituted by Christ, but that of the theology of the Word. They are communications through the presence of the Word; Augustine's concept of the sacraments as a material element to which the '*verbum* of God is applied receives a new and different emphasis. The scholastic concepts of matter (the visible action) and form (the ritual words) are straightjackets in their application to penance and matrimony which are not really signs, but verbal communications. Should we not say the same of the other five sacraments? Rahner is insistent that the 'grace of God is not merely spoken, but is an event brought about by verbal utterance'. His approach recommends itself in as much as the kerygma of salvation operates by means of the word of proclamation. We come to faith through acceptance of the word of proclamation, an acceptance entirely dependent on the enabling grace of God. The Word itself causes the loving belief that receives it. The Word of God is the arrival of its own message and the challenge creating the possibility of accepting it.

A further thesis notices that the Church employs these 'exhibitive words' in various degrees of intensity and focus, for there is an inner flexibility in God's self-communication, even in these 'exhibitive' words. Historical circumstances, the capacity of people to 'accept' the Word, differing degrees of fidelity to the word manifested by the preaching of the Church, an individual's engagement in his or her actual community and other factors all demonstrate that the Word of God is in *process* of development:

> [The word] can only realize its essence through an historical process, for it is not always and at every time its full self; it grows, it *becomes* what it is and must be, it can have the incompleteness of provisional and preparatory moments.[59]

Rahner therefore emphasizes the historicity of the Word of God. The Word, however, is basically one with the sacrament: Rahner does not start by distinguishing between word and sign; he rather asserts the signifying character of the word along with the verbal character of the sign. Both sign and word are symbolic realities in the preaching of the Church. The sign is a visible gesture of the Church and the word uttered conveys the authority of God's Word: 'Thus the whole sign of grace, no matter what form it takes, must partake of the character of the word',[60] whilst the words uttered along with the Church's action share in the sign-character of the visible gesture.

This basic oneness, however, contains dissimilarity. In arguing this dissimilarity, Rahner reintroduces his first insight proper to his own approach: he emphasizes the role of the Church. For instance, the prayer for a sick person in the name of Jesus, made by a group of believers, is different from the prayer of the presbyter who anoints him. Both have the promise of being heard, but the latter is a sacrament and the other is not. And what about penance, a sacrament lacking a material sign? Why is the forgiveness pronounced by a priest

The Sacramental Life of the Church 21

within the context of the confessional effective, and that of a penitential service outside the ritual not? Why too is a Mass celebrated with the consecration a sacrament and a service of the Word not? Rahner has to solve this problem while maintaining that the sacramental sign is basically a communication in which the word effects the grace proper to it. Should we then conclude that the position of the ritual sign makes the word pronounced by a person acting on behalf of the Church a true sacrament?

The essay *Word* contains a lengthly argument in pursuit of this difficulty and it concludes with the following thesis:

> The supreme realization of the efficacious word of God, as God's salvific action is the fundamental and 'radical' commitment of the Church ..., to situations decisive for the individual's salvation; here and here only we have the sacrament in its proper sense.[61]

Later, *Jüngel/Rahner* offers a more simple proof: the Church is the sign of God's presence within mankind's eschatological salvation; each sacrament is the activity of the Church for an individual within a decisive situation; therefore the crown of God's efficient word amongst us is the sacrament.[62] The explanation of this difference between sacramental word-events and other word-events lies in the fact that the sacramental word effects what it symbolizes with an objective certainty: the grace of salvation.[63]

Such words as 'supreme realization', 'radical commitment of the Church' may well at first glance puzzle the reader. Can the Church ever engage herself in a half-hearted or provisional manner? Is there a non-absolute self-realization of the Church? Can she fail in her mission as the true living sign of the eschatological triumph of God's mercy in Jesus Christ? Rahner tries to find an answer in the other half of his thesis in *Word* by investigating the human situation in which an individual faces salvific choice:

> The Church fully realizes herself [=*Grundvollzug*] by her proper commitment to each individual in as much as she becomes the merciful word of God in the concrete actual situation of salvation. Hence her word is not something provisional

or conditional, but the ultimate efficacious word of God in the dialogue of faith. It corresponds with Trent's *opus operatum*... [which gives an objective certainty of grace received].[64]

Just as the word preached may have its historical intensity, so is the sign dependent on the historical situation of the person. It is from this situation that Rahner deduces the single sacraments of the Roman Catholic Church: initiation – baptism; culpability – penance; choice of partner in love – marriage, and so on.[65] If God utters his word in such situations through the rites of the Church, we have a sacrament:

> All other actions through which the Church exercises her proper self as the permanence of of God's efficacious word of grace in the world, are insufficient [for the existence of a sacrament].[66]

Apart from these existential situations necessary to introduce the seven sacraments Rahner admits that there can exist other experiences which were capable of being graced by a like 'exhibitive' word of God. For this word can also be uttered in the sphere where sacramental words are not available, or simply unknown. He then offers his cherished topic: justification or 'engracement' outside the sacrament, in as much as all human beings, and not only believing Christians, are able to experience the critical situations necessary for the existence of the sacrament.

The question then arises: What is the difference between words outside and words inside the sacramental system? *Word*'s answer is a near anticipation of his later insight to 'anonymous Christianity' and in tune with his 'revolutionary' approach to the sacrament.[67] Efficacious words not of sacramental character (preaching, good example, existential experiences of goodness, for example) though not explicitly sacramental, yet are oriented and ordered to sacramental words proper. Rahner speaks of a *process* from the one to the other in phases throughout history, a process also present within the history of believers in that there is a movement towards a full and explicit manifestation of the Church's sacramental action on the individual. The consummation of this process is a sacrament:[68]

because the reality anticipated [salvation, justification] is already present, before its historical sacramental manifestation has been fully expressed, then it is called sacrament.[69]

What characterizes this process is that though salvation in some way is present in each of its phases the the fuller phase is never superfluous:

> They are phases of the self-realization and historical self-presentation of the one and the same essence of the one efficacious word of God, which, where and only where it attains under God and Christ its unambiguous, historical and ecclesiological presence, that perfectly embodied eschatological presence is called a sacrament.[70]

Sacraments are words of grace. They not only speak of or inform us about grace, but also enable our answer to the self-communication of God. The sacramental word is both offer and acceptance.

How may we characterize therefore Rahner's approach to sacramental theology, an approach which goes beyond what we may call 'sacramental absolutism', the dominant Roman Catholic mentality according to which sacraments are the almost exclusive means of gaining final salvation? I shall later refer to this absolute view of sacramental praxis as an aspect of post-Tridentine 'sacramentalism'. Rahner however links the idea of of sacrament with other notions less obviously implied in their concept.

1) By emphasizing the Church's unique role in the sacramental event, Rahner develops his firm conviction that the Church is an irrevocable eschatological sign of God's 'triumphant' saving will, and hence the necessary mediatory instrument in attaining the present grace of future salvation. As he writes in a later essay, 1983:

> The Church is the great and unique gesture of God *and* the gesture of acceptance of mankind through which divine love,

reconciliation, and the self-communication of God are forever manifested and imparted.[71]

Consequently the Church is the mediating moment of the sacramental process in which both sign and grace assert their presence, the *res et sacramentum* of medieval tradition. Rahner always keeps in mind that the Church is the primodial sacrament in which both sign and the grace signified are present.

2) Rahner chooses to describe sacraments as it were 'from below': material signs, community gestures, and human acts in sundry situations. He presupposes this human side of sacramental life as a *fore-grasp* or *'pre-apprehension'* (*Vorgriff*) to salvation. This, of course, presupposes the transcendental thrust of human action: each and every human being, even if unaware, 'is aiming for the immediacy of God',[72] our supernatural destiny. Human striving is met by the explicit will of God to save mankind through Jesus Christ, the incarnate Word of God. The 'material' element of the sacraments, therefore, now arises out of Rahner's anthropology; it is open to sacramental events and to salvation. This is the background, I believe, of his 'revolutionary' approach to sacraments.

3) By connecting sacramental praxis with the hearing of the Word of God, Rahner discovers a whole new area of consideration unexploited by the traditional theology of the Roman Church. His assertion that the sacraments are words of grace interprets them as a reciprocal *communication* between God and mankind, between faith and sacramental praxis. There is a dialectical oneness, a case of identity in difference in the relationship between faith and sacramental praxis. In confronting the dilemma, faith *or* sacrament, Rahner has the courage to state: 'Compared with faith, sacrament seems to play a secondary role, if any at all'.[73] This statement in itself is untrue, unless it is complemented by the traditional post-Tridentine view that faith alone (in baptism especially), is never complete, because:

> a sacrament in the traditional sense is but the most intensive instance of God's revealing word ... a peak in the moments of ... the life of faith.[74]

Faith in the Word of God is not therefore an addition to the sacrament, nor is the sacrament an addition to faith. Rahner says it would be naive to believe that there cannot be faith without baptism as though our first conscious act of faith were nothing more than the actualization of the grace of baptism received in infancy. On the other hand, it would be incorrect to assert that faith can be a *real and irreversible* option for God's word, when it is not expressed through a sacrament of the Church. Word and sacrament, Church and sacrament, divine will incarnate in human striving, characterize Rahner's sacramental theology.

These three features throw a light on the position adopted by Rahner concerning the necessity of an explicit sacramental praxis. Is it then true that sacramental praxis is not that vital for salvation, but it admits qualification? Karen Kilby's lucid presentation of Rahner's sacramental theology expresses the matter admirably:

> he [Rahner] denies that these sacraments are in any way unique in causing grace, or that they are always more effective than other 'merely sacramental' activities; something which is not strictly speaking a sacrament might in particular case 'work' better in actually bringing grace to the individual than a sacrament does.[75]

Nonetheless, sacraments are not only words but, so to speak, *deeds*, of grace. They do not only inform us about, but 'confer' in their own way the reality of salvation. Rahner's sacramental theology is founded firmly on the basis of Roman Catholic tradition; in reinterpreting the *permanent* features of that tradition he remains true to it.

1.2.2 Permanent Features

Rahner's examination of sacramental theology is in continuous dialogue with the features of traditional Catholic teaching: his criticism of its *permanent* elements and his re-interpretation of its formulations generate his own version. To be faithful to Catholic orthodoxy any sacramental theology has to fulfil at least three conditions: first, if and, only if, those 'new' statements which re-interpret tradition adequately answer the questions permanently posed by faith; secondly, if that relatively new answer to such *permanent* questions satisfies both the official interpreters of the deposit of faith (the Teaching Office) *and* the contemporary sense and *praxis* of the faithful; lastly, if these 'new' statements are not only rooted in past Catholic teaching and are presently intelligible, but are also open to future development and, perhaps, deeper understanding of the faith.[76]

The integrity of our faith in salvation through the agency of material or human realities poses fundamental doctrinal questions: how to envisage the relationship between two entirely different kinds of reality; how can a material element or human gesture be connected with the divinely granted, supernatural reality that is salvation? These general questions demand detailed answers. This present chapter examines Rahner's conception and reinterpretation of permanent features of Catholic tradition.

(A) *'Ex opere operato'*

Although it is not quite accurate to assert that Catholic sacramental theology originated in the decrees of the Council of Trent, it was that Council that had to resolve the question: whether the promised grace of salvation is granted by means of sacramental signs or human gestures, or whether salvation can be achieved by faith alone.

This question had already received a somewhat negative answer before Trent: neither the merit of the recipient nor the dignity of the person administering the sacrament determines the acquisition of the corresponding grace. Trent takes over this negative delimitation and gives an alternative answer: *sacramenta novae legis* **ex opere operato** *gratiam conferunt*: the sacraments of the New Law confer grace 'through the sacramental action itself' (sic Tanner).[77]

In almost all his essays concerning the sacraments, Rahner returns to this central and characteristic solution of Roman Catholic theology. *Kirche61*, which is concerned with the understanding of popular praxis, presents a twofold criticism of it: negatively, he asserts that *opus operatum* does not mean that sacraments work by an 'almost physical certainty', although positively 'one can certainly affirm that God has attached the unconditional promise of grace and help to other realities as well as to sacramental signs'.[78] Rahner includes within these 'other realities' such activities as a sincere prayer, a vow, a pilgrimage, and so forth made by an individual who trusts in God to fulfil his promises. Though these are technically subjective performances, *opera operantis*, and their objective counterparts are *opera operata*, Rahner does not consider these two aspects of the sacramental event as radically different:

> The (sacramental) sign has an unalterable eschatological validity; it is the established sign of the eternal irrevocable covenant of God with men, a sign which so shares in the eternity and irrevocability of God's salvific will, that the sign itself can never lose the quality of being a visible expression of God's compliant answer to man.[79]

To put it briefly: the eschatological nature of the sign is a participation in God's irrevocable and salvific will. This constitutes the difference between sincere prayer and sacramental action.

Rahner illustrates the point by the asking how the sacred rites of the Old Testament differ from those of the New Testament. The presupposition is that there has always been a salvific action of God concerning the individual and that rites and symbols are characteristic of all religions, especially that of the Old Testament. Circumcision is a prime example, for it would be incorrect to think that God would change the promise inherent in circumcision by transferring it to Christian baptism. Although Rahner holds that God has created the world 'with definite structures' and in an unalterable coherence of all that is, there is nevertheless a difference between the old and the new inasmuch as the new completes, fulfils and makes irrevocable the old. On the one hand:

> the old covenant as such ... was intrinsically fragile; of itself it was transitory, temporary, replaceable and destructible,

though capable of persisting outwardly when in truth it had ceased to exist.[80]

On the other hand:

'the signs of grace in the new covenant are always and permanently assurances of divine grace.'[81]

If we now apply this principle to the difference between sincere prayer and use of the sacraments we reach the positive content of *ex opere operato*: *opus operatum* 'means an unambiguous, abiding promise irrevocably made by God, and as such is a manifestly recognizable and historically valid occasion of grace for each individual human being, dependent upon the promise made by the God of the new and eternal covenant'.[82]

It is obvious that the individual can refuse to accept God's salvific action implicit in the sacramental sign, but (and I believe this to be Rahner's ultimate intention) that same acceptance is already in place within the context of the new covenant, or (as he adds without further explanation) within the Church:

It cannot be questioned that grace is truly received through these signs, for the Church as a whole incorporates the promise of her own subjective holiness, a holiness produced and preserved by efficacious grace.[83]

If the sacraments are instances of the Church herself at work, they share her redemptive grace, not only as something offered to, but also as something accepted by, the community of the faithful.

Was ist ein Sakrament (Rahner-Jüngel) presents, as has been already pointed out, Rahner's approach as coloured by his endeavour to fuse the word of God with sacramental praxis. The concept of 'exhibitive word' is now introduced and this concept is used to accommodate his Protestant partner in dialogue (E. Jüngel) with specifically Catholic views. This notion presupposes the effectiveness of the word common to all confessions, namely: God's 'predestining, efficient grace' is disclosed in that word; triumphant, eschatological grace is attributed to it. It is this word that is spoken over the sacramental elements, and as such it is effective. Its efficacy, however, leaves open the possibility of rejection by loveless unbelief.'[84] An individual refusal, however, does not annul the promise. *Hence* Rahner can say:

> [By admitting the possibility of refusal] we have explained what the notion *opus operatum* means in Catholic sacramental theology. Basically it refers to that same victorious power which comes to us from God in an exhibitive word of faith. The sacramental word attains its fulfilment in exactly the same manner.[85]

After making this identification, Rahner invariably associates *opus operatum* with the manifestation of God's victorious, eschatological grace, a manifestation *which is nothing other* than the Church, for this salvific word belongs to or becomes the word of the Church when she addresses the individual in her various sacramental words.[86] He adds in another place:

> Wherever the universal and permanent descent of grace into the world reaches the stage in history at which it becomes unalterable, that is the presence of the Church and the sacraments.[87]

The objective effectiveness of the Church's sacramental word (*opus operatum*) is equally expressed in the notion of sacramental causality.[88]

(B) *Ex genere signi*[89]

The faith of the Church has always been conscious that there are material signs or human gestures which are *intimately connected* with God's saving grace; the task of doctrinal theology is to explore the meaning of this connection. Rahner's philosophical and theological background points him in the direction of *symbolical causality*.

> A number of Roman Catholic fellow theologians may find the word 'connection' all too vague on the grounds that there is not only a 'connection' between sign and grace, but a definite and

active power, one granted by God's promise to *confer* grace by the sacraments. My vagueness was deliberate, however. Throughout tradition, whether ancient or recent, there have been manifold expressions of faith in the sacraments. Some sketches of sacramental theology borrowed the Greek word *mysterion*[90] in characterizing the celebration of sacred rites. The word, *mystery*, in the New Testament and early Christian usage denotes the hidden decrees of God as (in part) manifest through Christ's life, death and resurrection *and* their reception through faith. It is understandable, therefore, that mystery is not only communication of God with man, but at the same time man's reaction to it: at first with awe and admiration, followed by acceptance or refusal. Not only God's self-revelation, but also man's acceptance is somehow part of the mystery.

This wide general meaning of mystery became more and more restricted during the age of the Apologists (the second and third centuries): first to baptism and the Eucharist, and then to other sacred rites of the early Church. It was about this time, too, that the Greek *mysterion* was translated by the Latin *sacramentum* (in Jerome and Cyprian, for example).

At this earlier time, before medieval theologians employed Aristotelian philosophy, Platonist theory with its concept of *images* helped to envisage the working of the sacramental sign. An *image* does not only stand for a hidden reality, but is also, even if only imperfectly, the reality it signifies. The human reaction, therefore, was not only one of awe and reverence in face of the Mystery, but a belief that, owing to God's condescending self-revelation, the newly baptized were transformed into a 'new creation': they die the death of Jesus Christ and live the risen life promised by the Saviour; bread and wine, too, ritually consecrated in the Eucharist re-enact God's Incarnate arrival in the presence of the faithful. Such an image, contemplated in faith, led to a humanly unfathomable reality.

Aristotelian philosophy gave western minds (often it is believed conditioned by their Old English or Germanic mentality) a different approach to the relationship between sign and grace, and indeed, to the whole of reality. A sign was an entity apprehended by the senses, one which had reference to another entity beyond human understanding. Theological investigation was now concerned with defining the nature of the relationship between sign and grace.

In the third part of his *Summa Theologiae,* Thomas Aquinas introduces sacramental theology by affirming that a sacrament is *in genere signi* (within the category of sign). In the very first article of question 60 Thomas still seems to be wavering about assigning a definite *causal* category to the sign/grace relationship. Indeed, Sacrament, which according to him derives its name from sanctity, should in the first place be assigned to the category of *analogia* (analogy): by representing, by conserving, or even by effecting sanctity. Indeed, sacrament can either imply some hidden sanctity (*sacrum secretum*) or have some inner tendency, an *ordo* (constituent character) to the same as its cause or its *sign*. The contemporary Church, indeed, mainly used sacrament in this sense. In answering his first objection, Thomas does not confine himself to causality. If there is causality at all, one should rather speak of formal or final causality, but *non opportet quod sacramentum semper importet causalitatem* (a sacrament does not always imply causality).

Nonetheless subsequent questions addressed by Thomas cannot avoid the idea of sacramental causation; the 62nd question, indeed, opts for the kind of causality proper to a sacrament. Neither formal nor final causality is appropriate for explaining the sign/grace connection; *instrumentality* is, however: God, the principal agent in causing grace uses the sacramental signs.[91] Note, however, that Thomas regards sacrament (sign) and grace as two 'entities', and their relationship is characterized by God's agency as instrumental cause. This typical Aristotelian way of thinking confines, to my mind, his subsequent treatment of sacramental theology to meticulous questions concerning the material and formal elements in each and every sacrament, questions later resumed by the Council of Florence in the fifteenth and, partially, by Trent in the sixteenth century.

Rahner's *Kirche*[61] follows Thomas in exploring the various views and theories by means of which the causality of the sacraments was explained. Although the Council of Trent, the one most responsible for the details of sacramental theology, never opts for any particular theory, it does use causal terms. Rahner interprets Trent as describing the working of the sacraments in terms of transient causality, that is, cause and effect are 'quite distinct factors, almost as though they were material things'.[92] This 'sacramental cause', of course, cannot be that of *physical or efficient causation*, excluded even by Thomas. Can then the sacraments be regarded as 'instruments' in the hand of God, the ultimate Cause?

Later, some theologians postulated, in contrast, a *moral causality,* analogous to honouring a 'legal claim' by someone who had contracted to perform it; the sacrament would be considered as conferring a legal (juridical) title on the recipient in terms of which God would be obliged to grant the corresponding grace.

Kirche61 discusses the variants of these two different versions (efficient and moral) of sacramental causality. Rahner dismisses both on the grounds that it is unlikely that an inanimate, often material, thing can *physically* bring about a transcendent spiritual reality, namely, grace. The water of baptism, or the accompanying gesture or rite would be disproportionate to the effect produced. Rahner is equally unhappy with Thomas's instrumental causality: would God take something material 'into his hands' to produce grace in the soul of the individual? Even if that could be figured out by some means, what is to be attributed to the instrument and what to God? Any moral or juridical claim on God, too, even if it can be shown as God's promise, would put a constraint on God, an act of voodoo, forcing the hand of the godhead.

Nevertheless, Rahner's own solution to the problem incorporates something of both of these attempts to define sacramental causality. He feels at home in adopting the old axiom, *sacramenta significando efficiunt gratiam.* (Sacraments effect grace by signifying). He had worked out his theory of the symbol some three years before.[93] Without repeating his explanation of 'symbolism', we shall briefly recall the basic insight; there are two kinds of symbols: those perceived as indicating some outward reality or command (conventional signs); and those which are so intimately connected with what is symbolized that they make it present, *Realsymbolen* (real symbols). Thus the Logos is the symbol of the Father, and Christ's humanity is the symbol of his divine person. Rahner applies the same pattern to the sacraments: the sacraments are 'real symbols', and as such they make the grace signified really present.[94] In his own words:

> the grace of God constitutes itself actively present in the sacra-

ments by creating their expression, their historical tangibility in space and time, which is its own proper symbol.[95]

This abstract formulation of symbolic causality seems to amalgamate a somewhat physical with a moral causality. Rahner speaks of the sacraments as 'making', 'creating', their graced complements while at the same time admitting that the 'juridically established structure of the sacrament does not run counter to this view', inasmuch as the sacramental sign can be regarded as an appeal to the grace-giving God. On the one hand he will have to maintain that there is a certain sense in which the sacramental signs already 'contain' the grace which they confer onto the recipient and, on the other, that they are only 'reminding' God who alone, according to his promise, can give us that grace. The first represents the traditional formulation of Catholic theology, the view already proposed by Thomas Aquinas (*Summa* III, quest. 62 art. 3). The other alternative is contrary to the first: the sign itself is neutral with regard to grace, unless an 'extrinsic pronouncement' of God constitutes it as the carrier of God-given grace in the recipient. (In that case the sign itself is not a *Realsymbol*.) For Rahner, sign and signified, symbol and symbolized retain their own character: the baptismal water is washing *as well as* 'engracing' the recipient; bread and wine are really food *as well as* the source of sanctification; the words of absolution in response to repentance are both human reconciliation *and* divine justification; and so on. Symbol and symbolized are now in a *reciprocal relationship* with one another like body and soul, like the humanity and divinity of Christ. In Rahner's own words:

> that which (the sign) manifests generates its own reality and existence by a manifestation which is distinct from itself.[96]

To express the same idea by use of Rahner's more philosophical language: being has to be manifested in order to exist in the fullness of its reality. Whatsoever exists 'causes' its own self-expression, and whatever is thus expressed 'causes' the *existence* of some manifested reality. More specifically, God manifests, that is, expresses his salvific action, in the sacrament, and the sacrament causes, that is, realizes the existence of salvation in the recipient.

The last paragraph could not avoid employing Rahner's own abstract formulations. His theory is perhaps more understandable in the context of the ecclesiology of *Kirche61*. For it is, indeed, the Church, the symbol of God's saving grace, that attains her own self-expression or self-fulfilment in dispensing the sacraments; in other words the Church finds her fulfilment, her real and concrete existence through preaching the word of God and administering the sacraments, since the performance of both relate to the salvation of the world. The Church exists by God's will, but her existence is realized through these self-realizing activities. Similarly, the sacraments are indeed symbols of grace, but it is the administration of them that brings about the existence of Christ's grace in the recipient; to use Rahner's own words:

> The relation between the Church as the historical visible manifestation of grace and grace itself [which are *mutually conditioning reciprocal agencies. Their relationship*] extends into the relation between sacramental sign and grace conferred. The sign 'effects' grace, by grace producing the sacrament as sign of the sanctification 'effected'.[97]

This characteristic quotation illustrates Rahner's answer to the traditional question about the 'causality of sacramental grace'. Whether or not his reinterpretation will be acceptable to the official interpreters of Church teaching, or whether or not his argument is more meaningful to his contemporaries, remains to be seen. He claims both to be the case, a claim that I myself will re-examine in the Comment and Questions of a later chapter.

(C) 'A Christo ... Jesu instituta'

Rahner envisages the seven sacraments of the Roman Church as indeed attributable to Christ, however indirectly. He writes:

> Through a long history of reflection on her faith the Church has become aware that she has seven fundamental gestures to perform on behalf of individual Christians, gestures which effect what they signify by the power of God. The seven fundamental signs or gestures possessing this power are called sacraments ... The Church is aware that these gestures and signs have been given to her in virtue of the authority of Jesus.[98]

The above quotation is, of course, only a short summary of a lengthy treatment of the matter of the institution of the sacraments in *Kirche61*. He accepts the challenge of those sixteenth-century reformers who resolutely questioned the number seven. Four, or perhaps five, of the traditional seven cannot be traced back to the words of Christ. Apart from the Eucharist and baptism (and perhaps penance) we can produce neither the *ipsissima verba* nor an explicit intention of Christ in support of the other four (confirmation, holy orders, anointing of the sick and marriage). For Protestants they are human inventions introduced into the *praxis* and legislation of the later Church and not inherited from the Redeemer. In spite of some early wavering, Luther denied sacramentality to penance, in the form at least practised by the contemporary Church. None of these four were held to have been 'instituted' by Jesus Christ.

The Council of Trent merely repeated the long-standing conviction canonized, more than a century before, by the Council of Florence whose own decree was a summary of the sacramental theology of the tenth and eleventh centuries; the great scholastics of the time took it for granted that not only the two principal sacraments (baptism and Eucharist) but all seven were truly instituted by Christ. Thus the number seven (in itself, a sacred number) became rooted in subsequent Catholic *praxis* and mentality.

The decrees of Trent initiated a desperate search by post-Tridentine theologians for words in the Bible to counter Luther and the other reformers. If they did not find Christ's own words of institution, it was sufficient to point out other sayings and allusions in the Bible in support of Christ's intention to institute all seven sacraments. These words came from his apostles who through the evangelists wrote under the inspiration of the Holy Spirit. They must have remembered undocumented words of the Master, or they must have put his instructions into practice. The best examples of these scriptural arguments are: for the anointing of the sick (Mark 6:13; James 5:14ff), and for marriage (the Pauline Ephesians 5:32); and the praxis of the early Church (Acts 8:15–17) for the separate institution of confirmation. The evidence that the sacrament of penance came from Christ was evident, these theologians considered, from his preaching of *metanoia* (conversion from sin) from the very beginning of his mission, and too from the Matthean power of binding and loosing, as well as some sayings from John's writings (John 20:22ff and 1 John 1:9).

Recent theology is more careful in its handling of the scriptural evidence for the origin of the sacraments. Both the lack of a blind belief in verbal inspiration and the emergence of modern biblical scholarship have raised problems about the institution of the sacraments, even of baptism.[99] When scriptural evidence is lacking, the last resort becomes ancient tradition; after all there must have been a verbal, unwritten tradition by virtue of which the Church could attribute these sacraments to the Lord's institution. *Kirche61* argues that such an assumption is nothing more than an hypothesis. Furthermore, an argument based on tradition alone can no longer be used; neither the encyclical *Divino afflante Spiritu* (1943) nor the account of biblical scholarship given in Vatican II (see the 8th session on Revelation) permit it. Nevertheless Rahner, who is ostensibly arguing against the appeal to tradition, does something very similar. He tries to establish the seven sacraments as *implied in Christ's institution of the Church, the primordial sacrament*. The argumentation of *Kirche61* sustains this thesis.

The main premise of his long-winded and detailed argument is that the sacramental act 'activates the very nature of the Church with regard to an individual'. It would be superfluous therefore, if not mistaken, to try to find precise words or sayings which express the intention of Jesus to found each and every sacrament. They should certainly not be read *into* the Bible.

Accordingly Rahner's first argument is negative. He opposes the contrary position by trying to restate his adversary's words in confirmation of his own view: 'we have no saying of Jesus about these four (namely, matrimony, holy orders, anointing of the sick and confirmation) sacraments'. Even Jesus' command to remember him at the eucharistic assembly cannot be interpreted as the institution of *ordo*.[100] Even so the contrary argument is anachronistic, since the grace-giving signs of Jesus' time were not yet regarded as sacraments. Indeed, no objective effectiveness can be attributed to four sacraments, as it can be to the Eucharist and baptism, or even, to a certain extent, to penance, the effect of which is the remission of sins and a readmission of the penitent into communion with the Church. If Christ had uttered words to this effect, subsequent generations would certainly have appealed to them. Hence, it is most improbable that such sayings ever existed.

Rahner holds a similar position with regard to the institution of holy orders and its ritual transmission. Though it be true that ritual transmission through the imposition of hands had been practised, as Peter's and Paul's appointees to certain sees bear witness, the transmission of the office itself is not grace. The imposition of hands was also used in the penitential rite and even as a gesture of blessing between persons. Hypothetical assertions about 'lost' sayings are, therefore, not only improbable, but superfluous: imagining *dicta probantia* (hypothetical utterances) does not further theological reasoning.

Matrimony is the best illustration of the need for precision. Even the Council of Trent states cautiously that Paul's parallelism between marriage and Christ's relation to the Church (Ephesians 5:25ff) only 'suggests', 'hints at', a sacrament.[101] Furthermore, no patristic source of the first four centuries suggests the sacramental nature of marriage. They speak of matrimony's divine origin and of its holiness, even of the divine help needed in married life, of its illustrating the relationship between Christ and his Church, 'but none of this is an explicit assertion of the sacramentality of marriage'. Consequently there were no such assertions; the conclusion was rather laboriously *deduced* by using 'a conceptual apparatus' invented as one available to Paul (or the Pauline author of Ephesians). The conclusion had to be worked out through a historical process of doctrinal development and with the help of a premise that would sustain its correctness. Rahner's own premise is, of course, that the sacramental nature of the Church entails the institution of the seven sacraments. He speaks of the

> implicit institution of a sacrament through the explicit constituting of the Church as the historically visible form of

eschatologically victorious grace ... [for] the Church is the fundamental sacrament and ... the *opus operatum*: the radical self-expression and actualization of this Church.[102]

Rahner is now intent on reaching his own theory, one which is anticipated by the particular instance of matrimony. He does not hesitate to apply the same analysis to ministry, confirmation and the anointing of the sick.[103] Holy orders is treated thus: 'Jesus established a ministry in the Church, but no word of his concerning its sacramental nature has been handed down to us'. The rite, a sign of transmitting power, was well known before the time of Jesus, yet it was not regarded as a sacrament. Confirmation, indeed, is still with difficulty separated from baptism. It came about by the fact that the early Church administered Christian initiation with two rites, both of which were kept together: this is still the *praxis* of eastern Churches in which baptism is linked with confirmation, whereas a timelapse was introduced between them in the West. It is even more difficult to separate the two according to their respective effects. Whereas baptism confers the gift of the Spirit as well as receiving the subject into the bosom of the Church, confirmation seems to have the same effect; it emphasizes the same gift of the Spirit, and assigns a mission within the Church to the confirmed. The very same grace is effective though with a different emphasis.[104] The two are sacramental phases of one process of initiation. Note, however, that the distinction between the two originated, not from Christ, but from the Church, for 'the early Church was quite convinced that it was acting according to the mind of our Lord'. Christ's intention, therefore, was (to use a modern term) a kind of initiation into the community, while the decision to have two rites came from the Apostles. Their action was entirely legitimate: they acted on behalf of Christ and on their own authority.

The anointing of the sick as described by James (5:13-16) reflects the normal human behaviour of any believer. Prayer for the bodily and spiritual healing of the sick is certainly not a sign needing to be invented by Jesus as Healer. His promise that 'if you pray for anything *in my name*, it will be granted to you', was certainly not intended as the institution of a sacrament with its proper grace. Yet the prayer and accompanying anointing soon became regarded as a sacrament 'directly' instituted by Christ and the hypothesis that James was declaring openly what he had heard from the Lord earlier is superfluous. The text of course does not itself exclude the possibility of its being later understood as evidence for a sacrament, as indeed it was. How did this come about? Rahner's answer repeats the appeal to his premise, the sacramental nature of the Church. Is it not obvious, Rahner asks, that the situation which James describes is one in which the presence of the presbyter equates the prayer of faith with the prayer of the whole Church? That intervention alone allows us to regard the action of the praying and anointing community as a true sacrament, without proposing hypothetical words of Jesus.[105]

This last reflection on what used to be called extreme unction prompts Rahner to expand his theory in more detail. The situation which James describes links words (of prayer) and ritual actions together. If (a) this link is applied on behalf of an individual in a situation that is critical for his salvation, and if (b) the Church addresses this individual by engaging her whole character as a sign of God's eschatological victory in Christ, then the result is grace *ex opere operato*. Both conditions are required for true sacramental action. Rahner's concept of full engagement on the part of the Church is applicable to other sacraments and this concept is, I believe, the heart of his theory.

> When in baptism the Church receives a human being into her realm, when she reconciles him anew to herself and to God, when she celebrates the Eucharist as the highest actual fulfilment of her own being, and permits the individual to share in it, such actions are not merely actions of the Church, but really bring into actuality and functioning the very nature of the Church herself; her own self is involved totally and radically. Such activities share in the nature of the Church herself as the fundamental sacrament (*Ursakrament*).[106]

When the notion of Church as Sacrament has been stated, restated, expanded in different ways, illustrated, and argued with adversaries, Rahner can safely conclude that the dogmatic definition of Trent stands: Christ did institute all seven sacraments, immediately indeed, but through the mediation of the Church's very essence.[107]

❧

To sum up: in these last sections I have selected the most characteristic features of Roman Catholic sacramental theology and presented them in the context of Rahner's own approach. We have met the classical teaching, though with a Rahnerian twist. I shall again close with a remark of Karen Kilby taken from her presentation of the whole of Rahner's theology. There is an element of surprise in her treatment of the sacraments: although, she states, Rahner is most generous in claiming the real possibility of salvation for everyone, he also affirms that 'sacraments work *ex opere operato*' as visible signs which produce the grace of ultimate salvation. This view has always attracted the suspicion of being magic or salvation-automatism and seemed even more spurious when sacraments were regarded as the unique means of salvation. Kilby seems to expect from Rahner not the dialectics of 'on the one hand ... and on the other', but an 'either... or'. Should not Christ's triumphant grace and its universal presence be sufficient for salvation, rather than God's salvific will to save together with the use of sacraments? Rahner's choice, however, is to adhere to the traditional teaching of the Roman Church. He clearly appreciates the difficulties involved in explaining sacramental causality, the objective certainty of sacramental efficacy (*ex opere operato*), and the exact number seven.

> What makes him radical is that in trying to cope with these difficulties he is willing to rearrange radically many of his audience's ordinary ways of thinking. So the fixed points of Catholicism remain fixed, but the overall vision which emerges from Rahner's theology can be anything but familiar.[108]

This assessment remains true as we shall see when we address Rahner's treatment of each of the seven sacraments.

1.3 The Sevenfold Gift

Rahner's treatment of each of the seven sacraments is dispersed throughout various articles. Hitherto I have presented a general approach to *all* the sacraments in the 'Rahnerian' version and emphasized its conformity to the teaching of the Roman Catholic Church. The previous section imitated the sacramentology of the schoolbooks by offering a general treatment corresponding to their *De sacramentis in genere*. The discussion of each of the seven sacraments (*De sacramentis in specie*) usually followed. Whereas the first, general, approach clarified the idea of sacrament without regard to the existential circumstances of the individual person, the second specified the way in which each sacrament contributed to the sanctification of individual believers. Whereas the first laid down the principles according to which sacraments work, the second tried to define the specific effects of the single sacraments. Rahner must have had this general scheme in mind, one which was already prompted by Thomas Aquinas. Thomas, as we have seen, derived the word, sacrament, from 'sanctity' and dubbed its function as sanctification. Rahner, too, uses the same word though within his own general approach. For him the sacraments are strictly connected with the proto-sacrament, the Church. He writes:

> The Church in her function as an historical sign of victorious grace only attains fulfilment of her own nature when grace is victorious in an individual's sanctification.[109]

The sequence, however, in which Rahner will treat the seven sacraments and how he will envisage their coherence and divergence is not arbitrary. His basic premise makes it clear that each single sacrament inasmuch as it is a self-realization (or self-fulfilment) of the Church must resemble the others. This common quality is also evident in their effect, from the grace they impart, the scholastic *res sacramenti*, since it is that same grace which gives each sacrament its own special character.

Rahner's two works on the Church and sacraments (*Kirche55* and *Kirche61*) offer only incidental hints concerning the coherence of the seven sacraments. *Kirche55* uses the Bible in an attempt to envisage the genesis of the new community of the Church. His first consideration addresses the power with which the New Testament community (unlike the synagogue of old) is entrusted, namely the ability to forgive sins (a vague reference to penance?). This power of forgiveness, however, represents only the negative aspect of the new beginning. The essence of the new community becomes truly visible in the celebration of the Lord's Supper, the permanent celebration of which necessitates both new leaders and new members. The leaders seem to suggest a sacrament of holy orders and the members a sacrament of baptism. When the experience of Pentecost galvanizes this small community, they come to reflect that full membership entails not only the remission of sins but also the transmission of the Spirit. Is this realization perhaps the germ of the idea of confirmation? Much later, then, a similar reflection on marriage leads the Church community to realize that the union of man and woman is a powerful sign of Christ's love for the Church, and consequently carries an appropriate grace. Holy matrimony emerges as a state in which the Church herself is present in as much as marriage is the Church's 'self-realization' (or 'fulfilment'). Rahner offers a like hypothesis with regard to the anointing of the sick: the Church community is praying for members facing the danger of death; the rite of anointing by the presbyter guarantees that the sick person belongs forever to the one communion of the saved, even if death should ensue.[110]

However artificial this quasi-deduction seems, its intention is to show an historically based coherence of the seven: that there is no need to search for words of institution by Christ. Later in *Kirche61* Rahner summarizes the argument:

> Deductions of this kind are based on the actual nature of the Church. They are attempts to imitate and recapture insights into the Church's awareness of her own faith, something she gained throughout the course of her long history under the guidance of the Spirit.[111]

When, however, Rahner comes to treat of each of the sacraments he adopts another order. The two *Kirche* articles start with the Eucharist and baptism, whereas *Foundations* deals first with the sacraments of initiation (baptism and confirmation), then with the sacraments blessing a 'state of life' (*ordo*, marriage and penance). The Lord's Supper crowns them all, for it is the acme of the Church's sacramental self-realization.[112] Since both positions emphasize the paramount importance of the Eucharist, we begin by addressing Rahner's treatment of the Lord's Supper.

(A) *The Lord's Supper*

Rahner's contributions to the theology of the Eucharist are characterized by the three important features of his own approach to the sacraments; the emphasis is on the insights already made into the sacraments in general. The earlier *Kirche55* and *Kirche 61* stress the ecclesial elements in all the sacraments, including the Eucharist. Later, Rahner's preoccupation with the relationship between God's word and the sacraments modifies his treatment of the Eucharist. His 'revolutionary' approach to the sacraments forces him to re-evaluate the Lord's Supper in terms of its cosmic dimension. This threefold emphasis did not radically change, but rather enriched his teaching on the Eucharist. In addition to and parallel with these preoccupations, Rahner had to reflect on and reinterpret the Council of Trent, and in consequence some aspects of prior tradition including dogmatic-doctrinal statements together with eucharistic piety rooted in faith in the real presence of Our Lord within the sacrifice of the Mass.

Rahner does not immediately address the grace-imparting power of the Eucharist, but simply affirms that the first effect of the Eucharist is a 'more profound incorporation into the unity of the Body of Christ', that is, the Church.[113] The first effect of the sign (the rite of the Mass plus the bread and wine) is in the technical language of the scholastics *sacramentum et res*. It is not primarily the real presence of the Lord, but the incorporation of believers in Christ into the Church herself, into her unity and charity. Rahner here considers himself to be in good company; the *Didache*, Augustine, Thomas, as well as an early document of Pope Innocent III (1202 CE) have the same approach. All the different gifts offered to the communicant, the *res sacramenti,* depend on this sacramental mediation. He then takes a further step: the first effect of the words of consecration, the *anamnesis,* the recalling of Christ's command at the Last Supper, is not the real presence of the Lord, but the establishment of a Church in which the new covenant and Christ's sacrifice are present. By celebrating the Eucharist the Church becomes herself and is 'most clearly apparent in that she reaches the highest fulfilment of her own nature'.[114] All the essential and constitutive elements of the Church and her essential functions are encapsulated and made manifest. It is only on this presupposition that we can assert that Christ is really present in the eucharistic species. In other words, the Church, by celebrating the Eucharist, fulfils her own essential being; it is her main self-realization. Rahner, indeed, comes very near to the view that each eucharistic celebration constitutes the Church, and the whole Church, anew. If this be true, then it is also true that wherever the faithful participate in the Body and Blood of the Lord, the whole Church becomes present in that small congregation, reincarnate in the world.

An average Catholic education might lead to the conclusion that the real presence of Christ seems to be secondary in Rahner's account of the Lord's Supper, and that even though the real presence is presupposed and affirmed, it is nevertheless the establishment of the Church as the irrevocable presence of grace in the world which counts more, for this characteristic is the source of all other sacraments.

This impression, however, as we shall see, may well turn out to be false. Let us then turn to another aspect of the Eucharist, one based on the relationship between sacrament and the word of God. My section 1.2.1.C analysed *Word* (published in 1960) and there is a detailed study of *The Theology of the Symbol* (1959) in TI 4; both of these certainly guided him in the reinterpretation of the meaning of the real presence.

The first lengthy section of *Word* was as we have noted written with the Eucharist in mind. He starts his discourse with the real presence as an integral part of his teaching about the word of God: 'The Eucharist is "word", because the incarnate Logos of God is himself present in his substance ...'.[115] This statement is, however, an introduction only, for his interest is not primarily in the consecrated bread and wine, but in the whole mystery of Christ rendered present in the Mass. The *anamnesis* reminds the faithful (in Rahner's words) 'sacramentally' of the past, present and future of our salvation, that is, of Christ's death and resurrection, of his continued presence and his future coming. Hence

> the Eucharist is not only the major instance of those acts of self-realization [*Selbstvollzug*] of the Church which are called sacraments, it is too the real origin of all the other sacraments ... the Eucharist is in essence that word of God in the Church which supports and speaks all other words.[116]

If the Eucharist (and the whole action of the Mass) is the pre-eminent word of the Church, it follows that it relates, not only to the past and future, but also to the real presence of the Lord.

The consecrated species are the sacramental sign of this presence. A sign (that is, a 'real symbol') is not just the material element, but refers to all the elements of the eucharistic celebration including the words of *anamnesis*. Hence there is an inseparable unity between word and material element; both together are the signs of a real, but 'sacramental' existence:

> And thus the words of consecration remain as an element of the sacramental *sign* even 'after' the actual moment of consecration. [The material bread and wine as well as these words are needed] – both having the character of a sign and hence of a word – to form the one sign in this sacrament, through which he that is signified [can be] present.[117]

Rahner reasserts and extends this analysis by singling out an opinion attributed to Protestant theologians and condemned by the Council of Trent: it is false and heretical to say that the presence of the Lord in the Eucharist is not itself a reality, but that the presence depends on the faith of the individuals partaking in the rite. Rahner, too, of course would reject this view, but with modification. Yes, the Eucharist cannot fail to produce its effect without regard to the individual's faith and devotion, but this response in faith is required from the *whole community* of the faithful, since God's eucharistic word prompts and really effects that response. This is the sense in which we hold that the eucharistic word is conditioned by the faith of the whole Church; a reciprocal relationship between Word and faith is needed for the genesis of the Church and the Lord's presence. Rahner's emphasis on the faith of the *whole community* as a pre-condition for the celebration of the Lord's supper reinterprets Protestant (though probably not Luther's) teaching that access to the real presence is *'in usu tantum'* (only by usage).[118] The human face of the Church is not at issue; the appeal is to the faith of a Church which is 'the efficaciously predestined community of those embraced by the grace of God'. Rahner's conclusion, therefore, although it concentrates on the emergence of the Church, is a firm assertion of the Lord's real presence in the Eucharist:

> We have therefore a perfect right to say that the Lord is present in the essential word of the Church, that he is heard and believed in the Church. The Church herself is the word which proclaims the death of the Lord till he comes again: and with him redemption is present, as something granted to mankind absolutely and definitively, though the individual as such must still work out his salvation with fear and trembling.[119]

Sacraments are, indeed, about the individual person who 'must still work out his salvation with fear and trembling'. If this be so, what does an individual gain by reception of the sacraments, and in particular from the Lord's presence at the Lord's Supper? Rahner's answer to this question can, it seems to me, best be found by employing another characteristic of his approach to the sacraments. See his *Tablet* articles on secular life and the sacraments (in *Revolution* (1971) which renders part of *Active Role*).

In those articles Rahner states that grace is fundamental to our secular life and that humankind is already objectively redeemed by the event that is Jesus the Christ. This statement is universally valid. A sacrament is the precise means whereby this universal 'engracement' is offered to individual persons. It is through this

> small sign, which reminds *us* of the limitless presence of divine grace, that *this particular* kind of anamnesis and no other is constituted as an event in grace.[120]

The great memorable event of our redemption actualizes itself in this 'small' particular event in the life of an individual. We participate again in the awe-inspiring liturgy of the world and in the benefits of the grace resulting therefrom: each small community and each individual sharing in the celebration of the Lord's Supper.

Rahner here reasserts with high rhetoric the possibility of an experience of grace, with, perhaps, this difference: that the experience is now extended to include 'an experience of the grace of the world', the grace latent in secular history through which mankind 'senses the groaning of all creatures and their world, its demand for a more hopeful future'.[121] This experience includes that of Jesus Christ who lived our life and identified himself with humanity. He shared our human destiny, and the Mass invites the community which remembers this great truth to share his life.

A person attends Mass therefore, not to re-enact the bloody sacrifice of the Cross, but to 'allow something which is already alive in his heart to come out and proclaim itself'. Of course *anamnesis* entails not only the community's, but also the individual's assent to the self-offering of the Church.[122] Whoever goes to Mass offers up the whole world under the species of bread and wine, 'in the knowledge that the world is already continually offering itself up to the God beyond our understanding in its own proper way, namely the ecstasy of its joy and the bitterness of its sorrow' (ibid). The participant as a member of the community proclaims the death of the Lord 'inasmuch as this death, undergone once on our behalf, lives on in the world ... and is truly re-enacted in that mankind, whether or not it knows this explicitly, dies in the Lord' (ibid.). Each participant in the community liturgy proclaims the coming of the Lord, 'because the Lord is already accomplishing his coming'. When the communicant receives the real body of Christ he is in communion with '*that* body of God which is the world itself with its destiny'. Without that second communion, the first would be meaningless. Rahner has in mind 'two' bodies, that of the Logos and that of the world, and the communicant must be in communion with both, or his or her presence at the Mass has failed in its intention.[123] The cultic action of the Mass demands such an experience, lest it become a magic ritual at which the Church should forbid the reception of the sacrament. Rahner's own formulation is: 'to receive the sacrament without faith *that is without a belief experience*[124] seems to be the disposition which Paul rejects as a profanation 'of the body and blood of the Lord' (1 Cor. 11:27).

Roman Catholic tradition could raise a serious objection to Rahner's position as outlined above. By overemphasizing the 'belief experience of faith' in the reception of Eucharist he assigns two different objects of that faith: first, the body of Christ on the altar; and faith in an individual's belonging to the 'body of the world' already truly saved. Are both these objects necessary for valid participation in the Eucharist?

Rahner himself admits a similar difficulty putting an objection against his own view. What if somebody said 'is it only at Mass that [one] receives the Body of the Lord *really and substantially*'? Rahner's rejoinder is (to my mind) characteristic of his 'revolutionary' approach to the Eucharist: if the Mass were the exclusive contact with Christ's body, then some of those attending Mass might find themselves in the position of Judas and sitting near to the Lord at the Last Supper. Although Judas may have believed in Christ's presence at the Supper, he did not believe that the Lord's coming had already encountered the desire of the whole world. The Lord is truly amongst us *before his sacramental manifestation* in the Eucharist.[125]

Although the answer acknowledges the real and substantial presence of the Lord in the eucharistic meal, it equivalates it with belief in the objective salvation of the whole world. Indeed, Rahner affirms the harmony of these two theological truths:

> that of the grace which always already present and effective from within [the redeemed world] and that of the sacramental sign as posited from without [that is in the sacred rite] at a particular point in time. Any theology ... is faced with the task of showing that such harmony exists.[126]

Does that mean that Rahner proposes faith in the (already redeemed) 'body of the world' as the condition of our faith in the Lord's presence in the Eucharist; or is it rather the contrary: belief in the eucharistic presence is the condition of the belief in the objective redemption of mankind?

The Sacramental Life of the Church 49

Rahner's teaching on the harmony that exists between the 'redeemed body of the world' and the 'real presence' seems to fit in with his so-called 'Copernican revolution' concerning sacramental theology. Strangely, the (more or less systematic) *Foundations* contains hardly an echo of it; he chiefly stresses the scriptural background to the real presence and to the ritual re-presentation of Christ's sacrifice. Christ's bodily presence is, however, always regarded as part of a meal within which the body and blood of Jesus Christ is really food, not only for the individual, but, and much more, for the whole society that is the Church,[127] the insight that guides his interpretation of the Tridentine dogma concerning the real presence.

A lecture given by Rahner in 1959 in the presence of Protestant (mainly Lutheran) theologians presented his ecumenical audience with a detailed *and* critical analysis of Trent's doctrine on the real presence. Though it is not our task to repeat the substance, it is worth noting that he finds it difficult to summarise exactly what is explicit dogma binding for all Catholics and what is just theological opinion appearing perforce in the texts of the Magisterium. These texts are anything but lucid and simple statements of mandatory faith. The reason is:

> A new age, a new historical situation, can make a doctrinal proposition seem clearer or more obscure *quoad nos*, by the simple fact that it inserts it into a new context of knowledge – even when one was clear about how it was earlier understood.[128]

It is understandable that a lecturer with irenic intention towards a Lutheran audience could feel ill at ease in speaking about the real presence, and the way in which it was overemphasized in post-Tridentine praxis. Rahner had referred in passing to the whittled down individualistic approach to the Eucharist, elsewhere:

> It needs ... to be stressed repeatedly that the Mass ought not be understood by the faithful (The danger is far from remote.) as merely the production of Christ's real presence, as if the Eucharist were merely for the purpose of producing holy

communion. This individualistic narrowness must not be tolerated because it mutilates the faith, if not in theory, at least in practice.[129]

Post-Tridentine theology and *praxis* teaches that the first and foremost truth about the Eucharist is the affirmation of Christ's real presence, not that it is the sacramental representation of Christ's sacrifice for the life of the world. Rahner expresses the dilemma in these words: 'It is not because Christ is present that we offer him as our sacrifice, but the other way round.' He is really present because we remember him and share in his sacrifice at Mass.[130] This reversal of the relationship between important truths is but one of the 'obscurities' he finds in post-Tridentine tradition. There are others which need correction.[131] Firstly, the truth about the real presence needs to be stated in the context of another, more comprehensive truth:

> It is, for instance, the clear perception of average popular piety that, though the reality of the presence is not in doubt, the reception of the body of Christ remains only *res et sacramentum*. This belief replaces something that is essentially higher and more comprehensive, [namely] the union with Christ which takes place in grace and faith and love.[132]

To put it another way: salvific union with Christ (justification) is not exclusively bound to the eucharistic meal. It may *precede* our actual participation in the Lord's Supper. This statement will be significant also in the case of other sacraments.

Secondly, Rahner would like to throw light on the understanding of the word *transubstantiation*. Granted that it is difficult to change this consecrated term, by means of which the Council, following almost immemorial tradition, expressed the revealed truth of the real presence. This dogmatic statement binds us to believe that in receiving the consecrated species we do not consume bread and wine, but the body and blood of Christ under the mere appearances of bread and wine.

Modern natural science provides an odd context in which to speak of the *substance* of bread; we understand bread as a conglomerate of several substances. The notion of substance and accident or species is borrowed from Aristotelian metaphysics, a knowledge of which is hardly contemporary. If then we take this word as the sole explanation compatible with the wording of the dogma, we must hold either that the Church has defined Aristotelian metaphysics along with the real presence, or that we are free to express the same truth with another word more apt to the mentality of our contemporaries.

Rahner and most of his fellow-theologians exclude the first a priori. The alternative is equally precluded by Pius XII's encyclical *Humani Generis:* to alter the old term may impair its meaning.[133] A suggestion that may help to overcome the difficulty with 'transubstantiation' is not to employ the medieval understanding of substance,[134] but to use the term for the cluster of substances which constitute bread and wine. If all these 'clusters' can be commonly understood as bread or wine, why can we not speak of the transformation as if they were one substance taken over by the body of Christ? Their dissolution, too, could signal the cessation of Christ's sacramental presence. One wonders, however, whether this solution would be acceptable to modern men and women. Since the councils (apparently) refuse to tie themselves down to any particular philosophy, and ignore food-chemistry, Rahner tries another ploy. He introduces a conceptual distinction, valid not only for the Eucharist, but for any dogmatic statement of the Church. He supposes that the wording of dogmas which define revealed truths differs from the wording of the Bible. The dogmatic statements concerning the Eucharist explain and interpret correctly the faith of the apostles present at the Last Supper; when Christ gives his apostles a piece of bread and says that this is his body, the twelve are not eating a piece of bread, but the body of Christ. Of course, this simple faith can be expressed in several different forms. The councils have chosen one of these and dogmatized it.

In formulating a dogma there are two possibilities according to Rahner:[135] it is either an 'ontic' or a 'logical' statement in explanation of faith. It is the second, the logical one, that Rahner makes his own, it explains revealed fact without appealing to other, subsidiary, truths. The formulation may use terms commonly understood at the time of the definition. It can be supposed that 'transubstantiation' is such a term, one that was common at one time. Although it may depend on a settled philosophical vocabulary, its use is only meaningful in so far as it refers back to the reality found in the Bible. If this reference is lacking, the term employed can be true or false. The truth of the dogmatic proposition consists in this reference. Just as Christological definitions were formulated in the philosophical terms of the period, so too was 'transubstantiation'. In both cases the term (or terms) chosen establish these references safely – the Greek *ousia* of Nicea and the *physis* of Chalcedon were terms expressing the divinity and humanity of Christ. 'Substance' and 'species' express the change of bread and wine into the body and blood of the Redeemer. Both are 'logical' explanations of revealed fact.

The alternative 'ontic' explanation creates its own context; it transfers the content of faith into a different category of truth (or system) from that of revelation. It speculates about the origin of the revealed fact, and it explains its genesis and present meaning. Accordingly, it makes statements about the faith as dependent on *something other* than the words of revelation and by means of this 'ontic' methodology tries to render faith more intelligible, and exclude misunderstandings. In doing this, however, it restricts the word of God to one form of language within which the mystery of the dogma is translated into verbally clear-cut truth, for those, at least, who accept that approach. The dogma of the real presence is not an 'ontic', but a 'logical' explanation.

The significance of this Rahnerian distinction for theological thinking as a whole is that the character of revealed truth as a mystery can be approached only, as Rahner often says, in an 'asymptotic' way. In addressing Lutheran theologians, whose various schools display some plurality in their theological thinking, Rahner must have presupposed a like plurality in Roman Catholic faculties. He concludes:

> The difference between Catholic and Protestant theology seems to me to be this – an essential difference, to be sure – that the logical explanation of the words of Scripture by the Church can become a definite truth of faith for the Catholic theologian, whereas as matter of principle it remains theology for the Protestant theologian, and is always subject to revision.[136]

This subtle distinction is surely important today for ecumenical dialogue and too for contemporary ecclesiology. The difference between the two denominations is not so much in their respective understanding of faith in the real presence, but rather in the underlying concept of the Church. In interpreting the dogma of Trent, Rahner assumes that there were other terms that could have expressed the same belief. 'Transfinalization', 'transsignification' and even Rahner's own 'real symbol' could have, perhaps, been used for the very same faith. In view, however, of the variety of widely divergent terminology among Protestant theologians, the Church has decided on transubstantiation; it is, therefore our Catholic duty to use this term as an expression of *dogmatic* truth. If history has produced martyrs who were ready to die for this truth, their death was for the integrity of Catholic teaching and not for the term itself. For to believe that in the Eucharist bread and wine are the body and blood of Christ is, in Rahner's view, tantamount to 'belief in the Church'.

(B) *The Sacrament of Ordination*

Rahner's introduction to a sermon on the occasion of the first Mass of a newly ordained priest reads as follows:

> As the people redeemed in Jesus Christ, we offer the sacrifice of the new covenant on the altars of our Church ... For there is no greater deed than this, and there is no way in which its value can really be increased: the Lord of ages becomes present in our midst – He who is the heart of the world, and whose act of love moves the stars and takes up everything with Him into the glory of God.[137]

It is surprising that Rahner in the bold rhetoric of this *Primizfest* homily does not first mention the person of the newly ordained priest, but rather the people of God who offer the sacrifice of the New Covenant in which 'all earthly reality sees itself accepted before the infinite majesty of God' (ibid). The priest seems to be just one member of that people: he is not detached from the rest. He is nevertheless the one who is, on behalf of others, able to speak the words of consecration over the bread and wine.

In my analysis of Rahner's concept of the Church in volume 5[138] I could not avoid a reference to the sacred ministry, the concept of which implies also the genesis of those 'organs' that perform the functions of the Church. One of these functions is the ministry of the people of God. In Rahner's approach to the ministry, however, each and every member of the Church shares in this function: all the baptized belong to the universal priesthood that constitutes the visible Church, the 'proto-sacrament'. The priesthood of each single man and woman is the starting point from which one should try to understand the special gift given to those who are entrusted with the dispensing of God's mysteries. This extra quality can only be explained by the sacrament of ordination. Rahner's task is, therefore, to establish the 'sacramentality' of the priesthood over and above the general priesthood of the faithful.

It is not easy to determine Rahner's strategy for this. Had he continued with the insight of *Revolution* or of *Active Role*, in which he tried to explain sacraments as rites meeting human need, he could have stated simply that the Church, in common with any other society, needs to appoint functionaries within the assembly. These functionaries are the priests, and the visible, sacramental sign of their office is their commission by a higher authority. Rahner is, however, aware that this simple solution would only work if the Church were a mere human association, a sort of 'chess club', as he was wont to say. The sacraments, as such, are not altogether open to sociological treatment, since they belong to the sacred sphere, that of sanctification by grace.

In order to establish priestly ordination as a sacrament Rahner tries to apply the traditional requirements of all sacraments. Ordination, therefore, should be sacred sign conferring a corresponding grace in a objective sense (*ex opere operato*). Commissioning by higher authority cannot be the special sign that singles out an individual to the specific office of the priesthood, since those not ordained can also be commissioned to perform ecclesial or even ritual tasks. The transmission of an office, by itself, is not the same as conferring grace. Nor can the imposition of hands be such a sign, since it is used as a general symbol of forgiveness, of blessing, and of other religious encounters. Rahner does not even mention the tendering of the chalice and other instruments used in the celebration of the Mass as possible signs of sacramental ordination: those traditional signs now abandoned even within the liturgy of the Church.

The traditional way of retaining the triad in the analysis of the sacraments used to assign the *character indelebilis* resulting from ordination as the specific mark of the priesthood. It was regarded as its *sacramentum et res* which was supposed to confer on the ordained a quasi-ontological change. As I have shown in volume 5, Rahner has often expressed his doubts about this theory; for him the *character indelebilis* meant nothing more than the fact that priestly ordination cannot be repeated.[139] Nonetheless it may have been this conclusion that turned his attention to the third of the medieval triad: he sought the specific characteristic of ordination in the quality of priestly existence as something basically different from the life of those not ordained. In medieval terms, of course, it would be the *res tantum*, the ultimate result of the grace of ordination. The quality specific to priestly existence is nothing else but the holiness proper to the ordained.

Kirche61 presupposed that this holiness of priestly existence should be understood in terms of the holiness of the Church. This view is implied in Rahner's first premise according to which the Church 'actualizes' herself in preaching the Word of God and in administering the sacraments: if the Church is herself holy, and if she exists in her functions, the functionary should also share in this holiness. This does *not* mean that the priest preaching the Word of God must not express his personal spirituality. Neither does it mean that in administering the sacraments he must be the sole proper leader of any congregation, for unordained members of God's priestly people can be, and are, entrusted with similar tasks. Personal piety and sound spirituality cannot be the exclusive privilege of priests. There are, indeed, priests who excel in fulfilling the requirements of their office, yet clearly lack personal holiness. Nonetheless, the Church is not indifferent to the personal holiness of those ordained: it is, after all, the grace of this priestly holiness that is ultimately granted by the sacrament of ordination.

What then does the 'holiness' of an ordained minister actually mean? Following his basic insight that the sacraments are 'self-realizations' of the Church, Rahner first defines the 'holiness' of the Church herself:

> [The holiness of] holy Church ... can therefore only consist in the personal holiness of her members. If all were sinners who had fallen away from the grace of God, holy Church herself would not longer exist.[140]

If, however, we believe God's promise that this could never happen, we should trust that he sanctifies at least some members of his Church through efficacious grace. The same applies to the sacrament of holy order: 'a ministry impious throughout its exercise and a holy Church are incompatibles' (ibid). Accordingly, one could assume that this special holiness of the whole Church is imparted by ordination to the priesthood, without implying, of course, that each and every minister must be in the state of grace.

> It is not the efficacy of the actual administration of a single sacrament that depends on its minister's being in the state of grace, but the *perpetuation of sacraments in the Church as a whole and in the long run*.[141]

The very existence of the sacramental system is in some sense dependent on the holiness of (some) priests: 'for one who proclaims the word of God but not his own faith could not be a witness to that word unless he himself believes in it and lives by it'.[142] This sentence seems to imply that both holiness and living witness are enabled by the special grace of the sacrament of ordination. Although ministry and holiness are conceptually distinct, they are joined in the moment of exercise.

In technical terms the valid transmission of the priestly office is of objective value (*ex opere operato*), whereas the special grace of the priesthood, at least in its kernel, is conferred in accord with the subjective personal disposition of the ordained (*ex opere operantis*). Priestly existence is therefore the interplay between the authority of office received by ordination and the obligatory call to personal holiness. Rahner speaks elsewhere somewhat paradoxically about the renewal of ordination: 'the renewal of ordination is not indeed an *opus operatum*, but it is truly an *opus operantis Dei et hominis ex opere operato*'.[143] This play with words allows the human contribution (*hominis*) to refer either to the higher authority transmitting an office, or to the personal disposition of the recipient. It is the speciality of ordination that it connects the objective effect (*ex opere operato*), the power of the office, with the subjective piety (*ex opere operantis*) of the ordained priest.

In another contribution, which I shall discuss presently, Rahner returns to this coherence between the objective (*ex opere operato*) and subjective (*ex opere operantis*) aspects of priestly ordination and, indeed, of each and every sacrament. First of all, as he states in general: 'it is impossible that there be *valid* signs of the reality of salvation and of God's saving activity which touch no inner reality'.[144] God's salvific action through signs *must* in some way *affect* in some way the spiritual life of the priest. This is valid for all the sacraments, since 'the grace-giving action of God and man's reception of grace in faith and love, though they do not belong to the constitutive elements of the sacramental rite, essentially belong to the sacrament'.[145] Obviously the twofold use of the same verb 'belong' masks slightly different meanings: the first should be the 'kernel of grace' (my own coinage) conferred objectively, whereas its repetition migh denote the 'fruit' of that first conferral. This latter is at least partly due to the subjective piety of the recipient. If, however, this subjective contribution *essentially* 'belongs' to the sacrament it cannot be something additional. What Rahner must have in mind is the teaching of the Council of Trent: the reception of the sacraments requires some co-operation on the part of the recipient: 'those who place no obstacle' (*non ponunt obicem*), must refer to the recipient.[146] Another reference, this time to Trent's decree on justification, according to which the 'engracing' effect of the sacraments (called by me the 'kernel of grace') is implanted ('infused') in the recipient 'in view of each ones dispositions and cooperation'[147] enables Rahner to connect the subjective aspect with the objective, (*opus operatum*):

> ... there can be no competition in the spiritual life between the *opus operatum* and the *opus operantis*. Not only because the *opus operatum* demands in some measure the *opus operantis*, if the sacrament is to be in any way fruitful. But because the *opus operantis* reaches its proper climax in the *opus operatum*, i.e. its climax of outward, corporeal expression which corresponds to its proper and given nature.[148]

Leaving aside the technicalities of traditional discourse, however, Rahner's argument for the exclusive particularity of priestly ordination is not convincing. That obligatory holiness of the priest that shares the holiness of the Church may well be the fruit of ordination, but as such it is extra-sacramental. Any lay person who, by the grace of God, reaches that state which seems to be essential to the sacramental system of the Church, can substitute for the holiness of the ordained priest. To establish the 'sacramentality' of the priesthood, therefore, he has to explore other avenues. He will use the traditional connection between the Eucharist and priestly ordination, in particular: the essence of priestly ordination is not so much the exclusive power of the priest in consecrating bread and wine, but rather his priest's role in offering the *sacrifice* of Christ in the Mass is the speciality of priestly ordination.

> To argue, by the way, that the holiness of priestly existence essentially belongs to this sacrament, can leave one exposed to the error of the Donatists, John Wycliff and Jan Hus, who seem to have made holiness the condition of *validity* in administration of the sacraments: an 'unholy Priest' cannot validly consecrate the Eucharistic species, cannot absolve penitents, and so on. Rahner avoids this conclusion by emphasising that the holiness of the priest is not a constitutive part of the sacrament but rather its fruit. Asserting, however that this fruit of ordination is essential to the priesthood introduces some ambiguity into Rahner's position. An ordinand can validly receive the ministry as an office, he can validly administer the other sacraments, but if he is not in the state of grace, his ordination cannot be 'fruitful', that is, the grace special to the priesthood is lacking. How is then holiness *essential* to the sacrament of ordination?

In 1950 Rahner wrote a booklet, published in 1950, on the frequency of daily Masses celebrated by many priests, often in one place. It is derived from his earlier article published in ZKT, 1949, entitled 'The Many Masses and the One Sarifice'. The booklet eventually was published in English.[149] Rahner does something very similar therein by attributing the apparently subjective effect to an objective process.

In that pre-Vatican II situation *Celebration* had an almost explosive effect. Despite its complex Rahnerian style with all the technicalities of scholastic theology, it had a practical intention. It questioned the value of the frequency of Masses celebrated by priests who, very often, side by side at many side-altars, offered the one and unique sacrifice of Christ. Each Mass was obviously neither the repetition nor an increase of the infinite value of Christ's death on the Cross. What then was the value of such multiplicity of celebrations?[150]

This main question of *Celebration*, however, is not our present interest. I shall consider first his concept of the Mass as a *sacrifice*, and then the special role of the priest presiding over the liturgy of the Church representing our Lord's sacrifice on the Cross: does this role confer on the ordained minister some benefit particular to his priesthood?

In order to explain that the Mass is a sacrifice, which is Rahner's dogmatic presupposition, he has to state first how far the Cross of Christ can be called a sacrifice. Here he seems to anticipate the structural analysis of his sacramental theology: the Cross is a sacrifice consisting of two main elements, that is, the *exterior* suffering and death as a real symbol (*Realsymbol!*) and the *interior* will of self-offering. Neither of these two alone could be called a sacrifice: the sign (suffering and death) can be taken for a sacrifice, *because* it expresses voluntary self-offering and, conversely, that voluntary self-offering is a sacrifice insofar as it is manifested on the Cross. The exterior and interior elements in their unity and distinction are in different timescales: the one at a fixed point in history and the other outside ordinary time. A further quality is needed, however, without which the sacrifice of the Cross cannot enter the realm of the cultic and sacral. This quality is manifest in God's acceptance of the Cross as a sacrifice through Christ's resurrection from the dead. Rahner can, therefore, in parallelism with Old Testament sacrifices state:

> Since God himself promises possibilities of acceptance and produces them (by establishing a *priesthood*, and laws regarding worship), the offering of a sacrifice is itself grace. Even though the offering itself is a human action, it remains God's instutition.[151]

In the case of Jesus the resurrection belongs esentially to the notion of the sacrifice and his priesthood is implied therein.

In order to regard the Mass as a sacrifice we must assume a visible sign of offering, one that symbolizes an invisible reality granted by God alone. Although it obeys the command of Christ, the visible sign of offering is a human action of the Church *representing* Christ's sacrifice on the Cross. An appeal to the reality of Christ's presence under the species is insufficient to support the truth of this. The primary function of the Mass is *not* the consecration of bread and wine, but the sacramental representation of Christ's sacrifice on the cross. Because the Mass is a sacrifice, it is within this that the real presence of Christ is made available.[152] The double consecration (bread and wine to body and blood) symbolizes Christ's death on the Cross and makes him present under the sacramental signs as *Christus passus*.[153] The agent in the mass is, however, the Church that in re-enacting the sacrifice of the cross offers him to the Father for the salvation of mankind. In the sacrifice of the Mass these two different actions are brought into unity.

> Christ's visible act of sacrifice on the cross and the sacrificial offering, which occurs in the Mass are two different events, even so the sacrificial *victim* is the same.[154]

In other words, the Mass, the visible representation of the Cross, is a sacrament of the Church and, as such, a source of sacramental grace that is (or rather should be) an essential interior act my means of which the participating congregation assents 'to the movement of Christ's loving obedience to the Father'.[155]

This latter effect of the Mass as a sacrament, of course, does not belong to its objective validity; it is, nevertheless, as Rahner puts it, 'existentially' inseparable from its celebration. This indeed is the fruit of the Eucharist.[156] The Mass is, therefore, an 'engraced' human act of *Holy* Church as a corporate entity and, as was pointed out above, the holiness of the Church is dependent on the subjective sanctity of her members. This is true also of the priest who actually presides at the celebration. He, along with the other participants in a priestly people, is a 'co-offerer' of the Crucified Christ to the Father. Should their common contribution in faith and love cease *altogether*, the celebration of Mass would no longer be valid.

What then is the particular contribution of the priest to the sacrifice/sacrament of the Mass? According to Rahner it would be false to argue that it depends on the measure of grace enabling the priest's active participation in offering the sacrifice of Christ. It used to be held that a special fruit, a *fructus specialissimus*, is bestowed on the priest celebrating Mass by means of which his contribution is different from the rest of the congregation: whereas the participation of the faithful is based on the character of baptism, the priest, owing to his higher function, acts through the character of his ordination. Rahner rejects this argument in that the Mass is an act of the Church that has primarily the same general effect within any particular Eucharistic assembly, and that, therefore:

> All the forms of participation ... are essentially the same: everyone's readiness to allow the fruits of the sacrifice of the Cross to be bestowed on them by the Mass, a willingness which is carried into effect by taking part of the Mass.[157]

The celebrating priest receives grace in the same manner (and 'measure') as the faithful present; the grace received is not particular to the priestly office. The effect of Christ's sacrifice, is applied to the whole congregation, as one particular unit of the universal Church.

Secondly, even if the 'character of the priesthood' implies the exclusive power to consecrate the Eucharist species, that consecration alone would not be a meaningful celebration of the *sacrifice* of the Mass, 'of which the participation of the faithful (if only potential) is a part' (ibid. p. 58=71). The priest acts in the *service* of the Church and of his actual congregation, but the benefit of his action is on the same level as that of the other participants.

Nonetheless Rahner does maintain a difference between these two contributions. Remember: in arguing the sacrificial character of the Cross he emphasized that, as well as the visible act of suffering and death and Christ's permanent sacrificial attitude, there is a third aspect that makes the Cross a complete sacrifice. This aspect is the *acceptance* by the Father. If the Mass is the representation of the Cross and accepted as a sacrifice (resurrection), the validity of the Mass as a sacrifice depends on this acceptance. Note, however, this validity is *not* that of the consecration of the species, but of the whole liturgical action of the Mass. The priest's contribution is to guarantee the validity of the sacrifice. His function

> consists in the fact that the priest alone offers the sacrifice in the sense which makes the Mass *possible and valid* as sacrifice, though without detriment to the fact that all baptized truly cooperate in offering the sacrifice. In virtue of the *potestas offerendi* which belongs to the priest alone, the priest determines the *sacramental validity* of the liturgical oblation.[158]

The priest is, therefore, the guarantor that the Mass is indeed a sacrifice and this fact does not require any special grace, a *fructus specialissimus*, for the celebrant. Neither does it raise him above the rest of his congregation. Rahner's conclusion is therefore:

> the visible service of the official celebrating priest guarantees the Church's sacrifice of the Mass to be the *accepted sacrifice* of Christ ... [yet] The service of the priest is only one function within the celebration of the sacrifice which the whole Church must offer. He therefore does not obtain a benefit of an essentially different manner from any other participant.[159]

(C) *Initiation in the Spirit: Baptism and Confirmation*

The rite of Baptism is often used as a pattern for the theology of the rest of the sacraments. Although Rahner sees danger in this traditional approach, he begins *Sevenfold* with a meditation on baptism as a precondition of the possibility of man's whole sacramental life. He finds the verification of his own characteristic sacramental theology in the rite of incorporation into Christianity.

Kirche61 offers a short summary of the theology of baptism. The priest (or whoever administers this sacrament) ritually accepts a new member on behalf of the Church, and the whole Church is made present within a particular community. To use 'Rahnerese', the Church as 'the consecrated and socially organized people of God 'actualizes' herself by accepting a new member, for, the Church exists in time and space in the lives of her members. Without them she ceases to be what she really is. Consequently Rahner regards this act of incorporation into the Church to be the *'res et sacramentum'* (to use a technical term) by virtue of which the newly baptized transcend their previously held convictions and adhere to the Church's beliefs and way of life. The full effects of redemption can be experienced only *as a member of the Church.*

> The subject of redemption to which God's mercy is addressed is in the first place always the people, the nations, the Church as the partner in the covenant (which the individual as such cannot be), and the individual only shares in grace as a member of such a people of promise.[160]

The effect of baptism seems clear, therefore: the common good of all Christian denominations. A theologian, however, cannot refrain from raising certain pertinent questions concerning baptismal tradition. The first of these concerns the notion of baptismal character, the *signum spirituale et indelebile,*[161] which was regarded as the *res et sacramentum*. *Kirche61* had already broached the topic. The original meaning of 'signum' was the sign identifying a soldier belonging to the Roman army; this was adapted by Augustine as 'the enduring unique identity of the baptized, produced by a sacramental and historical event.[162] This identity is a particular status within the Church: it is not something visible, but is similar to the spiritual character of a ministry, or the dignity inherent in sharing the royal priesthood of Christ. It is a relationship which cannot be lost, not even by heresy, schism and (as increasingly happens) by 'leaving the Church'. An unbaptized person, even if he is justified, lacks this special relationship.

An essay of Rahner's published much later puts another question regarding baptismal theology on behalf of his contemporaries:

> why does baptism, and even baptism of infants exist, when we know, or at least hope, that God leads to eternal salvation every person of good will, hence also non-Christians, 'heathens' and even atheists (if they obey the voice of conscience).[163]

The difficulty emerges from Rahner's belief that no human being is ever excluded from God's offer of grace, and accordingly 'divine life lives in their innermost heart'. By its very nature, however, this unseen offer of grace longs to manifest itself, and needs to be expressed in a clear gesture like love between two persons. He is returning here to the basic concept of sacrament, for sacraments incorporate the grace of the Holy Spirit and make Christ's eschatological redemption present.

That Catholic tradition in the West is wedded to the notion of sacramental causality is the source of another problem connected with the previous one. According to this, it would be inadequate to regard baptism as just the disclosure, the manifestation of a reality already imparted. For Rahner, who holds that in our present situation God's justifying grace is offered and, in a way, already granted to every man and woman, it is difficult to explain how this causality works. Nonetheless Rahner's sacramental theology remains convinced that the outward manifestation by sign is a case of real causation: it must *become* an historical reality through some visible expression. This 'becoming' can also be interpreted as an effect due to a cause. This insight, I believe, is the origin of Rahner's symbolic causality.

The last difficulty, and one that is problematic for many contemporary Christians is the practice of infant baptism. Their objection to the practice is patent: it is a protest on behalf of a newly born infant who is not yet able to choose and decide what to believe, a protest in the name of freedom. For free decisions should be postponed to the age of reason.

Rahner's answer to this 'protest' is easy to foresee: he will defend the age-old practice of the Church, even though he allows that a Christian's obligation to baptise children is less certain than the obligation to baptise adults.[164] Baptism is not a matter for the child's personal decision. Just as no one can decide whether or not to be born, so God's purpose for the individual is beyond choosing. God's love in Christ always precedes our free decision; we are in fact already redeemed before we know and accept that redemption. Characteristically Rahner regards human freedom as something 'responsive'; 'it is always and unquestionably a reaction to something we have not chosen; it is not merely creative in an empty space.'[165]

Perhaps the insistence on the passive quality of 'responsive freedom' is exaggerated. Another emphasis, however, may serve to qualify it: to have been baptized as an infant is not so much a state, as the start of a process, for 'the baptism of children attains its full meaning and purpose only in adults'. It is 'ratified' throughout life. Responsive freedom is not merely passive: it lives, grows or diminishes, increases or decreases in our adult life. It follows that the renewal of baptismal vows is always to be desired.

Sevenfold, a sermon on the occasion of the baptism of a child, follows the same trend of thought with appropriate rhetoric. God is about to invite the new born baby into the number of the saved and

> we can believe that here where the grace of God is invoked over this child, our appeal does not remain unheard but is accepted and answered.[166]

Baptism is a twofold event. On the one hand, God's eternal purpose of love inserts itself into human history, and his Holy Spirit becomes really accessible in the Church 'of those who acknowledge Jesus Christ crucified and restored to life', and of those too in whom God has revealed himself as the one Lord who will come again to meet us at the end of the time. Put another way: the baptism of a human being enables the Church to proceed, though with infinitesimal small steps, towards her own self-fulfilment. On the other hand, baptism admits a human being into this history which is also the history of God himself. He or she becomes a member of holy Church which is the historical expression of God's saving purpose, the embodiment of his grace. At the very beginning of our lives we become sharers in the grace and righteousness of the Holy Spirit. The newly baptized receive God's sanctifying grace.[167]

Rahner becomes rhetorical in explaining the twofold nature of baptism to those present at baptism. He expounds the whole sense of the purpose of human existence. Man is a mystery to himself, because his pilgrimage is never ending. Everything we can achieve remains potential, provisional and temporary yet our longing suggests the presence of an eternal future fulfilment. Our quest implies that '... we are infinite potentialities, because we are called to an infinite perfection'; we know that our entire unending journey cannot end in a void; ' there is always a promise of a perfect end'. These figurative words anticipate Rahner's eschatology: 'we believe that all longing lives by the promise of truth, and no darkness or void could be recognised as such, unless somewhere there existed never-ending light'. Light and perfection are *already* present in our present existential situation; our fulfilment is not only in the future, it is *already* here,

> ... but still hidden, believed in, but not yet enjoyed. The future is *already* here, the life of God is *already* within us, the Holy Spirit is *already* poured out upon us, and we are *already* sons of God, so that now we need only to receive the revelation of what we already are.[168]

Sanctifying grace is not only the future fulfilment of our innermost desire, for our faith declares it as an eschatological reality, an *already and not yet*. We pray for a child at baptism, and that this child actually obtains a 'parting' gift to nurture and develop, to keep and enjoy throughout life and in the life to come.

Rahner's words are obviously addressed to adults concelebrating, as it were, the rebirth of a baby: 'this child is our brother', a fellow human being, to be loved not only for himself, but in God who accepted him in baptism as we were once accepted:

The Sacramental Life of the Church 67

In this moment, although as yet unaware, he is given the divine power to begin his endless journey to God, but this does not mean that he is taken away from us. In fact, he has come even closer to our love. The shortest way to all that is unique and inalienable in another human being whom we love is the way through God. It is not a round about way, but the shortest of all, in fact, the only way.[169]

The whole congregation becomes an integral part of the rite, not just the baptized and the baptizer: 'when we attend a baptism something happens in our own lives too'.[170] It holds for us too the divine promise of an strength to accept our responsibility for the one baptized. We can say to the child:

Now you belong to us, and we to you in a quite a new way ... What is happening is a re-incarnation of what we have already received in our own souls, and by our presence here we partcipate in this sacramental celebration, and witness to the gift of the Holy Spirit whose fruit ripens within us.[171]

We are tempted to chant a solemn *Amen* to Rahner's meditation, founded as it is in elements of his own theology. The sacrament of confirmation seals the maturing of the presence of the Holy Spirit received by the newly baptized.

What distinguishes confirmation from baptism? Both give us the Holy Spirit, both assign a task (and, I believe a ministry) within the Church, both confer sanctifying grace *ex opere operato*. Rahner's *Foundations* declares that, despite their separation in the decrees of Trent, both 'belong together in the single Christian initiation into human and Christian existence' they cannot be separated.[172] The two random (and somewhat odd) cases, reported in Acts of the Apostles (8:14–17 and 19:1–6) (where people had received the word of God and had been baptized without receiving the Spirit) do not provide a sufficient scriptural basis to justify another, different, sacrament within the process of initiation. We must follow Rahner therefore in search of a theological basis for *one* sacrament of initiation celebrated in two different rites, even if with different ministers.[173]

There seem to be two inter-related ways in which Rahner, tries to explain the difference between baptism and confirmation without denying their unity. His first appeal is to two trends of the work of grace: *Kirche61* declares that 'God's grace has a double direction'. The first of these is total dedication to Christ, sharing his death and burial (Rom. 6:1-4). The grace of the Cross liberates us from the yoke of the law and the rule of sin, and from the merely human values of this world. The second is the grace of the incarnate Lord, an acceptance of the world in gradual transformation; the grace indeed of Christ's eschatological victory as manifested in the world. Both aspects of grace assign a special task in accord with God's free intention, and both are accompanied with corresponding charismata, themselves 'nothing other than the special ways in which one and the same Spirit reveals its purposes'.[174]

It is not difficult to assign the first 'direction' to baptism and the second of confirmation. Another common feature of these two sacraments lies in the self-realization ('actualization') of the Church herself. She shares her existence and earthly mission with new members. Baptism therefore entails a more passive way of 'liberation' from sin and death, and a consecration to intimate communion with the faithful. Confirmation, on the other hand is ,

> the sacrament of giving witness to faith in its charismatic plenitude ... The grace of confirmation ... is properly the grace of the Church for fulfilling its mission to the world and for proclaiming the world's transfiguration in Christ.[175]

Rahner's meditations on the sacraments maintain the approach outlined above, both in distinguishing between the two and in asserting their basic unity in the Holy Spirit. The Spirit is presented as the common origin of both sacraments. Neither possesses 'founding words' in the Gospels, and both exist as the self-realization of the Church. Hence they are

> administered wherever the Church fulfils her mission within the individual salvation-situation of any man or woman, whenever she is able to communicate herself as the grace-giving word of salvation.[176]

Baptism and confirmation are the basic sacraments of initiation into the Christian life. Since they are sacraments of the Church, it is her decision under which outward signs, by whom and to which age group they are administered. Their visible signs (water and chrism) and the usage of Roman Catholicism, clearly differentiates the two. If both, however, confer the Holy Spirit with his gifts on the recipients in an objective manner (*ex opere operato*) such differentiation is not clearly definable. Who can observe the work of the Spirit and his various charismata, and know for what purpose they are granted? Baptism does more than delete the dubious reality of original sin in which we are all born, and confirmation is more than a mission to spread the Gospel and bear witness to Christ. Both are open to furthering the inscrutable work of God's Holy Spirit for the slavation of the individual, and for the benefit of Christian communities all over the world. Though they are received once for all and tolerate no repetition, both sacraments belong together as stages of a process that ends in our eschatological future.

(D) *You Are Forgiven: the Sacrament of Penance*

It is impossible to offer a short summary of Rahner's teaching on the sacrament of penance. Since Rahner's early studies and publications were focused on the history of penance, any account of it would require an equal historical erudition. To meet him, therefore, on his home ground would involve us in the re-examination of this history from its very beginning to the present crisis. His interest in the subject goes back to the thirties,[177] but it was mainly in the fifties that he gradually published his researches in various periodicals and produced those bulky manuals for students, the fourth typewritten edition of which extends beyond 400 pages. It was not until 1973 that most of these learned studies were published together in volume IX of *Schriften* (corresponding to TI 15.).

His dominant systematic insight into the sacrament of penance can be best expressed: *the sacrament results in remission of mortal sins, through the sinner's reconciliation with the Church.* This central insight enables Rahner to address a whole range of questions posed by the penitential *praxis* of the Church, ancient, medieval and modern.

Kirche61 (a work already well founded in historical research anticipated an important 1955 essay, 'Forgotten Truths concerning the Sacrament of Penance')[178] provides the best introduction. This works consists mainly in systematic observations, but he resumes the same topic in 'Penance as an Additional Act of Reconciliation with the Church',[179] in which he also gives a survey of his main Patristic authorities. A triumphant, even if muted, note can be detected in the essay, for Vatican II in its Constitution on the Church and on the Priesthood, clearly adopts (or at least, implies) his considered position contrary to that of most theologians.[180]

The Church is concerned with her members who grievously sin and thereby not only put themselves in contradiction to God, but also to the Church of Christ which 'in her members and by their holiness must be the prime sacramental sign of the victorious grace of God'.[181] Her concern is now put into action by 'binding' the sinner, by withdrawing herself from the sinner by a kind of exclusion. By this Rahner does not mean excommunication in the recent canonical sense, but an exclusion of the sinner from full membership of the holy community of the redeemed. Men or women in grave sin are excluded from communion within the eucharistic service, though they remain in the bosom of the Church. This 'binding' exclusion, however, is done with a view to the 'loosing' of sinners from their burden through the absolution of the priest. Binding and loosing are not an either-or, but two phases of the same process terminating in the remission of sins through reconciliation with the Church. Both belong inseparably to one and the same sacrament.

> In this last specific (reconciliation with the Church) Rahner extends the intermediary stage of the sacramental event (the *res et sacramentum* of medieval scholasticism) into the penitent's peace with the Church, the *pax cum ecclesia*. His view, to my mind, combines the *praxis* of the early Church with the medieval preoccupation with the inner acts of the penitent: the person's aversion from sin and conversion to Christ's grace, that is, his or her sincere 'attrition' or 'contrition'. Rahner takes these latter for the penitent's participation in the sacramental event itself: '... the

acts of the contrite penitent confessing to the Church are part of the sacramental sign itself.[182] God's forgiveness is then granted to the sinner on account of his of her reconciliation with the Church. The priest can now absolve the penitent: his or her sins are remitted also in heaven.

The elements of this short summary in *Kirche61* can be found, in a more expanded form in *Truth*, published sixteen years earlier. There, too, the first step in his approach, namely, the exclusion of the sinner from the Church is illustrated by the New Testamental usage of 'binding'. It never means a *total* exclusion, but rather a 'ban' imposed on the sinner, in as much as a baptized person always belongs to the Church. Yet this belonging is only on the surface for the sinner; his or her membership maybe 'valid', but not 'effective' and, in a way, a lie:

> you are precisely as a member of the Church not at all the person you appear to be by your visible membership; you have the appearance of being alive (...), but in reality you are dead.[183]

This approach implies that every grave sin has by necessity an ecclesiological aspect. Hence it will be the task of the Church to judge your state, to discern the guilt you have incurred and separate you from holy Church, to put you under a ban. Her task is not to condemn you, or to excommunicate you. It is rather a *krisis,* to distinguish and separate, just as Paul seems to have done with the incestuous member of the Corinthian Church 'whom he has already removed from among' the rest of the faithful:

> For though absent in body I am present in spirit, and as if present, I have already pronounced judgement in the name of the Lord Jesus ... When you are assembled ... you are to deliver this man to Satan for the destruction of the flesh, that his spirit may be saved in the day of the Lord Jesus. (1 Cor:5, 2-5)

Leaving aside what Paul meant by 'delivering' the sinner to Satan,[184] the ban is obviously not final, but its ultimate aim is salvation for the sinner.

This is exactly what Rahner understands by the opposite of 'binding': The Church 'binds in order to loose'. It is here that he draws upon the praxis of early public penance as transposed to present circumstances (Mt. 18:15-20). In varying forms the early Church has adopted various forms of the same and made it her own 'rite' of penance: forgiveness was an act of the Christian community. Without this ecclesiological approach to penance 'the penitential discipline and practice of the Christians of the early Church [would] remain ultimately incomprehensible'.[185] In Rahner's sense this early praxis is a continuation of the Jewish approach to public penance.

In spite of the ample testimony of ancient writers,[186] why have the majority of Catholic scholars up to Vatican II not been able to recognize peace with the Church as the constitutive element of the sacrament itself? Rahner thinks that this is connected with the radical alteration in penitential praxis roughly at the turn of the first millennium. In early scholasticism, auricular confession gradually made its way from the British Isles to the Continent: penance became something that could be repeated, satisfaction was relegated to an act after the absolution of the confessor, and the event of reconciliation, which used to be a liturgy within a Christian community, had become a private affair. This praxis made the subjective acts of the penitent the central moment of the penitential rite.

Reconciliation with the Church returned with the high scholasticism of the twelfth and thirteenth centuries, although in an entirely different form. Theologians applied the Aristotelian scheme of matter and form to all the sacraments. In order to decide, on the pattern of baptism, what the material element of penance was, they had to appeal to the words spoken by the penitent by means of which his or her contrite mind was to be signalled: a detailed confession was required before the absolution of the priest could be given. No one, in Rahner's opinion, attributed the remission of guilt to absolution only, as the cause of forgiveness. Thomas Aquinas regarded absolution as the formal and, with his immediate predecessors, the inner disposition of the penitent as the material element of one and the same sacrament. At that time the harmony of these two constituted the whole significance of the sacrament.[187] At this point the *pax cum ecclesia* motif could have been revived: the contrite penitent facing the priest as the representative of the Church obtains the main effect of his or her confession: reconciliation with God together with the additional effect of peace with the Church.[188]

The theology of penance of Thomas Aquinas is, however, much more complex. Thomas wanted to have it both ways. On the one hand, the perfection of repentance (*contritio perfecta*, even outside the sacrament) can be a sufficient ground of forgiveness; on the other, as Thomas implies in some texts, the sinner who so repents does not completely belong to the Church, unless he or she is absolved by her representative. According to Rahner's own interpretation of Thomas, the absolution of the priest thus revives the *pax cum ecclesia* motif: it is not just one of the additional effects of the sacrament, but is a constitutive part of the penitential event even as the sinner's subjective repentance and the satisfaction imposed. It is regrettable that later confessional praxis blurred this insight,[189] and with it a lesser awareness of the Church's true significance crept in:

> she is no longer regarded as being in herself that sacrament filled with the Spirit which brings about salvation and grace provided only that we do not close ourselves against her Spirit through our own fault.[190]

Furthermore he blames the individualism of our modern times in which salvation is an affair between the Ego and God which in turn leads to forgetting that holy Church is 'the sole medium of grace and the Spirit', the 'means of grace', indeed, 'the witness of God's sanctifying compassion in the darkness of the sinful world, the visible presence of the love of God in human history.[191] This is why, as Rahner explains, peace with the Church as the moment of mediation, the *res et sacramentum*, disappeared for a long time from Roman Catholic consciousness. *Reconciliation* was published in 1967. By 1980, however, Rahner was going to have to face shortcomings other than those arising from individualistic legalism: the total neglect of this sacrament in many countries. He published, therefore, a short essay in the periodical

Entschluss: 'All the same: why do we have to go to confession', *Warum man trotzdem beichten soll?*[192]

༄

Rahner's firm conviction about the role of the Church within the sacrament of penance, imposes a change in the concept of sin itself. Grave sin, the sole material element in the sacrament of reconciliation, is an offence against the Church. Granted, sin is an offence against God, against one's own nature, against man's supernatural destiny, but over and above these:

> Sin is also an offence against the holy communion of the redeemed, which the Church is. ... [Therefore] the Christian who sins offends against his own attachment to the Church (which is essential to him as a Christian) and against the Church herself.[193]

It is not easy to assign the origin of this ecclesiastical definition of guilt and sin. If it were something implicit in Rahner's general approach to the sacrament of penance, we might get the impression that his argument concerning sin moves in a vicious circle: since there is a sacrament of penance within the Church, sin therefore has an ecclesial structure. On the other hand, penitence within the Church is necessary, because sin is sin against the Church. I do not think, however, that Rahner can be saddled with this circular argument. Well before this interpretation had crystallized in his mind, he had worked out his ideas about sin and guilt, and his historical studies on penance, too, confirmed his earlier view concerning its ecclesial nature.

I once tried to introduce the reader to Rahner's theology of sin within a different context.[194] An early essay (1953), gives a long-winded discourse on guilt, sin and sinfulness, in which all his philosophical presuppositions are apparent.[195] Leaving details aside the article emphasizes that: guilt can only be committed by the free act of the whole person; and that the clear recognition of *real* guilt is rarely patent. 'Only through God can we be delivered from guilt in the strict sense'. Nevertheless this 'mystery' of *real* guilt can be known through listening to God's word announced to the sinner:

> by a man [the confessor] in so far as he can truly say that he has been appointed and sent to accomplish this word and be its servant. To the *'Tibi soli peccavi'* corresponds God's *'Ego te absolvo,* and this alone delivers from guilt.[196]

Thus, without stating it explicitly, Rahner is convinced that the remission of guilt can only happen within a dialogue recognised as effective by the Church.

The same subject is taken up again in 1962 in his lecture on 'Guilt – Responsibility – Punishment within the View of Catholic Theology'.[197] Here, without the philosophical run-up, Rahner works out why sin and guilt should be classified as mystery,[198] a theme that he resumes in *Sevenfold's* meditations about the sacrament of penance. A fatal decision against God makes the person guilty of such a grave sin that the consequence is eternal perdition. We do not know, however, with absolute certainty whether or not any individual is capable of such a decision. We cannot, so to speak, 'localize' guilt in ourselves or in others. Such statements, of course, do not mean that there is no guilt in the world at all. We do not know whether there is indeed *real* guilt behind the sinful actions that are often excused by means of modern psychology or sociology.[199] Therefore, though the Church's traditional distinction between mortal and venial sin is justifiable, it is in the concrete, just as difficult to tell the one from the other as to assign real guilt to a person.[200] When, in spite of this uncertainty, a person experiences guilt, he will also feel the uneasiness and hopelessness of his situation. Rahner's 'Guilt and its Remission' calls this feeling 'suffering', a state in which one 'desires to hear God's word of forgiveness'. God in his mercy answers the sinner's desperate call in the Church, 'the community of those believing in this forgiveness'. The Church *herself* indeed *is* this one word of forgiveness conveyed to man and woman in different forms, one of which is the sacrament of penance. It is the Church that answers us effectively in the despair of our guilt as she

> loosens the wrong that the guilt of man does to the Church. Indeed, one may say the Church forgives guilt through God's

word of forgiveness entrusted to her, in that she forgives us the wrong done to her.[201]

The sin of the Christian is, therefore, always in contradiction to the holy community of the Church. And it is the Church that can remit and forgive, as she does in baptism. Indeed, this word of forgiveness is very much like that pronounced at baptism, now, however, for those who have fallen into grave sin after baptism.

The grace of baptism and the nature of sin are in opposition, for sin is the loss of grace. The two sacraments of baptism and penance are parallel in this: baptism is incorporation into, penance cures the falling away from, the Church. Rahner develops the same insight within the context of the history of early Christian thought. In 'Sin as Loss of Grace in Early Church Literature' he distinguishes three possible approaches to the nature of sin. The first he calls juridical-ethical: 'by it sin is considered a transgression of the divine law ... one offends against God's holiness and justice, causes scandal' to his fellow Christians. According to the second, sin is an act or state by which the sinner incurs divine judgement on the last day: it is an eschatological approach that abandons the sinner to eternal death and perdition. The third, 'the person who sins destroys the life which he has received in baptism; he expels the Spirit from his innermost being and destroys the seal he has received in baptism'. In this last sense sin is the loss of grace with immediate consequences on the life of the sinner who is spiritually dead.[202]

If, indeed, this is the ultimate nature of sin, then it will be easier for Rahner to see the loss of grace as the loss or impairment of Church-membership, and mortal sin as an offence against the Church herself. A situation of grave sin not only impairs the grace of the Holy Spirit of God and Christ, but also the holiness of the Church. The power of sin is thus overcome by the even greater mercy of God's care for the sinner manifested in and through the community of the believers, the Church.

This very sketchy presentation of Rahner's writings about penance would be incomplete if I did not add two corollaries closely connected with the same topic: the anointing of the sick and the granting of indulgences. The first, the sacrament of the sick, once called extreme unction, is a sacrament in its own right, one which manifests God's merciful care through the Church for men and women in an actual situation of approaching death. The second, indulgences, will follow the discussion of the subject of anointing.

The sacrament of anointing is additional to the sacrament of reconciliation in as much as sinfulness, or rather, its traces in human life (even if guilt has been remitted) remain. Christian tradition believes that death, to which the seriously ill person is exposed, is connected with sin, according to Paul the 'cause of death'. The loneliness experienced by those facing possible death needs the help of the Church.

Kirche61 touches but summarily on the doctrine of the sacrament of anointing. Rahner's treatment is concerned mainly with the characteristic traits of that ultimate (eschatological) situation of men and women for whom 'serious illnesses ... [are] the harbingers signalling the approach of death'.[203] The Church, present through her members, accompanies and supports the sick in their loneliness.[204] A grave illness is, indeed, a time for decision and part of a person's salvation history. As the sign of Christ's eschatological victory embodied in time and history, the Church announces the hope that she represents by dispensing the Body of Christ, the *viaticum,* to those in danger of death, a signal that his or her eventual death is configured to the death of Christ, the gateway to resurrection and to life eternal.[205] The connection between the Eucharist and anointing is obvious. Patristic heritage, however, prompts the recognition of the connection between anointing with the sacrament of penance. Trent tells us that it is a completion, a *consummativum,* of the whole penitential procedure.[206] *Kirche61* he dwells no further on this matter. Rahner contents himself by arguing that there must be a sacrament of eschatological hope conveyed to those in danger of death by a representative of the Church, a sacrament in addition to the Eucharist (the daily nourishment of Christians) and penance (the function of which relates to guilt).

In *Kirche61* Rahner does not develop the theme that the

anointing of the sick is pre-eminently the sacrament of the Church's effective prayer over a person whose trust is being put to the test. This topic gains more emphasis in his meditations on the sacrament; he refers to anointing as 'Trusting and Healing', *Bergend und heilend*.[207] The passage in the epistle of James (5:14-15), usually considered to be proof or illustrative text for the institution of anointing, is an exhortation to prayer addressed, not only to the person concerned, but also to the elders of the holy community. And James had no doubt about the efficacy of this prayer:

> Is any among you sick? Let him call the elders of the church, and let them pray over him, anointing him with oil in the name of the Lord; and the prayer of faith will save the sick man, and the Lord will raise him up; and if he has committed sins, then he will be forgiven them.

Trent, of course, recalling the sending of the twelve in Mark 6:13, finds in this passage the constitutive elements of each and every sacrament: institution by Christ; matter and form; the minister proper to its performance; the efficacy *ex opere operato* and the grace of the Holy Spirit conferred on the recipient (so that extreme unction 'wipes away any sins that may still be unabsolved'). This doctrinal exegesis of the Tridentine Fathers can carry conviction even today. Rahner, however, dwells rather on the mystery of grace and its embodiment in the words of Jesus and of the Church accompanying ritual actions. The bedside prayer of the presbyter (or bishop) together with a ritual gesture of anointing is a word of salvation for the sick (including the forgiveness of sins and release from its consequences), one that also intends the recovery of bodily health or strength for those who face the inevitable with courage and due submission. That this liturgical rite is truly a sacrament in its own right depends not only on the promise of the Lord, but more profoundly: the Church anticipates her eschatological fulfilment in her prayer for those in danger of death.[208]

The teaching of the Tridentine Church is that one of the effects of the sacrament is the remission of the remnants or consequences of sins. The elder in anointing the senses of the sick person appeals for forgiveness: 'let the Lord forgive you whatever sins you have committed through your sense of sight, of hearing ...' and so on. Rahner understands the word 'sins' in these formulae, not so much as punishments still operative, but as a reference to the person's contact with a material environment contaminated by the 'sins' of the world.[209] The sacrament expunges all these 'remnants'. Those in danger of death are reassured by the sacrament of the sick that their sins with all their consequences are forgiven: the dying can face their Maker with a clear conscience.

❧

The long-standing praxis of the Church in granting indulgences envisages a similar action: not for those in danger of death, but for the living. Indulgences remit the remnants of sin.

Rahner's *Investigations* discusses the, nowadays too often misunderstood, topic of indulgences in no less than three major essays. To the uninformed, indulgences may appear as a heavenly bank-deposit through which the Church and her Head dispense the benefits of divine grace to Christians who, after their presumed conversion in the confessional, are still in debt to God and neighbour. Moreover, indulgences seem to effect the partial or total remission of punishments due to sins already confessed and absolved. It is thought that such punishments that still remain are due to God's 'vindictive' justice. The Church's jurisdictional power grants these indulgences to the converted, those in state of sanctifying grace who fulfil some good deeds. Some devout souls, indeed, believe that indulgences are payments on behalf of their deceased loved ones in order to 'shorten' their sufferings in purgatory (conceived often as a heavenly concentration camp after the 'absolution' of a prison sentence, an idea well known to people who have lived under a Communist regime). Those who have some slight knowledge of Christian tradition concerning penance, see indulgences as relics of a former praxis when Church authorities reduced or absolved penitential satisfaction, either before or after their solemn absolution.

To grasp what indulgences should mean within present,

radically altered, penitential practice today is a problem also for the *Magisterium*, and even more a problem for theologians who have the burdensome task of explaining the constant teaching of the Church.[210] Rahner had to face this task and in a review of 1949, he accepted almost entirely A. Poschmann's account[211] of the historical origin of indulgences. Both theologians place the origin of indulgences at the time of transition from the praxis of public to that of private penance. A contribution to *Sacramentum Mundi* summarizes what the official Church then meant by indulgences:

> [it] is the remission before God of a temporal punishment for sins of which guilt has been forgiven ... granted by ecclesiastical authority out of the Treasury of the Church to the living by way of absolution, to the dead by way of suffrage.[212]

This definition itself is not an infallible doctrine; single concepts, therefore, implied in it can be interpreted (as they always have been) in different ways. It is, however, defined that the Church has received authority from Christ to grant indulgences salutary for the faithful.[213] Without going into the various decrees, regulations and clarifications about indulgences promulgated by the *Magisterium* and Canon Law I single out, as did Rahner, the main concepts operative in this official doctrine of the Church:

- *Punishment* due for sin (even after guilt has been blotted out).
- The *efficacy* of an indulgence granted *ex opere operato* or some other objective way. The relationship of the recipients' subjective *contribution* towards gaining the effect of an indulgence.
- The so-called *Treasury of the Church* in virtue of which indulgences are granted.
- The power committed to the Church's authority to dispense indulgences.
- The status of the *dead in purgatory* who are (*per suffragium*) beneficiaries of indulgences.

It is clear that the doctrine concerning indulgences is complex,

The Sacramental Life of the Church 81

and it is no wonder, therefore, that the terms employed to expound it underwent changes throughout the years, both changes of theological approach, and changes of meaning. Rahner is correct in advocating a 'new' understanding, one somewhat different from the medieval concept and, to a certain extent, from the official doctrine concerning indulgences. The novelty of Rahner's exposition in 'A Brief Theological Study on Indulgence',[214] can be summarized up in three points:

a) it concentrates rather on the effective prayer of the Church and not on her juridical power;
b) it regards punishment of sins as interior consequences of guilt (already blotted out by absolution) hence avoiding the false idea of a 'vindictive' God revenging himself on crimes committed;
c) instead of supposing a 'storehouse' of merits accumulated by the just to be dispensed by the Church, it simply identifies the so-called Treasury of the Church with the sacrifice of Jesus Christ, the source of God's salvific will and activity.

Rahner affirms first of all, that the consequences of sins after absolution cannot simply be removed by a juridical act. The older practice of public penance made such juridical intervention by the Church understandable. Since such acts involved punishments imposed by Church authorities themselves, they could withdraw, diminish or even alter the nature of the satisfaction required from the penitent (for example alms, instead of fasting, and forth). The new order of private penance, however, changes the emphasis: 'punishments' are not imposed by the Church, but are the 'remnants' of already absolved sins. Since the Church has not imposed them, any appeal to her juridical power would be rather odd. Is the Church any longer capable of deleting these 'remnants' consequent upon sin after absolution? The answer to this question is the doctrine of indulgences.

What exactly then are these remnants of sins? From the early days of medieval scholasticism theologians became increasingly conscious of the subjective state of the penitent;

the remnants of sin were regarded, therefore, as an interior suffering introduced by the sin that had been absolved. The Church was able to offer some relief to the faithful, not, however, by a juridical act, but by effective prayer and intercession.

This, of course, makes non-sacramental indulgences similar to anointing, in which the prayer of the presbyter and of the congregation creates a true sacrament. An indulgence granted through the prayerful intercession of the Church does indeed have a certain degree of objective efficacy, for this intercession is constantly made by the Church for 'a benefit which is ... in harmony with the will of God': 'there is nothing to prevent our granting (to a certain degree) the character of *opus operatum* to an indulgence'.[215] The *opus operatum* of the sacraments of the sick and of reconciliation is due to God's free gift of love. The initial love regained by the sinner in penance is increased and perfected with the aid of indulgences that enable the suppression of the consequences of the guilt removed by the sacrament of penance:

> an indulgence can be nothing other than a (very important) aid accorded to the repentant sinner to enable him to reach a state of love that removes all imperfection. It is an (intercessory) aid for the gaining of the grace needed for such charity (ibid.).

The prayer and intercession of the Church, indeed, assists the increase of love initiated by the penitent's conversion in the sacrament of reconciliation.

Rahner's approach to indulgences rejects the idea of a *'vindictive'* God who imposes punishment on the sinner. The consequences of sin derive from the fact that our conversion is never complete. Reconciliation does not simply, and immediately, correct all the ingrained attitudes and encumbrances of previous life. One often has to say, 'I am in many respects the same as I ever was'. In one sentence:

> Springing as these do from sin, they live on after it and constitute a just judgement upon it. We Christians call them 'the temporal punishments due to sin'.[216]

In other words, there is a tension between the conversion

worked at the 'kernel', the innermost centre of personhood and its outside manifestation: a contradiction 'productive of pain' and tangible suffering. For:

> Who has not suffered from his own inability to turn himself into a different man?[217]

This 'impotence' is a lack of personal integration: we never realize fully the good intentions to which we are committed. If this inability is recognized as due to a guilty past, it will be the cause of inner suffering. The process of full integration, Rahner holds, it is not in our power, 'it has to be bestowed upon us'. This bestowal is not, of course, a juridical act, a sort of legal amnesty. It is that same love of God that works our 'maturing' even after death when the time of new decisions is over. It still continues

> to take effect even after death by permeating and shaping all those levels in the human person which are less immediate to actual personhood.[218]

We can entreat God that he will grant throughout life favourable circumstances on our way to full integration. We Christians are not left to do this on our own. To those who prayerfully find their way through the labyrinth of life God's providence manifests itself within the Church of Christ:

> she is the one Body of Christ in which all the members live for one another, suffer for one another and are brought to perfection for one another. When God regards an individual he always sees him in his place in the whole, as one with Christ the head and as one with the brethren of one Christ.[219]

Since this is the case, then our prayer for God's help is not limited to ourselves. I can pray for my fellows, since my progress can help theirs and vice versa. To such 'prayer the Church can lend her support'.

Tradition refers to this help of the Church as the treasury entrusted to her. The word expresses the past, present and future merits of her saintly members available to the Church to dispense to those in need: 'we can say that God gives the individual that which the Church implores on his behalf for his salvation'. If, however, these merits are ultimately due to God's salvific will, manifested and realised by Christ's unique sacrifice, we can identify the treasury of the Church with this unique act of divine condescension. She, on behalf of all her members, pronounces this intercession

> that draws down a remission of the 'punishments' due to sin. Now, provided that we understand this *special* prayer in the right way ... we can say: this is precisely what takes place in what we call an indulgence.[220]

Moreover, the Church can validly perform this special intercession for the living as well as for the dead. The necessary prior conditions are some specified good works, even if they are only symbolic.

This is the practice of the Church. She offers many indulgences. Whether or not they are all 'gained' is another question. The important fact is the belief that the Church's intercession, owing to God's promise, achieves, in one way or other, its purpose. The most consoling thought behind this praxis is that the Church supports the maturation of love in each and every repentant sinner. That love is born in the sacrament of penance and is fulfilled through the laborious process of moving towards perfection. For

> those who believe in the meaning of prayer, and who know what is meant by the Church, can be seized with awe at the ... idea: the holy community of the redeemed, the Bride of Christ, stands at the throne of grace on my behalf! From her heart ... prayer rises up on my behalf ... she does this not merely in general terms or implicitly, but explicitly, and as pledged by an act of her supreme authority to pray on my behalf.[221]

Rahner's interpretation of the relationship between indulgences and the sacrament of the sick asserts the fulfilment of conversion gained in the sacrament of penance. Whereas penance and anointing are instances of the Church's sacramental power, *ex opere operato,* indulgences are an instance of the Church's prayerful intercession for pilgrims on the way to final salvation.

(E) *Marriage: the Mystery of Human Love*

For us Christians marriage is a sacred reality. It was called a *sacramentum*,[222] though not in the later technical sense of that word. Of course, biblical references to the union of man and woman abound, but none of these seems to have sufficiently regarded it as a cultic human action within the Church, one that symbolizes and works the salvation of the spouses. The only exception is the text of Ephesians 5:21–33, in which matrimony is a mystery that models the even greater mystery of Christ's love for his Church. Since the Vulgate translated mystery as *sacramentum*, it became inevitable that theological reflection should regard the union of two baptized persons, not only as a biological necessity and a social institution, or even as a remedy against sexual desires, but something much more. When we reach the age of high-scholasticism with its clear definition of the sacraments, there is no longer any doubt that marriage must be one of the seven sacred signs symbolizing the mystery of Christ and the salvation of the spouses.

This development did not have a smooth passage. Several factors impeded the recognition of matrimony as a true sacrament. First, theologians were unable to point to any sayings of the Lord about matrimony, other than his radical opposition to divorce (like some of the prophets[223]) which, in itself, did not argue for its grace-giving power. Then there was the problem of fitting marriage into the cultic life of Christianity; in its secular setting it was always a form of contract between families according to the laws and customs of the land. When marriage was adopted into the Church's liturgy, its coming-to-be at the actual wedding could be understood as a religious action, but the state of matrimony could not then be recognized as a constant source of grace for the spouses. In the first Christian centuries the relative newness of unmarried chastity (later virginity) for the sake of the Kingdom threw a shadow on the married state in which sexual relations were practised; perhaps for this latter reason one could not assign a special grace belonging to marriage. The practice by which husband and wife vowed chastity was far from rare in the early Church and when a clear cut general definition of the sacraments came into vogue, theologians had to decide: what was the material and what the formal element in marriage; and who was really competent to administer this sacrament which had made its way into the group of sacred signs effecting the grace of salvation *ex opere operato*.

Anyone trying to establish the sacramental nature of marriage has to be aware of this wearisome development. It is no wonder that the Reformers denied that marriage was a sacrament: Luther, indeed, considered it a merely secular affair. They were later obliged to give marriage more status than had Luther.[224] More ecumenically minded theologians now regard matrimony as a state closely associated with the sacraments: it is a 'sacramental'.[225] Marriage must have been instituted, if not by Christ, then by the Creator himself: Genesis 1:27 'male and female he created them' and Genesis chapter 2 on Adam's 'marriage' with Eve were texts quoted or referred to by the evangelists and St Paul. By the end of the thirteenth century Catholics were convinced that marriage was one of the seven sacraments; the Council of Trent defined it as a dogma of the Church. At the same time Trent anathematized those who do not accept the difference between major and minor sacraments.[226] Marriage was, no doubt, thought to belong to this latter group.

Rahner wrote very little about marriage. In *Kirche61* there is a short section that is little more than an outline of a proper theological treatment of marriage as a sacrament. His approach to this sacrament is based on Ephesians chapter 5 with its comparison between marital love and Christ's love for his Church. Rahner's interpretation does not regard this comparison as allegory, but as a symbol that the Creator intends as an expression of the symbolized reality (*Realsymbol*),

> We must say that this will of God is operative in the reality itself, in marriage, and gives it a definite intrinsic characteristic which fits it for the function of a symbol.[227]

Rahner has to show, of course, that if marriage is to be a sacrament must it be a *Realsymbol*. To do this he has first to analyze the genuine relationships between persons, one of which is conjugal love. This love was prefigured in the Old

Testament in Jahweh's marital love for the people of Israel. 'Male and female he created them'; it follows, then, that the very possibility of being human rests on the bisexuality of mankind. This provides a sufficient ground on which to build a certain analogy between the human reality of marriage and the love of Yahweh for his people. Therefore:

> it might perhaps be possible to grasp why authentic matrimony at all times has a value truly representative for God's unitive love in Christ for mankind.[228]

Conjugal love, however, can only function as a *Realsymbol*, if the incarnation becomes a fact: Christ is embodied into this *one* ('monogenetic') humanity ('which is one through conjugal love').[229] Before this event the union of the spouses was not such a 'unitive' symbol: when, however, the Church is 'visibly and manifestly the beloved bride of Christ', then

> such symbolism of a fundamental kind, established in the very essence of the Church, is truly a fundamental act in which the Church fulfils her very nature, and ... is a sign which produces what it signifies, ... and therefore, since it signifies grace, is a *sacrament*.[230]

If this reasoning is valid, we can accept two more of Rahner's conclusions. First, if marriage partakes of the love of Christ for his Church, this relationship is convertible: marriage itself contributes to the life of the Church. Secondly, a Christian marriage is an infinitesimally small, but real, unit of the Church; it is the Church in miniature.

Rahner is convinced that the idea of marriage as a sacrament can and must be approached through an analysis of interpersonal love. A wedding sermon of his tries to show his audience how the unconditional love of the spouses implies God's knowledge, supernatural wisdom and grace. It is a grace that does not just help the bearing of each other's burdens and the fulfilment of those duties to one another that are expected by society. Grace means divine life, a share in the divine nature: in other words, grace is God himself in his desire to give himself to spiritual creatures. Since mutual love is endowed with this grace, it cannot be anything but a sacrament. Marital communion is, therefore, a mystery and those who live this mystery fully will understand that God himself is love.[231]

One wonders if any young couple could comprehend Rahner's sermon about their mutual love being a source of the indwelling of divine grace. He puts it more convincingly, however, in a major essay, in which he again tried to argue the sacramental character of marriage.[232] Of the five parts of *Marriage* the first three mobilize his whole philosophico-theological system.[233] All the basic notions of his system are cited in explanation of the first premise of his argument, such as: the identity between love of God and love of neighbour as based on the transcendental implication of mutual human love, the orientation of which leads the lovers into the 'immediacy' of God; the much debated principle of Rahner's system according to which in the present order of salvation every good human act is also a salvific act by virtue of the grace implied in it (It follows that 'genuine love is de facto always the theological virtue of charity sustained by God's grace'.[234]); the social dimension of mutual human love that 'signifies at the same time a unity with mankind as a whole' even within the partners' exclusivity (a concept qualified as 'susceptible to alteration'); the belief that their mutual love 'opens itself to *all, to a wider community*' of mankind.[235]

Since, however, this 'wider community' is the Church, which is the primordial sacrament, she is 'realized' in marriage as in the other sacraments and fulfilled through the mutual relationship between the spouses. Marriage is therefore a sacrament. This conclusion can be converted: whereas the sacramental nature of marriage can be deduced from the primary sacrament that is the Church, the mystery of conjugal union 'realizes' the mystery of the Church.

This same convertibility implies that all that we say of marriage as a real sign of marital love can also be asserted of the Church:

> The same 'sign' (that functions) in marriage is also present in the Church. For the Church is, in Christ, the basic sacrament:

in her the love of God for mankind in his act of self-bestowal achieves its historical manifestation through grace in the loving unity of mankind.[236]

In other words, every human being is in relation with the community of mankind, a community that depends on a unity of love binding each free, unique individual into the unity of one assembly, of one 'communion'. This indeed is the objective of the Church and also of her individual members. It is, however impossible for human beings to realize this final unity, unless through smaller units whose basis is or should be the union of spouses. If then a Christian marriage fulfils this purpose, it has achieved what the Church is supposed to achieve: the union evidences, realizes the Church.

The basic parallelism drawn by Rahner between the Church and marriage is only valid up to a point. There is this difference: whereas the sign that is the Church by indicating a humanity consecrated and united in grace, extends beyond the social organism of the visible Church, the love of couples is a sign of the unity of two individuals where sign and signified can irretrievably break down. While 'in the Church the intrinsic connection between sign and reality signified can no longer radically be destroyed *in virtue of the eschatological victory of grace in Christ*', the sign function in marriage can be sinfully 'degraded into a lie', if the grace-given love and unity is destroyed. Nonetheless, like marriage, the Church is a sign:

> at the palpable level of historical and social human life, of the fact that *that* love is being made *effective and victorious* ... which is the love of God for us and of us for God, the love which comprehends and unifies all so long as no-one sinfully denies it.[237]

Rahner asserts, nevertheless, that the love that unites married couples and contributes to the unity of the Church is one and the same: marriage is one of the ways in which this unification of humankind in love is made actual: the same love is constitutive of both matrimony and of the Church.[238] The idea that marriage is the Church in miniature is thus justifiable.

In marriage the Church is made present. It is really the

smallest community, the smallest, but at the same time the true community of the redeemed and sanctified.[239]

This 'profoundly significant theological dimension' characterizes the unity in which two baptised individuals voluntarily bind themselves in marriage. The grace that it signifies needs no words of Christ in institution. It is implicit in the fact that the religious relevance of marriage is recognized by Jesus (for instance in his rejection of divorce). It is held in high esteem by the Church 'as *an eschatological sign of salvation for the Kingdom of God* (considered as the absolute proximity of God to man)'.[240] The spouses love for one another (as expressed in their mutual consent) is not only the sign of their lasting union, but the sacramental event of grace which works objectively (*ex opere operato*) at least in the case of two baptized individuals in the Church.

This last statement does not mean that the marriage of the non-baptized is a merely secular affair. Ephesians 5 does not restrict the parallel cited above exclusively to Christians. The marriage of the non-baptized, too, is something sacred, whether they are aware of it or not. Rahner risks characterizing the relationship between Christian and secular marriage as the difference between *opus operatum* and *opus operantis,* or as of being justified *prior to baptism* and *through* it (that is through the objective efficacy of a sacrament). No matter the form of marriage in various periods and in different regions, the parties are striving towards a union, a being together, even through a way of life entirely foreign to us. This is why Ephesians refers to Genesis 2, in which man and woman, exemplified by the marriage of Adam and Eve, are an integral part of the order of creation. If we adopt Rahner's assumption that, from the very beginning, this natural order foreshadows the order of grace and redemption, then all activity that honestly strives towards (any kind of) unity has 'the significance of pointing forwards to' a hidden relationship with Christ. In 'Christ's being and work ... the imparting of grace finds its eschatological culmination'.[241] This imparting of grace happened in fact through God's covenant with mankind, and it is symbolized by the covenant between man and woman. The same grace is at work in both covenants, though

The Sacramental Life of the Church 91

in a different way. Thus one can say with St Paul: 'This is a great mystery, and I am applying it to Christ and the Church' (Eph. 5:32).

❧

Rahner's *Marriage* intended to give a sketch only of a dogmatic and systematic theology and not to enter into the many other aspects of this sacrament. The present crisis affecting the union of man and woman renders, indeed, his teaching on marriage somewhat inadequate for many of our contemporaries. Questions urgent to them are not even addressed.

> He never discusses the main characteristics of marriage: its monogamous nature, its indissolubility with an absolute rejection of divorce. He never faces the problems involved in mixed marriages between different Christian denominations and between baptized and non-baptized persons. He never even mentions the traditional and modern debate about the purpose of natural and sacramental marriage. From what he writes the mutual love of the partners prevails over and above procreation as an essential goal of marriage. If this latter is altogether neglected or only piously mentioned, as in *Sevenfold*,[242] and the mutual love of the spouses is overemphasized, then some kind of marriage between homosexuals ought to be equally valid. For, after all, gay and lesbian people also strive to achieve union with one another. Is such love, their 'covenant', not a sign of grace-giving union between Christ and his Church?
>
> Finally, there is an important question that should have been raised even in a sketchy theology of marriage: in what sense is the sacrament a *cultic performance*.[243] Since all other sacraments represent a definite celebration within the Church, is it the actual wedding only that is the sacramental event, and is the spouses' life together, in which the resulting grace operates, only a consequence? If Rahner starts and ends his 'treatise' on marriage with interpersonal human love, then in what sense is married life an ongoing sacramental sign? Is the fact that both partners should be baptized Christians sufficient for regarding, not only the nuptials (*matrimonium in fieri*, as it was called), but also the spouses' everyday life, their struggles and pleasures, their fidelity in spite of occasional faithlessness, their separations and reunions (*matri-*

92 *The Sacrament of the Future*

monium in facto esse), to be a permanent celebration of Christ's indissoluble union in love with his Church?

If all these questions are validly asked by modern men and women, as well as from a theological (dogmatic and systematic) viewpoint, then Rahner's article, *Marriage*, has only a limited value, one limited to an argument for the sacramental nature of Christian matrimony. As in Rahner's discussions of the other six sacraments, there emerges again and again the image of the Church. He 'believes' in this Church, in its ideal shape as a mystery of our faith in which all the seven sacraments, and marriage explicitly, are mysteries of Christ's definitive and irretrievably victorious, eschatological grace. Rahner's sacramental theology is profoundly ecclesiological, or rather, a eulogy of the mystical and eschatological aspect of the Church.

Nevertheless Rahner's treatment of marriage, more than the presentation of the other sacraments, gives us several clues by means of which we can reflect upon and extend his sacramental theology. Marriage is the sacrament that is best able to characterize the reciprocal relationship between the essential features of merely human life and those of the Church in both her sociological and 'mystery' aspects. Is this insight not valid for the rest of the sacraments of the Roman Catholic Church? Is Rahner's whole sacramental theology not an 'Ecclesiology of the Sacraments'?

This question leads us straight into our Comments and Questions.

Chapter 2

Comments and Questions: The Ecclesiology of the Sacraments

Rahner's theology of the sacraments is too widely scattered throughout his work to enable easy reflection. Apart from *Kirche61*, it is dispersed within various lectures and articles, as incidental remarks, and especially in his *Handbook*.[1] It is from these writings that I have tried to tease out his own particular approach to the sacraments: his reinterpretation of the permanent elements in the sacramental theology of the Roman Catholic Church as well as his remarks on each of the seven sacraments. This chapter does not attempt to summarize the approval or criticism of his thought by other authors. Nevertheless, like many other theologians who grew up in the Roman Church prior to Vatican II, I could not help being impressed by the novelty of Rahner's concept of sacrament, a fascination, however, that does not stop me from raising fundamental questions about and from suggesting alternative or corrective lines to his sacramental theology.

In what follows I shall address three matters proper to Rahner's approach, the first of which deals inevitably with the transfer of sacramental theology into that of the Church. The second confronts the reader with Rahner's anthropological approach to the sacraments which I have expounded through the discussion of his *Revolution* and *Active Role*. Since I discern some disharmony between these two approaches, I shall then suggest a view that may reconcile them and may provide a solid basis for developing a sacramental theology of a kind so much needed in our present situation.

2.1 The Sacraments and the Doctrine of the Church

It was only in the second half of the twentieth century that Roman Catholic scholars began treating sacramental theology within the theology of the Church. This approach had not been altogether alien to the East[2] and the Western Church seems to have followed it: sacraments were no longer to be regarded as mere instruments in the 'hands' of the Church (or rather of those who were legally authorized to administer them), but part and parcel of her mystery. It was a bold decision of the Second Vatican Council that its decree on the Church (*Lumen Gentium*) brought together the two concepts of Church and sacrament,

> Since the Church is in Christ as a sacrament (*veluti sacramentum*) or an instrumental sign of intimate union with God and the unity of all humanity, the council ... intends to declare ... the nature of the Church.[3]

Does this mean that any consideration of the notion sacrament in general or about single sacraments in particular cannot omit that of the Church, and *vice versa* that the sacramental nature of the Church is now an essential element of all ecclesiological statements?

(A) *The Church as the Primordial Sacrament*

The proposition of the Council, however divergent its interpretations, was accepted by most Catholic scholars[4] and Rahner, though with his own particular angle, was one of them. To recapitulate his thought: he argues first of all that the whole economy of salvation following from the incarnation of the Logos is first realized by the *genesis* of the Church. Then, if the Church in her historical nature *is* the eschatological manifestation of God's grace she must be a symbol of salvation for the whole world. Since, however, the Church cannot be separated from her actions in the world, she must realize herself in her members by means of the sacraments. For Rahner, therefore, there seems to be an unbroken line of descent from the incarnation of the Logos to the seven sacraments of the Roman Church: they are implied in the very institution of the Church.[5] There is no need for an explicit word of Christ for the institution of each and every sacrament. The Church herself *is* a sacrament in as much as she lives by distributing salvific grace to its recipients. This therefore is Rahner's own 'particular angle' on the interpretation of the Council's suggestion that the Church is 'like a sacrament or an instrumental sign of salvation'.

That the Church is a sacrament is not a concept unknown to *non-Catholic theologians*. Although their ecumenical aspirations permit them to admit, albeit gingerly, that the Church could be called sacrament or sacramental, they would prefer to drop this concept and reserve sacramentality to Christ alone, or rather to designate the Kingdom (*Herrschaft*) of God or God's hidden plans for the history of mankind as the promise to which the sacramentality of the Church refers.[6] They seem to fear any identification between God and the Church.

Let us illustrate this critical reaction first by E. Jüngel.[7] He accepts in principle the idea of treating the Church as a sacrament, since even Protestant theology (with marked resistance by K. Barth) speaks of the Church as a 'representation' or a 'display' (*Darstellung)* of Christ. Such theology insists, however, that in dispensing the sacraments, the Church is not the principal agent but that Christ himself awakens faith by means of a sacramental reality. This faith, however, is a passive reception of God's word. Once, however, some positive representation or display of Christ is accepted, both confessions are bound to presuppose some function and/or even action (*Handlung*) proper to the Church herself. Catholics, too, would admit that the ultimate subject of this action is God through Christ, but they seem to conceive it as *one* action (*eine Handlungsidentität*) both of Christ and of his Church. Protestant understanding, however, would interpret this to mean that the Church has something to 'perform': she has an *opus perficiendum* which is not directly due to God's saving action. For a Protestant the *opus operatum* of Catholic theology is not connected with the performance of the sacramental rite: Christ himself is the unique *opus operatum*. The Church represents this divine action in human fashion and may contribute to the circumstances in which the believer's faith is generated in order to accept the reality of man's justification in Christ. For Jüngel the Church in representing Christ, who is the one and only real sacrament, is only an *analogatum* about which we cannot assert that she *continues* the Mystery of Christ.[8] Consequently, he would prefer to call the Church not the primordial-sacrament (*Grundsakrament*), but rather the 'great sacramental sign' representing Jesus the Christ.[9]

Jüngel's *analogatum* is, indeed, a possible interpretation of *Lumen Gentium 1,* which recognizes a *similarity* between Church and sacrament: *veluti sacramentum et instrumentum.* It depends on the strength Jüngel attributes to this analogy. It seems, however, that his 'great sacramental sign' is only an exterior pointer to the one and only mystery that is Christ. Consequently his fundamental criticism of Rahner's view is that the Church is not a mystery in herself, but a possible pointer to God's plan of salvation in and through Jesus the Christ. This is, indeed, the proper sense of biblical notion of *mysterion.*

W. Pannenberg, on the other hand, is prepared to understand the council's use of the words *sacramentum ecclesiae* in a wider biblical sense: the Church is a mystery that represents the mystery of Christ by her very nature. He would, however, disagree that the sacramental system of the Roman Church can be 'deduced' from the mystery of Christ. This latter position is not covered by the biblical notion of *mysterion*. The Church can be called a sacrament only in so far as Christ, *the* sacrament, is present in her.[10]

Contrary to these cautious attempts of two eminent Protestant theologians, W. Kasper seems to agree with Rahner's association of both the mystery of Christ and that of the Church, while preserving the difference between the two:

> Karl Rahner stressed the inner connection between the realisation of God's saving mystery in Jesus Christ and the Church ... So the Church, the fellowship of the believers, is an essential element in the implementation of the divine will for salvation.[11]

What separates Jüngel's interpretation of *Lumen Gentium* from that of Rahner is, I believe, the different ecclesiology of two

Christian denominations. His *analogatum* is incapable of accommodating Rahner's theory of symbol according to which a symbol shares in the reality of the symbolized (*mysterium Christi*). Pannenberg's refusal to extend the sacramentality of the Church to sacramental praxis is in opposition to Rahner's insight that the Church finds her own 'self-actualization' as the *sacramentum ecclesiae* in administering sacraments. One suspects, however, that the objections of both Protestant theologians are due to a difference arising from their basic conviction about man's justification. Luther's fears of human self-justification by means of sacramental praxis, as well as Protestant anxiety about an overemphatic power of the Church are still latent. I shall take these criticisms as a warning: to speak of the Church as a mystery in addition to that of Christ, and of the sacramental rites as enabling the acceptance of God's saving plan for the world, must not lead to an identification of Christ and the Church.

Rahner, too, tried to avoid this pitfall in his attempt to approach the notion of the sacrament by means of the word of God. The Church *is*, that is, she 'actualizes' or 'realizes' herself in both world and sacrament.

(B) *The Sacraments and the Self-Realization of the Church*

Rahner's attempt in *Word* and in other smaller essays to lay the foundation of a hitherto missing Catholic theology of the word was welcomed by Protestant theologians. On the whole, it was taken as an ecumenical opening, a move towards a cherished principle of Protestant theology. Already before Vatican II, G. Ebeling in his essay on Christian existence as something ruled by God's word in contrast to the sacraments[12] regarded it as a slight advance, however insufficient, in ecumenical dialogue. Although Rahner envisaged the word as being on the same level as the sacraments, he held onto the necessity of expressing its content by some visible sign, i.e. a sacrament. Their equivalence rested in their common effect: both word and sacrament offer an opportunity for faith to arise or to be strengthened in an individual. Rahner defined the preached word using terminology resembling the definition of the sacraments: the word as a sign effects what it signifies. The inequality between word and sacrament lies only in the definiteness and irrevocability of a sacramental event. Remember: a Catholic theology of the word has to affirm the eucharistic transformation of the species into the reality of Christ's presence. If the words pronounced over the bread and wine do not really bring about the body and blood of the Saviour, the Eucharist remains just a hint of spiritual imagination. Ebeling summary reaction to Rahner's attempt was, however, that he was starting off from a common basis in order to arrive at the traditional Catholic priority of the sacrament over and above the word of God.

I have already pointed out the premises for Rahner's theology of the Word. It was based on two principles: one is the incarnational structure of the whole economy of salvation; the other, more proximate, is the self-realization of the Church in existentially decisive human situations. It implies, indeed, that the Church would not be herself if she did not express her very nature by meaningful actions. The same theology also entails that God's word requires a fully human answer manifested in such manner that the word uttering a confession of faith is incarnated in the material expression of a visible rite.[13] On this basis Rahner equivalates the 'incarnational' with the 'sacramental', and the fear of an identification between the incarnation of the Logos and the Church's sacramental action could be read into his thought.

A small book by M. Köhnlein challenges precisely this identification. Can we in any way compare the structure of a sacrament with the 'structure' of the incarnate Christ?[14] According to him, whereas in the incarnation a pre-existent Logos unites himself with the human nature of Jesus of Nazareth, in the sacrament (of the Eucharist) it is not the pre-existent but the triumphant Christ who is united with the material species. The One really present in the Eucharist is the risen Christ as the source of grace and eventually of final salvation. Of course Köhnlein's comparison between the incarnation and the sacrament is not a view generally accepted by Protestant theologians, and is obviously questionable for Catholic ones. Rahner's own view of Christ is holistic; it comprises the whole reality of the incarnation, for otherwise the eucharistic celebration would not be at the same time a representation of Christ's sacrifice on the Cross. However, Köhnlein's suspicion is understandable: the analogy between incarnation and sacrament rejected by him can be misunderstood as identification. The same argument could also be applied in objection to Rahner's 'incarnational' concept of grace, and even to the concept of man's final deification at which man's progressive sanctification aims. This fear of 'deification' is another ground for the denominational divide.

(C) *The 'Deification' of the Church through her Sacraments?*

This subtitle is obviously a question and not a statement. Nonetheless the suspicion may well arise in the mind of anyone who has followed Rahner's thought. Jüngel's article has already hinted at the danger but, strangely enough, it is Paul Wess, a Catholic theologian, who has recently questioned some of the statements of Vatican II, and with them Rahner's theology.[15] His work in pastoral theology contains some objections the background of which is very different from those based on reformed principles. As far as I understand him, he is concerned to prevent a possible conclusion from the texts of the Council, one which asserts not only the absolute infallibility of the scriptures, but also that of the Magisterium and the power of the hierarchy.[16] Wess affirms that the theological basis of this possible misinterpretation comes from the idea of 'deification'.

> Wess's criticism is directed at transcendental philosophy and theology of which, among others, Rahner was an eminent exponent. Transcendental theology is based on the infinite 'foregrasp' or 'preapprehension' (*Vorgriff*) of man's spirit, which at the horizon of its dynamism acknowledges God as its ultimate goal, even if one cannot know him in the same way as any other objects of everyday experience.[17] This infinite transcendence of man's spirit can only gain its fulfilment in his ongoing deification for which he must have a capacity. If we take this transcendental approach to God as our entry to theology, then we shall not be able to assert God's absolute transcendence. And indeed this deification of the Athanasian tradition governs Rahner's theological (already 'graced') anthropology which, as he affirms, is a minor case of Christology. Rahner's doctrine of the Church is built on this Christology.

If the Church is the continuance of the incarnation, she will be divinized just as Christ's humanity is through the hypostatic union. Wess disagrees with this concept and affirms the full and contingent humanity of Jesus to the extent that for him, too, the absolute transcendence and the incomprehensibility of God are equally valid. This therefore should also be the case with the Church: any intermingling of human and divine elements is a mistaken concept. God's absolute transcendence is equally valid for Christ's humanity and for the Church: the administration of the sacraments does not confer grace infallibly; neither the consecrated hierarchy nor the recipients of the sacraments are endowed with divine qualities.[18] According to Wess, therefore, sacramental grace itself does not itself contain any divine element, but God's saving work is prayerfully anticipated with a view to its eschatological fulfilment.[19] Otherwise we are committed to believe in a divine capacity conferred – at least – to the partakers in the sacramental event.[20] I shall return to Wess' conclusion concerning the nature of sacramental grace.

These critical remarks have been chosen to represent some reactions both to Rahner's concept of the Church as a sacrament (Jüngel and to some extent Wess) as well as to locating the sacraments within the mystery of the Church (Pannenberg). To these I added the cautious reception of Rahner's attempt to mediate between the two mentalities by means of his theology of the word (Ebeling). For if Jesus Christ is also acknowledged as the sovereign Word of God towards the world and, if the Word is equivalent to sacrament, then the sacramentality of the Church should also be accepted. Although I do not myself identify with these critical remarks, they give me the task of re-examining the relationship between God's plan in Christ and the Church on the one hand and the same between the Church and the sacraments, on the other. These tasks, however, can only be faced after the consideration of Rahner's other approach to the relationship between Church and sacrament. I shall call this latter 'anthropological or ascendant', in contradistinction to 'theological or descendant'. The above criticisms were directed against the latter.

2.2 The 'Sacramentalization' of the World and the Sacraments

I began my reflections on Rahner's 'sacramentology' with some points of criticism raised by Protestant theologians. The reason was obvious: medieval thought had worked out the system of sacramental theology in detail; the Reformation in the sixteenth century was a radical challenge to Roman Catholic theory and praxis of the same; and the Council of Trent was a defence of this medieval achievement.

This does not mean that Protestant (especially Lutheran) theology did not have its own approach to the sacraments in many respects similar to Catholic tradition. The administration of the sacraments is an essential task for both Churches. Though with different emphasis, Catholic and Protestant understanding of the sacraments has one thing in common: they both adopt a 'descendant' line, that is, both regard the sacraments as a gift from above, as the practical application of God's grace in Jesus Christ to the individual believer. The sacraments arise from and have to be attributed to the direct will of Christ who in justifying the sinner fulfils God's word of promise. The most obvious difference between the two traditions is that Protestant theologians want to reserve the word 'sacrament' for baptism and the Eucharist only. Even W. Pannenberg, one of the most ecumenical minded Protestant theologians maintains this reformed tradition and calls the other five 'sacramentals' – a term borrowed from Roman Catholic usage.[21]

Rahner's approach, at first sight, follows this 'descendant' line. Nonetheless a closer examination of his thought may well extend this last statement in as much as his sacramental theology leans heavily on his anthropological insights. To his 'deduction' of sacraments from the fact of Incarnation and the nature of the Church there corresponds (if I may so put it) an 'adduction' of the same founded on the human predicament: sacraments in their proper sense occur in an already 'sacralized' world.

(A) *From 'Sacralization' to the Sacraments*

For Rahner, therefore, a sacrament is the actualization of the Church as the basic sacrament. That the Church, however, claims to have seven sacraments to administer to the individual faithful is not a logical consequence of this ecclesiological insight. In order to follow his own tradition Rahner must hold, too, that confirmation, the anointing of the sick, marriage and ordination to the priesthood (as 'minor sacraments') confer grace infallibly on those who do not explicitly refuse to accept God's self-communication. The grace-giving efficacy of these *sacramenta minora* is, therefore, on the same level as that of penance, baptism and the Eucharist. They, too, are sacred rites and their effect is *ex opere operato*. The mere fact, however, that the activity of the Church is required for the existence of the sacraments already indicates the presence of an anthropological factor. The Church is a two-faceted reality in which the divine will to save co-exists with the social nature of mankind. It follows that the actual situation of men and women in society can co-determine the nature of sacraments.

Rahner is by now convinced that the whole of mankind is fundamentally redeemed through Christ's redemption; it has thereby gained such a 'sacred' quality that sharing the human condition is already necessary for individual salvation. This follows from his whole system: God's will to save is a call to the whole of mankind and demands an answer. This answer, though given in principle by Christ's redemptive death, has to be complemented by the answer of the visible Church and her individual members. Is, however, human nature on its own capable of that response? Christian theology has always denied this possibility in order to avoid Pelagianism.

Nevertheless Rahner has his own solution: owing to Christ's redemption God bestows himself on mankind by setting it in an existential situation that ensures the possibility that each man and woman is able to acknowledge and love him. In order to explain this Rahner resumes his theorem of the *supernatural existential*; it is not a new quality due to human nature, but an 'opportunity', a 'chance' that makes salvation available for each and every human being living in the new existential situation of a basically redeemed mankind.[22] Even though unaware of it, everybody lives within a fundamentally 'sacralized' humanity. This tenet is further extended from mankind to the whole world. Not only do we live in a basically 'sacralized' humanity, but also in a world which possesses a sacred character behind its merely secular face. I believe this must have been the presupposition of Rahner's essays on *Revolution*, *Active Role* and *Worship* in which every word, every gesture, every rite can express an answer to God's call. He could speak of the 'liturgy of the world' where the purely secular is now raised to the realm of the history of salvation; it is 'sacralized'. It follows that all created things, including the events of human history, are consecrated by God's blessing and become means by which his providence is exercised. The various forms of the traditionally so-called *sacramentalia* can be based on this sacred character of the world.

These, however, may or may not confer redeeming grace: they do not work by force of the rite itself, *ex opere operato*, but according to the measure of our subjective devotion, *ex opere operantis*. Rites and symbols are ambiguous; they can be misused, or regarded as an attempt to force God to grant man's desires. They can appear to be magical. In history the use of symbolic rites did inspire the so-called mystery religions, contemporaneous with emergent Christianity, and in the Age of Enlightenment some even considered them the very source of the sacramental system in the Church. Even if this hypothesis has been shown to be wrong in detail, yet emended by Rahner's theorem of the *supernatural existential* it could indeed be the basis of the sacramental system. The development of a religious culture based on earthly realities could create sacramental signs and connect them to God's promise of salvation. We could speak then of a process of 'sacramentalization'.

The question is, however, in what sense do we apply Rahner's theorem to this process. I have expressed my doubts elsewhere:[23] Does it imply that God's condescension effects an ontological change in the reality of the world? Nevertheless, if Rahner's *supernatural existential* is understood as the perception of earthly realities from the viewpoint of religious faith, our world can be regarded as God's gift, a 'sacralized' universe.

In this latter sense Judaic religious beliefs and practices can be the immediate origin of a sacramental system. It is enough to mention only the ceremony of circumcision, the celebration of Yom Kippur and the annual feast of the paschal meal. The rites of the Old Law prefigure at least baptism, penance and the Eucharist. In Old Testament times they were introduced not as magical incantations, but as trust and faith in God's word of promise; and from the point of view of Christian dispensation they can be regarded as sacramentals. When, however, salvation has become a real possibility through Christ's redemption and the Church has been founded, these rites of the New Testament were believed to be sacraments in their proper sense. This consideration, however, does not exclude the remote origin of the present sacramental system, something founded in the prehistory of other religious cultures.

Against this background it is easy to see how the rites of the so-called minor sacraments, too, have developed through the mediation of Judaism and have gained their status in the Roman Catholic Church. Confirmation, anointing and of the sick, ordination and marriage must have had their own prehistory in ancient religions.

> The best example of this is marriage: its natural biological significance was usually celebrated as a religious sign within ancient cultures. Marriage rites in later Judaism, including the time of Jesus, were not only social customs, but also predominantly religious occasions. Although John has little interest in the wedding feast at Cana as a ritual, nevertheless a later theology of marriage interpreting the pericope would say that Christ, has 'raised' this very human reality to the rank of a sacrament in its proper sense. Something similar could be said of three other sacraments, those celebrating the age of majority, initiation into ministry and prayerful presence at dangerous sickness.

A similar argument was, of course, already current in the Middle Ages in explanation of the emergence of all seven sacraments of the Roman Church, viz: the beginning and growth of life in human community (baptism, confirmation); the impasses of a lifetime, sin (penance), and the menace of dissolution and death (anointing); the social need for guidance and unity (ministry); the need for exclusive, mutual love between the sexes (marriage); and lastly, and most importantly, the nourishment of a life which persists beyond the present into an unknown eternity (Eucharist). These existential occasions in secular history are implicit in the human situation that demand God's succour. The common denominator of these is our incapacity to help ourselves and to meet the needs of human life. We need, on the one hand, to rely on help; we need, on the other, some tangible expression of our deep-seated aspirations in face of the obstacles presented by the humanly impossible. Yet our incapacity is not total; we attempt to realize the impossible. The religious person asks for the incursion of the divine into secular life and, more often than not, takes refuge in rites and symbols in the efficacy of which he puts his faith and trust. The argument is based on this very human need.

These considerations, however, are proposed only in exposition of what we have termed the 'ascending' approach, for what constitutes the transition from a sacred sign to a sacrament properly so called is not human religiosity, but the word of God pronounced by Jesus Christ. In certain existential situations we express our prayerful entreaty for God's benevolent help, and open ourselves to his word of promise. Even as God's will is ever ready to save mankind, man's existential need is the demand for God's blessing and help within human life. This is, I believe, the main anthropological factor that Rahner exploits and interprets the sacramental system of the *Roman Church*. Whereas Protestant theology of the sacraments insists on Christ's *ipsissima verba* for the institution of a sacrament, Rahner believes that Christ's will is entrusted to his Church. The Church is the primary sacrament, the medium of the 'descending line' through which true sacraments emerge. The choice and definition of the sacraments by the Church creates the passage from the sacral to sacrament.

We have still to question the legitimacy of this procedure, which also connects Rahner's 'descending' and 'ascending' approaches to the sacraments.

(B) 'Sacramentalism' and Sacramental Existence

Rahner's fundamental theology presents the human person as the hearer of the word. No wonder then that in approaching the sacraments he appeals to the word of God, the *bara Jahweh* of the Old Testament, and to the *logos* of God addressing us in his incarnate Son. This word is mighty and creative: for God did create our universe with his word; he did speak through his prophets: 'Like the rain and the snow come down from heaven and return not thither ... making the earth bring forth and sprout, so shall my word be that goes forth my mouth' (Isaiah 55:10f). Whenever we encounter this word and listen to it, we can trust that its result will happen. This is why Rahner's sacramental theology regards this word as the equivalent source of the seven sacraments. In this basically 'descending' approach he is, to some extent, on common ground with his Protestant colleagues. This 'to some extent', however, betrays Rahner's Catholic background, according to which humanity demands and faith responds to God's word. Both must be expressed by means of sacred gestures and rites. Listening to the word of God becomes efficacious through sacramental practice.

> What do I mean by a Roman Catholic background? Its origin is, without doubt, the long-standing *praxis* of the average Catholic who practises his or her religion more in terms of the reception of sacraments than by listening to the preaching of the word. To this corresponds the overemphasis of the ministry of the sacraments as the primary action of the Church. In well-established parishes, everything that happens is a 'Mass': the feast of first communion is a solemnity (a quasi-sacrament) for the whole community; special occasions cannot take place without the celebration of the Eucharist; newly born children must be christened; church weddings and church funerals are likewise a 'must'; so too 'extreme unction' before or even after death. All are requirements, not only for practising, but also for nominal Catholics.

Trent's teaching, however, on the absolute necessity of the major sacraments reinforces this attitude doctrinally. Without intending any pejorative undertone, I shall term this attitude and mentality as 'sacramentalism'. Sacramentalism is therefore the conviction that God's will to save is *only* operative through our performance of certain rites within the Church. Although it may acknowledge that we are justified in one single moment by God's gratuitous grace, yet the process of sanctification, through which God aids our human effort, must follow this event. Sacramental practice is a 'divine routine', for through this process God fulfils the promise of his word and realises it irrevocably within an objective, historical reality i.e. *ex opere operato*. It is this sacramentalism that offers the security of the saving force of the God's word.

Is it 'sacramentalism' that stands behind Rahner's sacramental theology of the Word?

I believe there is a twofold answer to this question. On the one hand, Rahner's anthropological approach to the sacraments could not condone an attitude of mere sacramentalism. Indeed his is an attempt to overcome it; for, if the world and everything in it is material with potential for sacramental action, his system can hardly support the absolute necessity of the seven sacraments. He postulates, indeed, a much wider range of Church membership, and defends the possibility of achieving salvation and sanctification without the use of the sacraments; he holds that faith and love are alternatives to the sacraments and he could even assert that what happens in baptism is a disclosure, the manifestation of something that has already taken place.[24] Rahner agrees with Thomas Aquinas in asserting that forgiveness can take place by means of perfect contrition, even before the penitential act and sacramental absolution.[25] Any word of the Church is the depository and mediation of God's grace and can have a similar effect to that of a sacrament.[26] It follows that the individual's use of the sacraments is not always an absolute necessity.

On the other hand, the above is one facet only of his doctrine. Karen Kilby points out that those statements of Rahner that seemingly deviate from Tridentine tradition are reintroduced at the level of human existence.[27] An objectively redeemed creation requires the use of sacraments as an unavoidable process for advancing towards ultimate union with God. This process towards final sanctification is not an absolute necessity, but it can be an existential need, even though an unconscious one. This existential need is determined by those events in human life that I have already listed, not only for those who are already justified by listening obediently to God's word, but also for every individual. Life in a radically redeemed, and hence 'sacral', world is 'signposted' by the waymarks of the sacraments. To avail oneself of them is no longer a dubious *sacramentalism*, but a true sacramental existence.

Whether or not this answer would satisfy those of Rahner's Protestant colleagues who insist on the efficacy of the word alone is another question. Would, for instance, Pannenberg and Ebeling agree that Rahner's quasi-equating the Word with sacrament implies a quasi-identity? For Ebeling seems to take back with the right hand what he gives with the left.

(C) *The Sacraments and the 'Self' of the Church*

Listening to the word and the sacramental life are an existential necessity, not only for individuals, but for the whole Church whose ideal nature is realized, not only through the preaching of the word, but also by the administration of sacraments. The Church's *'Self'* is realized in these activities. In this Rahner and Protestant theologians may be in basic agreement, Rahner, however, understands the existential need for the sacraments shared by human beings and that of the Church as strictly complementary. The Church becomes an existential reality through the administration of the sacraments, but the individual's situation determines what kind of sacraments are needed.

To my mind, this position creates a problem in sacramental theology alongside another, an ecclesiological one. As for this latter: what happens, if by hypothesis the Church does not (or cannot) administer her sacraments; is she then no longer herself? Or conversely: if there are no men and women who accept and use the seven sacraments, can the Church survive? If the Church does not or cannot realize herself by preaching the word and administering the sacraments, can she still exist as a 'sign for the nations', that is, as the primordial sacrament of salvation? Even if these difficulties can be explained satisfactorily (as I shall later), there remains the first problem, one of sacramental theology. Supposing that there are indeed some prominent existential situations in human life that demand God's sacramental grace, one can always ask why they should be seven in number. Are there not other important occasions of human need for sacramental support? (For instance, Catholics have often wondered why the final profession of religious is not a sacrament.) The individual situation of every man and woman is, surely, different and there can emerge occasions in life that, in the terminology of Martin Heidegger, are 'existentials'. In one sentence: can the existential need of human beings alone determine the seven sacraments of the Roman Church?

The two problems are complementary: on the one hand, if human need alone cannot determine the number of the sacraments, how can the Church do the same? If, on the other hand, the Church is capable of defining sacraments as rites of the Christian community, why does she restrict herself to the number seven?

There is, therefore, a dilemma for Roman Catholic theology: it must either limit, with the Reformation, the original sacraments to baptism and the Eucharist (and perhaps to penance) for which the words of Christ are patent, or to learn to live with the possibility that the Church could of her own account 'institute' sacraments besides the two (or three?) evangelical ones in keeping with the historically changing situations of the individual faithful.

> This latter position is somewhat similar to W. Pannenberg's solution: as mentioned above, he acknowledges baptism and the Eucharist as genuine sacraments and relegates the rest to *sacramentalia*. G. Ebeling's book, *The Word of God and Tradition*,[28] stands even nearer to Rahner's theology of the word. For Ebeling, too, sacraments derive from God's word and from the kerygma of the Church. The criterion, however, for what constitutes an individual sacrament is not first and foremost the human situation of need, but how these sacramental actions and rites illuminate and interpret the word of the Gospel. For him the word retains priority, but it can be helped by a rite to convey its full meaning. He comes even nearer to the Catholic position when he suggests that the sacrament, as the 'interpreter' of God's word, is at the same time interpreting a human situation. For him, however, the sacrament is aiming at faith, the sole basis of man's justification.

In spite of the similarity between the three theologians' approaches, Rahner can hardly accept Pannenberg's or Ebeling's position. In following Catholic tradition, Rahner has to hold that even the 'minor' sacraments work also through the rite itself – *ex opere operato,* hence they are sacraments in their proper sense. Furthermore, Ebeling's sacramental theology does not demand, either the Church as the intermediary in the origin of the sacraments, or even the number seven. A solitary reading of the word of the Bible could, in certain circumstances, be 'sacramental'.

It is obvious that the solution of the above dilemma cannot, without qualification, imply an arbitrary institution of a sacrament by the Church. An answer, however, could be built on Rahner's insight about the *Selbstvollzug* of the Church. The existential need of any individual must encounter the Church's own need to 'realize', to 'actualise' herself through administering the sacraments. The rather clumsy English translations of this term, *Selbstvollzug,* emphasize the first tag: 'self': *self*-actualization, *self*-realization, *self*-performance, *self*-fulfilment, *self*-constitution, and so on. The Church's response to human need demanding sacramental action establishes her own existential self; she makes herself present: in the twofold initiation of the individual (baptism and confirmation); in the eucharistic assembly of the faithful by re-enacting the sacrifice of Christ, and feeding it with the bread of life eternal; in rendering the sinner innocent (penance); in the love of the spouses (marriage); in *hora mortis* by raising the sick to health in body and soul (sacrament of the sick). It is presupposed, of course, that through these sacramental self-realizations the Church speaks or interprets the word of God and does not act arbitrarily.

What or who is this 'self' of the Church that acts not only in preaching the word and in administering the sacraments, but also constitutes her*self* by this very activity? In other words: what or who is the *subject* of the Church's proper action? Can we say that the Church is a 'self', a personal agent like ourselves? Rahner states repeatedly that though, on the one hand the Church is not a person in the same sense as a human subject, on the other she is more than the sum-total of her individual members. I now believe that this 'more' enables us to speak of the Church, not only as the logical subject of certain activities, but also as an entity to which we can attribute various qualities. She can be regarded as an *hypostasis* (as 'standing under', the literal translation of this term), that is, the subject of her own actions and possessing her own qualities. She cannot, however, act without her members. Thus the holiness of the Church (one of her classical attributes) is resplendent, not only in the holiness of just some of her members, but also in her 'sinfulness' (of which Rahner also speaks[29]), since her sinful members can be recognized as part of the Church as a whole.[30] One cannot come to such a statement without a certain 'hypostatization'.

What or who then is the 'self' of the Church that thus actively realizes herself? She can be regarded as a collective entity, as a collective person or personality. The notion is not unknown in biblical usage in as much as to call the Church a 'corporate person' means that any individual member of the Church cannot regard her, as it were, from the outside. What the Church does, in a certain sense, is *our* responsibility too; praise of the Church is self-praise; and criticism of the Church is self-criticism: 'we are the Church'. The self-realization (that is – the Rahnerian *Selbstvollzug*) of the Church in administering the sacraments should be attributed to this 'corporate person'. She is the socially organized assembly of individual selves who confess the mystery of Christ together, and thereby define themselves as Christians; or from another angle: she is one personal unit realizing, 'actualizing' itself in the *community* of her members.

> Before entering into an explanation of the above statement I need further to specify what 'corporate person' means. Rahner speaks of the *self*-realization of the Church. The 'self', however, is not the same as a 'person'. By 'self' I mean the way in which I am *aware* of myself, and by 'person' how I actually relate to my human environment, for to be a person is to be in an existential relationship with others. (I shall return to this distinction later). I understand Rahner's *Selbstvollzug* according to this distinction: the 'self' of the Church is the way in which her members are *aware* of the Church with all her qualities and attributes, and the 'person' is the way in which she actively *exists* within her context. Whereas it might seem odd to think of the Church as a 'collective-self' she can surely be a 'collective person or person-

ality' in the way in which she takes responsibility for her actions whether among her members (*ad intra*) or on behalf of the rest of mankind (*ad extra*). The 'self' is constituted through its permanent qualities; a 'person', however, is never a 'given', ready-made subject, but the result of a continuous process of development in and through self-realization. If the Church as a corporate person realizes herself in preaching the word and administering the sacraments, she is in the process of becoming more and more a collective person, until she reaches her fulfilment in the eschatological communion of the saints in heaven. If, therefore, by hypothesis the Church does not or cannot act, she can still be herself, but not that 'collective person', the bride who is going to encounter her heavenly bridegroom.

If indeed we regard the administration of the sacraments as the action of this corporate personality it will be more likely that we can defend the traditional number of seven sacraments. The advantage of this approach is that the concrete and existential being of the Church becomes manifest in communitarian acts, in religious rites and ceremonies, and not only in the private lives of individuals. The kerygma is not preached to individual souls only; the sacraments, though they work an individual salvation, are never a private affair; salvation touches the whole of mankind. This is the context in which the Church 'actualizes' herself and becomes a corporate person out of her own essential self.

> In dealing with the ministry of the Church I have in fact already made use of this distinction: the Church *is* identical with her ministry, and this actual ministry *is* the Church; with Rahner's teaching as my foundation, instead of equating the Church with her ordained officials (who may or may not preach the word and dispense the sacraments, i.e. with the hierarchy), I have insisted that the Church as a whole only exists if she performs her ministry, a ministry common to all believers. Thus priestly ordination is not just a private transaction between the ordaining bishop and the individual candidate, but an event through which the Church also becomes herself. Likewise, in asserting that marriage 'creates' the smallest unit of the Church, I have presupposed Rahner's *Selbsvollzug:* the communion of the spouses affects the reality of the whole Church. Furthermore, the whole Church is existentially present in the small community of the Mass; the whole Church is acting as a community in receiving a

newly baptized child; the whole Church supports the dangerously ill through the prayer of the presbyter; the communitarian aspect of penance (now gradually returning into the praxis of the Church) means that the whole Church acts on behalf of the penitent through sacramental absolution, and so on. In these assertions I have *de facto* identified the Church with her function. This function realizes, makes the Church present and, at the same time, interprets God's word promising salvation to the individual. The Church does not exist in herself, but in her self-realization as a corporate person.

Would it not be easier to comprehend the existing seven sacraments in these terms? The criterion becomes, not the existential need of the individual, but also the self-testimony of the *whole* Church in which she makes herself present, defines herself in the recipient of each of the sacraments.[31] This, of course, does not exclude the outside possibility of self-actualization through further actions when historical circumstances call forth the full engagement of the whole Church. (It is conceivable that a general council, or even a local assembly of a particular church in given circumstances, in whatever form it takes, can be believed to be a sacramental self-realization of the whole Church.)

Using, however, this concept of the Church can we also maintain that in a hypothetical case, the Church is even then herself, a corporate person, when she does not or cannot fulfil her essential functions in, preaching the word of God and administering the sacraments? For this, however, we must further develop the different ways of her self-realization in word and sacrament.

2.3. The Church is a Sacramental Event

My analysis of Rahner's sacramental theology was implicitly *en face* of his Protestant critics, who either disagreed with Rahner's understanding of the sacramental nature of the Church (Jüngel) or doubted that the concept of the Church entails the sacramental praxis of Roman Catholicism (Pannenberg). Rahner's answer to both of these objections was to show the basic unity-in-difference between God's saving plan and the reality of the Church on the one hand, and the self-'actualization' of the Church in the sevenfold praxis of the sacraments, on the other. The operative concept in his answer was that of *Selbstvollzug*. God's plan to save mankind realizes itself in the Church, and the Church in her sacramental praxis. *Selbstvollzug*, however, presupposes a functional notion of the Church:[32] her existence depends on the actual preaching of God's word and the administration of the sacraments. The Church is an *event* and her 'selfhood' (understood as the collective personality of her members) must be engaged in these activities. This position serves as a bridge between Rahner's descendent and ascendant approach to sacramental theology, and is supported by a theoretical scheme that can give systematic coherence to the whole of his theology. It is his theory of the symbol.

(A) *The 'Ontology' of the Symbol*

I submit, therefore, that the systematic core of Rahner's view of the Church and sacraments is his *ontology of the symbol*. His 'symbolism' was presented as an instance of 'symbolic causality', one of the features of his own approach to the sacraments.[33] I shall now resume this theory beginning with its application to the notion of God. For Rahner the God of Christian revelation, the Trinity, is the template of an all-pervading symbolism valid for being in general: he is the 'supreme Being'. This Supreme Being is not a lonely God, for the Father *communicates* his own being to the Logos and returns to himself in the Spirit.[34] If this God freely wills the world to emerge by an eternal decree, creation will have the same ontological structure as his own Trinitarian life. This means, as I understand it, that the Creator relates himself to the world according to the 'structure' of his eternal and necessary self-bestowal on the Son and the Spirit.[35] The world, though it is essentially different from God, is his own. This would explain why the whole world, in its very secularity, can be open to God's free creative 'action' and the creature can become a symbol of God.

If this (Trinitarian) God is the 'supreme Being', then being as such is not a static fact, but an 'act' in relation to another.

Indeed, *really* to exist is to be in relationship with others. A symbol is exactly this relationship. In other terms, being is *relational* by its very nature, and not, what we might call, a substantial entity.

What does it mean, therefore, to be a symbol? The answer in everyday parlance would refer to a reality which is more than itself: it points at something else, it is a *sign*. Rahner's distinction is already well known: there are signs that not only indicate, but also partake of that reality which they symbolize. He speaks of a *'Realsymbol'* as different from a mere sign, which is 'artificial' in the sense of being defined by human beings within a special context outside of which it is meaningless. The case is different with 'real-symbols': just as within the Triunity of God, the 'supreme Being'. To be is a dynamic event in three stages: the Father communicates himself to the Son in order to become himself again in the Spirit. We can generalize this pattern and say: a real-symbol points to another by means of 'self-bestowal' and thus relates itself to the symbolized; it expresses itself, and in this self-expression it 'sets itself over and again', that is, it reaffirms itself continually.

I come to the same from another angle: A real-symbol has the capacity to indicate an entity it symbolizes and by expressing that entity, reasserts its own existence (or, as Rahner puts it: *fulfils* itself). Not only, however, does the symbol 'act', but that which is symbolized does too, by reference to the symbol: it 'needs' the other to be what it really is. There is an interaction between symbol and symbolized which implies a true 'participation' in each other. Someone in expressing love is in an active relationship with the beloved and, conversely, the beloved is in 'need' of the lover in order to express his or her intimate feeling. In the case of the Trinity, the Father is only the Father if he expresses himself in the Son and the Spirit. Conversely, the Son and the Spirit are only Son and Spirit in their relationship with the Father. So too the Creator would not be creator without a created world, and Christ the redeemer would not be redeemer without the redeemed. Nor would the Church be the Church without the preaching of the word and the actual administration of the sacraments; she finds her self-expression in these actions. The Church acts as a symbol by her *kerygma* and sacraments and in doing so she continually fulfils herself by becoming the Church in her existential reality. This is why the Church is a sacrament, and the sacraments are the Church. Church and sacrament achieve their unity in difference.

If this speculative scheme is acceptable, we can better understand, not only the structure of a symbol, but also the structure of all that is. Rahner's ontology of the symbol seems to be an all-inclusive theory. Such theories, however, should be regarded as working hypotheses and their use as heuristic. Consequently, they can be further refined, extended, and exploited.

A short article by J. Buckley[36] points out an important feature in Rahner's ontology of the symbol. He makes a distinction between symbolism with a 'horizontal' and 'vertical', dimension and asserts that Rahner's theory of symbolism can be applied in these different ways. 'Horizontal' symbolism is restricted to the transient functioning of a sign: it is only valid in connection with the signified. 'Vertical' symbolism, on the other hand is more flexible: in expressing itself with regard to a symbolized reality it can alter its significance. A 'vertical' symbol is, so to speak, a 'symbol in itself'.

For example, it is our everyday experience that religious symbols i.e., signs and rites including the Church and her sacraments, are losing significance for many of our contemporaries – a cherished topic for criticism in a modern sociology of religion. Pastors, who are engaged in proclaiming and using them in their ministry, are in a quandary: how to find new and meaningful words and symbols, while at the same time, preserving the traditional meaning. The expression 'Lamb of God' in our Mass liturgy does not symbolize anything for most people today unless the appropriate biblical texts are known and understood: it is a symbolism with a 'horizontal' dimension that has lost its signifying power. A 'vertical' symbol, on the other hand can signify a variety of things. For instance a kiss, as a symbol, can be expression of intimate love, of sexual desire or Judas' betrayal. Dependent on the context it becomes, in a way, different; even if its symbolizing function towards the symbolized is impaired or ceases, it always remains a symbol in its own self-expression. Thus a festival meal, by remaining what it is, can symbolize a variety of things: its meaning can change according to its changing context. The rite of baptism can symbolize the washing away of the stains of original sin (which is nowadays out of 'fashion') or can be sign of receiving a new member into the community of the Church. The whole liturgy of the Mass can symbolize the sacrifice of Christ and/or the anticipation of an eschatological meal: it is a symbol with a vertical dimension.

Buckley, therefore, holds that Rahner's symbolism entails this 'vertical' dimension too, and that it can explain several difficulties, not only in Rahner's system, but also in Christian theology. If the Church is herself a symbol in Buckley's 'vertical' sense, then her *Selbstvollzug* is not confined to her activity in preaching the word and administering the sacraments. The Church can exist because of her relationship with God and Christ, even if no one listens to the preaching of the Word, and no one receives the sacraments. She can be, as Jüngel admitted, the 'great sign' of Christ's redemption; an *analogatum* of God's eternal plans. She is, however, truly herself if God's word is preached and listened to and the sacraments are administered to and received by the faithful. At the same time she can symbolize an alternative way of life to an unbelieving world. Her full reality is manifold: 'church' has the ability to denote different aspects in which the unity-in-difference between God and Church, or Church and sacrament are far from obvious.

Buckley's amendment of Rahner's symbolism seems to overcome at least two questionable points in his own system. First of all, it forestalls the misunderstanding that the notion of the Church is merely functional. Her *Selbstvollzug* in word and sacrament coexists with that 'vertical' dimension in which the Church is herself a symbol. She, so to speak, stands for God even in a world of unbelief and indifference. Secondly, by retaining the word 'symbol', instead of postulating a substantial reality for the Church, Buckley underlines Rahner's premise: an entity with a symbolic structure 'completes', 'fulfils' itself in something *other* than its original selfhood. In other words, it can be centre of possible activity: an *actus* (with immanent dynamism) as well as an *actio*.[37] The Church as a symbol in this 'vertical' sense can be the subject of her attributes and qualities without regard to her activities. Rahner's *Selbstvollzug*, therefore, satisfies both tags of the word: she is both a 'self' in the vertical sense, and a 'realization' in Buckley's horizontal sense.

I believe, however, that Buckley, even with this amendment, remains Rahnerian: the examples through which he illustrates the usefulness of his distinction for addressing some of the problems in Christian theology do not seem to require the abandonment of Rahner's unity-in-difference, both between God and the Church, and between the Church and sacrament. Neither of the two Roman Catholic theologians would satisfy their Protestant objectors. They fear any identification between God and Church as well as between Church and sacrament as smacking of *synergism*, that is, the working of divine action in conjunction with a corresponding human one. Take an example: if a person performs a good and salvific action, such an action is also God's, in as much as that person is in union with and difference from God.[38] Has the person, then, contributed something to his own salvation? God does not work *in* man, but rather *on* man, who then does his own good deeds, i.e. *human* actions. May one, perhaps, apply the same distinction to Buckley's understanding of the reception of sacraments: if an adult receives the sacrament of baptism with full devotion, the grace conferred is also the grace of the Church, for baptism is a rite in union with, yet different from the Church. The grace received is surely due in part to the person's devotion. The whole liturgy of the Mass is a symbol of Christ's sacrifice. If we apply Rahner's *ontology* of the symbol the celebration of the Eucharist may become a repetition of, or something additional to Christ's unique and once-for-all sacrifice. Even if we do not agree with the objectors' counter position, Rahner's theory of the symbol remains open to further examination.

At the end of his essay Buckley himself admits that his amendment of Rahner's ontology of the symbol in a 'vertical' dimension is only a hypothesis. That something is itself a symbol cannot be verified by comparison with the symbolized. The same can be said of my attempt to understand the Church herself as a symbol of God's presence. The assertion, therefore, that every being is a symbol, and can possibly function as one, has only a speculative value. It can be used as a *paradigm* in aid of theoretical understanding, but lacks any claim to truth. In order to avoid any possible discrepancy between a hypothesis and its verification, I shall have to find another way of interpreting Rahner's symbolism.

(B) *Symbols and 'Performatives'*

I shall now restrict our discussion to the sacraments of the Church and suppose that both Church and sacrament have a symbolic structure. The hypothetical statement 'some signs can be symbolic in themselves', can be better understood (Buckley), if we follow Rahner's approach to Church and sacrament through his theology of the word of God. I believe that Rahner, too, sensing perhaps the inadequacy of his analysis of symbol, introduced the notion of 'exhibitive' word. Whether or not he was acquainted with J. L. Austin's 'performatives' or D. Evans 'Logic of Self-Involvement',[39] his 'exhibitives' were invented to fulfil the same requirement. I shall interpret Rahner's 'exhibitive' in the light of the works of Austin and Evans.

Take a statement like 'God gives grace with no corresponding merit on the part of the recipient'. It is a statement with which all Christian denominations would agree. Austin would call it a 'constative' statement, since it communicates to the listener that which it states. Such constatives can be true or false in themselves. Made, however, in the context of a Christian community they demand something more, namely, the attitude of those who hear them and believe in their truth. Apart from being 'constatives' such a statement can effect something in those who accept them. Austin would call such statements 'performatives'. Thus Rahner's exhibitive and Austin's performative utterances do change things. They make clearer what sort of appraisal[40] is appropriate. This appraisal also reveals that they are valid or invalid: the listener should respond. They determine behaviour in addition to one's consent to or dissent from what it states. Because they involve the self of the one who utters them, and the self of those to whom they are addressed, such statements can also be called 'self-involving' ones (Evans).

Apply this same consideration to God's word, usually received through the kerygma of the Church. A performative statement not only informs the listener but, in a transferred sense, 'causes' something in him. This 'something' can be expressed by a simple verbal acceptance, 'I believe', or it can 'affect' an attitude that determines the future behaviour of the respondent concerning the utterance heard. The case of sacramental events is similar. The acceptance of the word as true and valid will be present and dominant in the whole life of the hearer. Or to put it differently, the listener *obeys* the word which he or she has heard. This is the word's performative force answered in belief or religious rite. The single sacraments can be considered as exhibitive words or signs which effect in those who perceive what they purport, namely, the promise of grace.

> This consideration harmonizes with Augustine's thought which still rules the sacramental theology of both denominations, Catholic or Reformed. For him the sacramental event is in the word spoken over the elements. It is an insight which will be translated in the Middle Ages into the two ontological principles of the form and matter of the sacraments. Both the word and the non-verbal rite become thereby equally constitutive for what the sacraments are supposed to effect. The discussion as to which of these is primary (as in the case of Ebeling *versus* Rahner) is superfluous.

A question still remains: to whom should we attribute the words used and the performance of the sacramental rite. If we accept Rahner's theory of *Selbstvollzug*, we can assume that Christ 'actualizes' himself in the Church which, in her turn, is also a symbol and entails the sacraments. It is unlikely that Christ's command to baptize provided the exact form of the rite, nor is it probable that he determined exactly how to celebrate his remembrance in the Eucharist. It is most likely, indeed, that he did not invent a novel rite for the symbol of baptism. His use of the word 'baptism with water and the Spirit' and the verbal 'being baptized' meant the initiation of a new attitude: he may have thought of the ceremonial washing for the remission of sins, as practised by John the Baptist or by the Essenes; he may have referred to the future of his apostles who are about to be 'baptized' into the same life of suffering and martyrdom which he himself was to undergo.[41] So it was with the Eucharist: the paschal meal with his friends at the Last Supper may have been an anticipation of a triumphant *convivium* of the finally redeemed in his eschatological kingdom. Within it he established the sign of bread and wine and identified them with his body and blood.

His words, apart from being a statement (Austin's 'constative') were a real reference to this eschatological meal ('performative') of that fulfilment.

Likewise, with regard to the minor sacraments, the Church, in the absence of Christ's definitive words of 'institution' in the Gospels, has adopted Jesus' attitude: to marriage (which he ruled to be indissoluble); to sinners (whose sins he forgave); to the mortally sick (whom he healed, or prayed for, and recommended their anointing); to his apostles (some of whom he regarded as leaders, or took all of them as his beloved friends; John 14:14–16). In other words, the later Church has taken Christ's non-verbal attitudes as performatives at the same level as his verbal command: 'Go therefore and make disciples of all nations, baptizing them ...' (Matthew 28:19, if it is genuine). The institution of seven sacraments by the Roman Church is due to the words or attitudes of Christ *and* to the response of his Church under the guidance of the Spirit. This Church believes that within these sacramental events God's promise of grace becomes a reality. It is a truth of our faith.

(C) *Sacramental Grace: Promise and/or Reality*

I have, hitherto, regarded the Church as a corporate personality and have, therefore, passed over the individual reception of the sacraments: the sacraments are specifically for the individual members of the Church. The recipient of them must become a 'member' of the Church, even in its large Rahnerian sense; he or she has to go through a process of initiation into the Christian life. It is a process, one which starts by attention to the word of God as preached by the Church, an attention which evokes a response: he or she accepts the word by believing and taking up a corresponding attitude which is authentically expressed by an action made available by the Church. One class of such actions is the use of the sacraments.

We can borrow here the terminology of Evans' self-involving logic: all sacraments mirror God's word as 'performative'; the recipient responds with an active acceptance: an attitude or behaviour. This response is itself 'performative', an action which is animated by the promise of God's grace in this life and ends in the eschatological fulfilment of the believer. God's promise, his grace, and the final consummation of a Christian life are moments of one and the same process of initiation.

I can sum up, then, my version of sacramental grace in terms of the process of initiation in the form of a thesis: *the promise of God, as heard by faith, is the free gift of grace; and sacramental grace is the promise of our future in God.* Let me explain this in more detail.

To say that grace is the promise *only* of eternal life, would not define its true nature. Likewise, to affirm that grace is an entity, some sort of power superadded to a Christian life striving towards a final consummation in heaven, would be to insert another supernatural reality between human activity and divine condescension (the *gratia creata sanctificans* indeed, of traditional theology.) Grace is rather a relationship which God grants, and with it, initiates a process the end of which is eternal life. This divine/human relationship can, indeed, be rightly understood as a promise that is already grace.

> We can reach greater precision by taking over from process theology the distinction between external and internal relationship: the first does *not* and the other *does* become a constitutive element in the life-process of an existent individual. The environment of an existent being is the context without which no process is possible, yet some aspects of this environment can 'enter' into a more intimate relationship with the individual, without destroying either the identity of the individual or the assumed aspect. For example, I may know *about* the Chinese language through living in Asia, but learning to speak it will be my own accomplishment. I have 'interiorized' the language without altering it.

The advance from promise to its fulfilment is similar: hope in God's promise is the modifying 'aspect' of an individual's situation which becomes part and parcel of the process of sanctification and manifests itself as the person's firm orientation towards the acquisition of an intimate love of God. This new orientation of our Christian life, however, still remains the promise of an ultimate fulfilment in the eschatological consummation of the whole of creation; at that stage love is fulfilled, and that is the true meaning of grace.

Sacramental grace is, then, a true constitutive relationship within our pilgrimage to eternal life; it is the grace of God appropriate for our initiation into the Christian life. Official entry into the Church, and with it the commission to some degree of ministry within the community, is bestowed by the sacraments of baptism and confirmation, as two sacraments in one. Even though the commission to priestly service remains selective, it too can be regarded as a further initiation of members of a priestly people into action in accord with the Church's priestly purpose. These sacraments, conferred once and for all, (and therefore unrepeatable) enable the recipient's participation in the continual celebration of the eucharistic sacrifice, and consequently in the celebration of mankind's ultimate destiny; a truth which indicates the central position of the Eucharist among the other sacraments.

> To place *ordo* among the sacraments of initiation may seem unusual in the context of traditional theology. In explanation: One can deduce the necessity of ordination not only from the 'institution' of the Eucharist, but rather assign its purpose as a function of eucharistic celebration within the Church; a way of thinking which follows from the proper understanding of the universal priesthood of all believers. Furthermore, I regard, too, baptism and confirmation as ministry within the Church, for even non-ordained members are potential priests capable of presiding at the eucharistic assembly when commissioned by the symbolic act of ordination. The Eucharist does, indeed, give sense and meaning to all the other sacraments.

The central position of the eucharistic assembly derives from the fact that the Eucharist is not just one of the 'seven', but at once the purpose and sacramental drive of the progressive sanctification of the faithful. It is, therefore too, an initiation which celebrates the real presence of Christ's sacrifice and with it, anticipates future fulfilment in the eschatological meal of the kingdom. The history of Christ and the history of the believer embrace the promised future when Christ in the midst of his followers will eat bread and drink wine in the glory of final resurrection (Luke 22:16). The

Eucharist so understood is an initiation into the *parousia* of the Lord as a future event anticipated now in our time.

A similar conclusion can be drawn, if we consider the traditional structure of the Mass. It is itself a process: it starts with the proclamation of the word of God and continues as the remembrance of Christ's life, death, and resurrection, celebrated in the expectation of his second coming. There are two main symbolic actions involved: in the first, the real transformation of the species re-enacts Christ's whole life, starting with the eternity of his Trinitarian origin, resuming the stages of his earthly existence, and ending with the anticipation of the eschatological meal, the apotheosis of the kingdom of God. At Mass the consecration of the species aptly symbolizes the incarnation, but even as Bethlehem does not predict Calvary, so Christ's real presence is not of itself the sacrifice we celebrate. That is expressed by our participation in another symbol: by 'eating his body and drinking his blood' we celebrate the fruit of Calvary through our communion with the Redeemer who has died and risen again on our behalf. Attendance at Mass, therefore, should detach the participant from the run of 'common' time into that 'special' time in which past, present and future are one, that is an 'eternity' which really affects our present, transient life. The Eucharist makes present the life implicit in an inscrutable future eschatological completeness.

The communicants at Mass, however, have not yet reached that state. They take their past into the Lord's presence, and, strengthened by the promise of eternal life, look forward to the hidden future of their earthly life. Their past may have been marked by the struggle not to turn away from God (and from the Church, according to Rahner), or indeed burdened by sins committed and absolved by the sacrament of reconciliation. This sacrament, too, is provided with the Eucharist in mind. The sacrament of matrimony, likewise, blesses the desire for an intimate communion of love with another person; a faithful love 'till death us do part', is itself a symbol of the Eucharist. Like Christ in the eucharistic sacrifice the spouses abandon their own lives for the sake of each other, thus, by growing together as man and wife re-enact the change of elements into presence of Christ in the Eucharist. Relying on

God's promise they can face a future which, though it ends in death, is preceded by the symbol of final anointing and the last *viaticum* as an initiation into everlasting life.

Let me summarize my initial thesis. The introduction of the concept of a process of gradual initiation as basic to the sacramental system, in which promise as grace and grace as promise actually happen, does not, I believe, involve the abandonment of the technical analysis made in the Middle Ages, for that analysis can also be envisaged as a process. This process began with the sacramental sign (*sacramentum tantum*), continued through the mediation of the moment of actual administration (*sacramentum et res*) and finished with the proper result of this event (*gratia tantum*). It is true that I conceive of this event as a happening in time, one which momentarily unites the promise to its fulfilment in grace, and that I can agree with Rahner's interpretation that this is the moment in which the recipient of the sacrament participates in the action of the Church for the sanctification of mankind. This 'fleeting moment' (the *res et sacramentum* of medieval tradition) is part of the whole process which mediates between sign and grace, and generates hope in the promise which has not yet reached its fulfilment in love.[42] The self is now in the process of gradual growth and is becoming more and more a person in communion with the Church on earth and through her with the risen life of the Lord of eternal life.

The seven sacraments of the Church, individually considered, are particular events of this process towards an ultimate fulfilment which transcends human capacity. They are not, therefore entirely separate ('punctual') miraculous events which infallibly produce personal grace. They are a kind of gradual initiation: baptism is the start of growth into the ministry explicitly conferred by confirmation and for some develops further by ordination into the office of deacons, priests and bishops; marriage is not finalized with the mutual consent of the spouses, but needs to be 'consummated', not by some random act of sexual intercourse, but by the process of maturing in interpersonal love; a good confession is never complete unless it withstands the subsequent test of a life converted to God; and the anointing of the sick has to be crowned by the gift of death in the Lord. The whole process in all its stages gains its coherence in the celebration of the

Eucharist which in turn, is the anticipation of and trust in God's pledge which bestows a new direction in a life destined to end in the eschatological consummation of all creation.

That mystery of that eternal future must now engage our attention.

Chapter 3

The Eternal Future

The topic that now imposes itself for discussion leads us into the very heart of Christianity: the doctrine of the last things, known to Christian tradition as *eschatology*. Not that this subject was untouched in our previous discussions. On the contrary, it has occurred mainly as an adjective, 'eschatological', usually connected with the noun 'dimension'. It has emerged that all the realities of revelation can be expressed in terms of their 'eschatological' dimension. Theological statements have implicitly entailed such a consideration, at least by reference to the finality and irrevocability of their content in the state of fulfilment and consummation. The very fact that such statements are to be read in the context of final salvation demonstrates the universality of eschatological belief.

This 'eschatological' tag seems to have been a *conditio sine qua non* of statements in the various fields of theological discourse: the Church is regarded as the final assembly of people called to salvation in Jesus Christ; redemption is the ultimate and unsurpassable fulfilment of mankind's relationship with God; Jesus the Christ himself is seen as God's complete and final self-revelation; and the gift of grace mediated to the Church and her members through his Spirit is a foretaste of the beatific vision – regarded by Rahner as the goal of man's pilgrimage and the *eschaton* of his eternal future. It is then more than plausible that sacraments anticipate an eschatological fulfilment.

If we seriously regard this eschatological dimension as an essential prerequisite of our whole theology, its absence would reduce Christianity to just another attempt by mankind to understand itself in face of the absolute mystery of God.

Contrary to the conviction of our faith, it would be one religion among many others. This is why I can safely introduce this present topic as the heart of our theological discourse.

So far, however, I have merely pointed out the importance of the 'eschatological' without exploring the content of what used to be the theological treatise of eschatology. This is what I must do in the following pages. As will be seen, however, I shall avoid entering into a detailed treatment of all its various aspects. Neither did Rahner who, to my knowledge, never taught eschatology as part of his students' theological training, although references to it abound in his writings. Apart from a short summary in *Foundations*[1] there is no systematic presentation of it, and this is why 'eschatology' or even 'eschatological' does not feature in the title of this chapter. I have instead summed up what follows under 'future' with the attached adjective 'eternal' to express the strictly eschatological material. In the concept, 'future', I shall also include what comes next in the flow of our natural time until this time is swallowed by God's eternity.

This time, I do not intend to add a separate section for Comments and Questions, but rather to raise them in the course of presenting Rahner's thought. My investigation, in the absence of any systematic eschatology therein, will proceed from question to question, from concept to concept, until it reaches its last topic: our common pilgrimage into the mystery of God.

3.1. Eschatology and 'Eschatological'

Of all the treatises of traditional theology that underwent basic change in the last century the most affected was that of eschatology. The usual treatment of the last things gradually lost importance, viz., the fate of the individual after death: particular judgement-purgatory-hell-heaven and the consummation of the whole history by God's universal judgement. This change was partly due to Protestant liberal theology in the nineteenth century according to which the failure of an immediate parousia in early Christian communities developed into the idea of an eschatology realized in the present of each and every individual believer.² Although Catholic theologians only gradually accepted this interpretation, they nonetheless came to be critical of their own tradition in dealing with the last things. It was recognized that an older eschatology's concentration on the individual's future destiny was very different from one that emphasised the promised universal consummation of our world's time and history. It became, too, more and more obvious that our knowledge of the last things is an extrapolation of our present situation, which is already 'eschatological'.³ Rahner's *Foundations* treats the first point by distinguishing between individual and collective eschatology, and he repeatedly returns to the second.

The first time Rahner tackled this latter topic was in 1960.⁴ *Hermeneutics* discusses in detail all the different approaches which help theologians in handling statements (in the Bible and tradition) concerning man's and the world's future. His purpose is not to discuss the content of these statements but to find an appropriate method for the theological treatment of what may lie in a yet unknown world to come. Older eschatology had regarded future facts as metaphysical objects identical in character with present ones, as if they were 'part of the world like any other so that knowledge of them presents no particular problems apart from ... [those of] theological realities in general'.⁵ Such a course is unacceptable after the modern change of an approach to reality ('the turn to the subject'). Rahner in fact appeals to a metaphysic of knowledge in which it is not difficult to recognise the traits of his own philosophical premises in *Spirit in the World*.

Hermeneutics, however, is a theological essay on the nature of eschatological statements. Rahner claims that their content is grounded in the present situation, but that they point to a genuine future reality: 'in a very ordinary, empirical sense of the world to come'. Hence to regard them as mythical, or merely the affirmations of something in man's present situation, would be contrary to Scripture: were this the case, such statements should be 'demythologized' or 'existentialized' in the established faith of the Church.

We should note here, parenthetically, that *Hermeneutics* raises another theological point, one which is not mentioned in Rahner's later treatments of the same topic. He appeals to God's omniscience which *de se* could communicate information concerning events or things of the future. Note, however, that whatever God may reveal to man in this way 'is also determined by the structure [nature] of the hearer, which is finite and conditioned' (a 'turn to the subject'!).[6] He does not of course intend to limit God's freedom to reveal whatever he decides to. This 'restriction', however, is necessary because either such communications would not have an existential significance, or would lack, too, the (so to speak) 'futurity' of divine utterances. It would be like reporting an event in a time-to-come, as though it were a past happening. It is therefore necessary 'to define an a priori sphere of eschatological assertions, a framework within which they are to be understood'.[7]

One element of nineteenth-century liberal theology remains in Rahner's *Hemeneutics*. It is quite clear from the Gospels that Jesus did not know, (or rather refused to say?) *when* the last day would occur: 'It is not for you to know the times or seasons which the Father has fixed by his own authority' (Acts 1:7), for 'of that day or that hour no one knows, not even the angels in heaven, nor the Son, but only the Father' (Mark 13:32). This statement implies for Rahner the essential hiddenness of eschatological events. The emphasis here is on 'essential', that is that everything which will occur at the end of time is now and forever a hidden, mysterious reality. If it were otherwise, faith and hope would never cease as Paul says in 1 Cor.13:13. The future therefore is essentially concealed.[8] His statement of course runs parallel with the affirmation that God remains a hidden mystery even in the state of fulfilment, just as any other eschatological event.

This position gives Rahner the first firm criterion for dealing with eschatological statements. Any detailed assertion about future events is an *apocalyptic* projection and not a genuine eschatological statement. Although the two kinds can be similar in form, eschatology and apocalyptic are different in what they affirm.[9]

Another criterion in *Hermeneutics* follows from the principle already proposed by Rahner: God's revelation must use words about the 'fulfilment' in such a way that mankind in history can understand their meaning. He is now back to his anthropology which presupposes two 'existentials' in man's historical nature:[10] both anamnesis (recall) and prognosis (forecast) are basic human attitudes (*Befindlichkeiten*). Their presence in man and mankind is inevitable. And this entails:

> If the 'presentness' of man's being is in reference to his futurity, the future, remaining the future as such, is not just something spoken in advance ... [it is rather] an inner moment of the self-understanding of man in his present hour of existence – *and grows out of it*.[11]

It follows from this that the meaning of eschatological assertions refers to the present or, as Rahner paradoxically puts it:

> Knowledge of the future will be knowledge of the futurity of the present: eschatological knowledge is knowledge of the eschatological present.[12]

The obvious fact that Scripture and the Church make such eschatological statements renders it easy for Rahner to determine their source. In affirming the feature of future fulfilment, they assert something already present, namely, the perfection of salvation already granted by God in Jesus the Christ. The Redeemer's work, at the very least, is already the beginning. Any other statements firmly asserting things (events, facts, judgements) about the future that are not at the same time about man, mankind and Jesus Christ cannot be taken as genuine eschatological assertions. They originate as anthropological or Christological assertions, even if they are often clad in the imagery of human language. There is, therefore, a rule: what is revealed about the future as future can only be disseminated figuratively through the use of imaginative human thought. If one mistakes this outward form for content one preaches mere apocalypsis. Eschatology, on the contrary

> tries to describe our situation in terms of its present intrinsic *possibilities* as they look to the future. It does no more than this.[13]

Or to use his other skilful formulation:

> To extrapolate from the present into the future is eschatology, to interpolate from the future into the present is apocalypsis.[14]

These insights from Rahner's substantial essay, *Hermeneutics*, (to which he constantly returns), lead him to reconsider the usual themes of eschatology. He faces the questions of universal apocatastasis[15] and the possibility of awareness about individual salvation before death. Insisting on one and single predestination, he demonstrates the inequality between the sure promise of salvation and the possibility of eternal damnation. Both of these will feature in his particular eschatology in *Foundations*. His emphasis on the unity of body and spirit of the person in its final fulfilment questions the doctrine of the immortality of the soul, as proposed in traditional Christian theology: it is the whole person who is going to be saved or damned. He resolves also the dispute about the difference between an imminent and distant expectation of the parousia in the early Church: if indeed eschatological assertions are grounded in and disclose the present, the *imminent* fulfilment of God's promised salvation is one possible form and expression of the human desire that animated primitive communities to look forward to the end of the world. (Paul's letter to the Thessalonians is no exception.) Then as now imminence gives urgency to present Christian life. Our Lord did exactly that in his discourse about vigilance: we do not know the day and the hour of his coming.

One might well ask: what scriptural and dogmatic statements concerning our eschatological future remain binding for Catholic belief? It seems that, apart from the fact that there is a definite end to history, we are left with only one firm stance:

> Eschatological assertions of Scripture are and are intended to be (at least in so far as dogmatic principles establish them as affirmed for certain) no more than assertions about Christology and anthropology in terms of the final fulfilment.[16]

Eschatology, therefore, does not proffer 'anticipatory, eyewitness accounts of a future which is still outstanding'. Its statements are not additional to the rest of theology, but rather 'give expression once again to humankind, as Christianity understands it: a being who "ex-ists" from out of his present "now" towards his future'.[17]

This is a convenient moment to add some reflections on Rahner's gnoseology of eschatological statements.[18] It is correct to state that his approach is basically different from what we call 'demythologization' or 'existentialization', both of which can be ascribed to Bultmann's purview. Without entering into details, Bultmann's programme regarded statements about the last things as mythical expressions arising from the cosmology and worldview of biblical authors. Yet I do not believe that Bultmann used the word 'myth' in a pejorative sense. On the contrary, mythical statements expressed for him profound reflections on human existence. They indicate, as they do for Rahner, constant features of mankind's behaviour (*Grundbefindlichkeiten*), or are similar to Heidegger's existentials. Only in this sense could one say that Rahner demythologizes and 'existentializes' the Bible's eschatological statements.

Yet Rahner, as we have seen, skilfully fends off any reductionism in the very first thesis of *Hermeneutics:*[19] eschatological statements are time bound in so far as they genuinely look to the future from the past and present. In asserting this, however, he has made his analysis more difficult. Future in the above sense (if I am correct) is a category of natural time, and not a time-transcendent state: it does not escape the relativity of a continuous process. And this is exactly what Rahner tries to avoid in speaking of irreversibility, an eternity of fulfilment. Thus as a next step I shall have to re-examine his analyses of time and eternity, of immanent (time bound) and transcendent consummation in a world to come.

Before attempting this, however, I must offer a reservation about one aspect of Rahner's approach. The reader of *Hermeneutics* and other parallel essays may have been, rightly or wrongly, given the impression that 'apocalyptic' is for him a term referring only to an emotive version of otherwise present, existential facts and events. 'Apocalyptic' images and notions, whether or not the term is pejorative, do not, according to Rahner, belong to Christian eschatology. On this ground one could hold that the apocalyptic images with which popular Christianity lived for centuries are now reducible to almost zero. Dante's universe has disappeared, enclosed as it was by heaven and hell, peopled by angels and demons and by men and women struggling against eternal damnation and yearning for heavenly bliss. It is no longer binding in faith. That can be a relief for some, but is it not a loss for the devout? (It is granted of course that a constant appeal to, or rather the threat of final judgement and condemnation, can be interpreted as the exercise of 'religious' [clerical?] power in order to achieve discipline in the present, methods that should now belong to the past.)

Although the apocalyptic deflected attention from the essentials of Christian faith, it can hardly be neglected. Jesus of Nazareth *was* an apocalyptic prophet with a contemporary Jewish religiosity and John, his late interpreter, employs dualistic categories (characteristic of the apocalyptic) in his Gospel to present man's ultimate fate: either salvation or damnation beyond time. It seems that Rahner should have retained a more positive estimate of apocalyptic literature in his eschatological 'gnoseology'.

Rahner is right to state that an anticipatory image of the last things is constructed from the material of present or past experience. Nonetheless reflection upon our everyday dreams and parlance about things to come should not be omitted from theological considerations. This does not mean of course that we should confuse eschatology with apocalypsis. I therefore suggest a fine distinction between a goal and its realization, between *finis and eschaton*. We regard the goal or purpose[20] of our actions, of our whole existence even, as the inner motivating force of our conscious or unconscious self. A goal is everywhere present, even when it is ignored by awareness or frustrated by free will. It was this universality which was regarded as the *causa finalis* in ancient philosophy. If we speak of a goal of a work we are about to perform we can obviously circumscribe or define it. Cautiously though, we can talk about mankind or the universe as existing for, or aiming at a definable goal. Yet can we predict what the realized achievement of such a goal might be? By its very nature the goal that we are aiming at is, and to a certain extent remains, abstract even if it is a real force for our action. If we knew in detail how our accepted targets were going to be realized, we would hardly be aware of the freedom of our actions. It is incorrect to call the knowledge of the goal or ultimate aim of our existence an 'anticipation'. We understand that goal by reflecting on the nature of our present actions, but the grasp of the concrete circumstances of its realization is a matter for our imagination: it cannot be 'anticipated' or 'planned'.

Rahner certainly presupposes the above when he repeatedly distinguishes between the content and the expression of eschatological statements. Yet I do not think that his writings were clear about the other half of our distinction: that between goal and *eschaton*. We can scheme and plan in our present life, but we can only guess, we can only dream about the concrete form of its realization. It is by no means in our power to achieve it. The goal, the purpose and aim are different from, what I call, the *eschaton*. And this is exactly where anticipatory knowledge can function. It does not deal with existing objectives but with probabilities and possibilities; it has to resort to imagination, to parables and poetry. I believe, however, the possible to be the smallest unit of reality, just as promise is the basic tool of religion, even theology. But whereas the goal can be presented in its very abstraction, the *eschaton* remains the child of hope. It would be fatal to identify or mix up the two: *finis* and *eschaton*. What is more, it would be incorrect to reduce the *eschaton* to a goal as yet unrealized, for it does not depend on our yearning, but on other related possibilities with which it is connected. It depends not on the subsequent life of one who has 'reached' the goal, but on circumstances in which other people's actions are also at work. I would prefer to confine anticipatory knowledge to this meaning.

One more remark to close this section. As our opening paragraph suggested, we should distinguish between 'eschatology' and 'eschatological'. 'Eschatological' is a special adjective having reference to the present constitution of mankind and the world. The eschatological, however, is only possible if we presuppose 'eschatology', that is, the tradition of theological doctrine about the last things. Whereas 'eschatological' is the modality[21] of the present, eschatology is the 'science of the possible'. It is unavoidable that the apocalyptic (even in Rahner's sense) will be part and parcel of it.

3.2. Time and Eternity

Although it is a modality of present human existence, the 'eschatological' has a clear reference to what is beyond time. Eschatology, as I have proposed, should be the 'science of the possible', that is of a state in which time is fulfilled, a state apparently without further possibilities to be reckoned with. Eschatology is, in this sense, also the 'science of eternity'. The relationship between time and eternity is fundamental for eschatological discourse. Rahner's basic position is that eternity is not the indefinite continuation of time, even though time and eternity are notions in correlation: although time could not exist without eternity, eternity is experienced within the course of time.

Eternity from Time[22] (1979) is one of Rahner's late essays. It is not a scholarly treatment but the meditation of an ageing theologian at a time when the word 'eternity' is declining in significance. 'We are', he writes, living under 'the tyranny of our concept of time'. And this tyranny seems to influence contemporary thought about the possibility of life after death. It entails the illegitimate transfer of time into an eternity running on and on indefinitely, one section following another and thus enduring forever. In this conceptualization of eternity, as a never-ending continuum, Rahner suspects a pious yearning for the possibility of change, including perhaps, repentance after death, or reaching a perfection unattainable in time. Is this not a mistaken desire? Is not this kind of eternity:

> the damnation of Ahasuerus, the wandering Jew, doomed always to roam without ever finally arriving anywhere. Under the tyranny of this concept time, is not the eternal heaven dissolved into an eternal hell, and vice versa?[23]

Eternity is therefore not the indefinite continuation of time. That would be Hegel's 'wrong eternity'.

Yet the concept of eternity, if we are to speak about it, has to convey something semantically significant. Shall it be 'no-time' i.e. the negation of all that was time-bound? Will our experiences in this present time irretrievably perish in eternity? Or should we say that a certain permanence of what has been is part of its content, lest the concept of eternity remains totally empty? If there is a 'now' in the flow of time, have we, besides the immediate experience of time, another concomitant one, which 'combines past present and future in unity'? Indeed, the concept of eternity seems to be a paradox, unless we can find some permanence within the continuation of time. This is what Rahner tries to explore in his meditation.

Concomitant to the experience of time we are also aware of something that is permanent. Such a permanence is our

> free personal decision which, by its very nature, does not permit what it has posited purely and simply to disappear into the void of nothingness.[24]

One can, therefore, assert that 'there is something in time that is not identical with time itself' (ibid.). The 'mental experience' of free decisions, Rahner affirms, transcends time and manifests eternity. Furthermore, in free decisions one does not passively succumb to the tyranny of time but tries in a way to be its master. Rahner illustrates this by the notion of a fundamental option through which we are capable of directing our whole life. These

> ultimate personal decisions, at least when they involve life in its totality, are irrevocable , they are truly eternity coming to be in time.[25]

Were it not so we could not speak of responsibility which is part of personal human freedom. For

> freedom in the last resort ... wills and posits finality and irreversibility ... Here time really *creates* eternity and eternity is experienced in time.[26]

By using these adumbrations of eternity Rahner seems to assert that there ought in fact to be such a state as eternity. Were it not so, philosophers could not state concerning material objects that 'there is some permanent substance constituting iron, silver and gold' – or even 'there is a structure and logic in history'. Along with irreversible decisions these, too, are intimations of eternity. These hints, however, only point to a possible 'state of eternity', and one cannot say, for instance, that a 'real' state of eternity will begin after a future final consummation, an eternity in which God is clearly seen in all his attributes, and man's whole being is experienced in its finality. No, the truth lies in the humble acceptance that our knowledge of eternity does not exceed the possible and the probable:

> For we are actually going into the unknown, the unimaginable, and, properly speaking, know only that [eternity] is filled with the incomprehensibility of God and [that] his love is final.[27]

If therefore the last word about the 'experience' of eternity in time declares its incomprehensibility, time itself with all its hints of permanence is a mystery also.

This incomprehensibility becomes even more obvious concerning our future. Perhaps the past can be preserved in personal decisions (or in the phenomenon of memory, through which Augustine tried to approach eternity), but these decisions, however firm they are, cannot determine the future. Evolutionary ideas, as Rahner affirms in an article written some thirteen years before (1966), cannot help:

> The future is that which does not evolve, that which is not planned, that which is not under control ... [it] is that which silently lies in wait, and which when it springs upon us, rips up the nets of all our plans ... so as to make a nonsense of that which we have planned or foreseen'.[28]

The future cannot be controlled or calculated; yet it exists as a mystery with which we have to come to terms. The distinction between *finis* and *eschaton,* which I have introduced in the last section, could be useful here: the permanent elements in time enable us to aim at this definitive state (*finis*), but its realization remains a mystery, *eschaton.* The only way to master this coming future is a hope that can trust, an attitude which

> would in fact not exist at all if there were no reference to the [infinite], absolute future ... [which] is present as presiding over us in some way; ... it is made over to us as the 'material' of the future.[29]

We shall see in our next section that this 'absolute future' is a leading idea in Rahner's thought, but the short article here considered only hints at an eternity within which the fulfilment of our desires and our plans can find a permanent home. 'It comes to meet us', Rahner asserts, 'it is intended to be imparted to us as the incomprehensible mystery'.[30] This mystery, even as mystery, can none the less be experienced in our present time.

Another article of Rahner's treats the concept of time in a more scholarly and theological way.[31] Though I do not believe that he made a thorough study of the immense literature available, he was certainly aware of the massive reappearance of the concept in contemporary thought: physics and cosmology cannot neglect the fourth dimension of our universe and philosophy has needed to address the matter, time and time again: from Aristotle through Augustine, Thomas and Kant (especially his treatment of the antinomies of this concept) to Kierkegaard. Rahner, however, avoids involvement in the never-ending speculation about the concept of time in secular learning.

His overview offered in *Time* seems to be more modest: he examines the defined doctrine of the Church which speaks about creation 'at the beginning of time' and looks forward to a point when time will end and be replaced by eternity.[32] He is aware that this assertion is debatable: Aquinas accepts it as a revealed truth at which philosophy can only hint and cannot prove; others, like Bonaventure and his school hold the contrary. Thus the meaning of the dogma itself is not unambiguously clear.[33] What is clear, given the historical setting of Lateran IV and Vatican I Councils, is the intention of rejecting the Platonic view according to which the world is everlasting i.e. 'eternal', in as much as this would militate against the first article of the creed. This negativity cannot, however, be the only intention of the dogma. Neither is that explanation correct that postulates a point in time before which the world did not exist and after which it had come to be. To imagine the 'earlier' or 'later' of the actual world is an illusion, or a kind of Kantian 'transcendental fantasy'

> which fails to understand that the world actually *has* time as the specification of itself, but as a whole does not in turn exist *in* time.[34]

In other words, time is not a receptacle in which the world is located, but rather the quality of all that exists. Does this assertion specify nothing more than the finitude of a world contingent in its total dependence on God? Rahner sees something more in it than the mere reassertion of the contingency implied in the first article of our creed. The minimal content that the dogma affirms is 'a temporality inherent' in man as well a 'discrete extrapolation of this temporal factor into the world as a whole'.[35] But what do we understand by this intrinsic temporality? The aforementioned 'transcendental fantasy' could lead one to imagine that there ought to be a clockwork mechanism outside the universe by means of which one could measure the temporal succession of events. It would presuppose a world apart from, and co-existent with the world we know. This assumption could only prove that there is a finite succession between some events, but not the succession of the totality of events. Such a concept does not imply the 'temporality inherent' in *all* creation, and the concept of time remains unexplained.

As a dogmatic theologian Rahner's only theoretical contribution at this level is to hold that the notion of time is best approached through man's awareness of it, an awareness then extrapolated into the world as a whole. Beyond this the concept of time seems to remain ambiguous in its non-religious context. The meaning of the dogma, although it does not solve the puzzle of time, gives a clear content to temporality. Like other dogmatic statements it pronounces a salutary truth

> addressed to men and ... an appeal to their free decision ... to accept 'irrevocably' the definitive salvation in a definitive exercise of freedom.[36]

He adds: because man, as unity of spirit and matter, is an element in the world, the world itself is drawn into his destiny, namely, 'the resurrection of the flesh and the consummation of the world in the "new heaven and the new earth"'.[37] In other words, he can state:

> that the world must be such that man can be that which he really is: a being endowed with freedom to be exercised in time and history, [a freedom] which attains the definitive finality of God in the definitive finality of its own decision (ibid).

We are back now to the previous statement that man is a being who can determine in time the eternal validity of his life. This is the experience concomitant with that of eternity that manifests our own temporality and that of the world. As is clearly implied in the Old and New Testaments: a continuous line stretches from the 'foundation of the world' to the consummation of man's history within a new world.[38] For the history of the world, with its consecutive 'modes of existence' is an intrinsic part of *our* history. It follows too that any idea about an infinite, everlasting world can only be false, and the assertion of a beginning and end of the world, its 'temporality', can be true. At the very least, it would be fair to say that man, by experiencing eternity, even though as something concomitant, also perceives his own and the world's time-bound existence. To put it briefly: the dogma declares time to be a salvific history of 'personal freedom engaged in dialogue with the God of grace'. What is more, this 'content' of time as saving history is primary, since

> it provides a standard of measurement in the light of which, as far as the theologian is concerned, all other time has to be considered, and that too in such a way that the 'content' of this kind of time also specifies the modality of time as such.[39]

It seems, therefore, that the concomitant experience of eternity has become the criterion of the immediate experience of time. Furthermore, that the same experience is also an experience of personal history acted out within the history of the world in its totality. Mankind in history, in the Christian view, is that of a free spirit in dialogue with the God of grace. This is true, in a sense, of the history of nature. Hence:

> The material time of the world is to be conceived of as an element in the material time of [the] history of the free spirit.[40]

If therefore man and his world have, according to the dogma, a beginning and an end, then time must be an intrinsic specification of both. For the history of the free spirit, which is in a real ontological relationship with the world, could not achieve its promised fulfilment without the universe. We cannot assert the temporality of humans within a static, never

142 *The Sacrament of the Future*

changing universe. The reality of finite freedom could not be involved in such a world.

Rahner's is not a philosophical account of time and eternity. He tries to grasp the meaning of time as it is tied to our freedom in face of the God of grace and attempts to solve the relationship between temporality (of free human agents and that of the world) and the eternity of God with a theological analogy. This analogy is similar to the one between nature and grace.

> At this point we should recall one of Rahner's earlier insights. According to him the 'nature' of free human beings and that of the world cannot be experienced without God's grace as a concomitant to creation. Nonetheless the 'pure nature' of traditional scholasticism remains a postulate demanded by the need that grace should be what it is: the *gratis* gift of God. 'Pure nature' is therefore a 'remainder concept', a condition of grace.

Like 'pure nature' material time is an abstraction rendered necessary by man's grace-given temporal constitution. It is a 'remainder-concept'.[41] It follows therefore that time, i.e. temporality, is a variable modality inherent within the particular constitution of each created being. For just as 'pure nature', which we cannot directly experience, is the condition of the possibility of grace, so the time of the world is the condition of eternity. Grace encounters man's freedom and makes dialogue with God possible. This dialogue is enacted in time.

To sum up: in analysing the concept of time Rahner offers a solution to an unending debate in ancient and contemporary science and philosophy as based on his own theology of the supernatural. Christian faith reduces the solution to the simple statement: because God 'gives' time to us to work freely towards our ultimate destiny, we must be part of a world which is intrinsically temporal, in order to allow our passage from beginning to end in a time which either hints at or contains eternity.

> Just as grace wills the world to be worldly within its own autonomous sphere, so too the 'time implicit in grace', is a

unique kind of time ... that derives its own ultimate quality from the eternity of God, who positively wills the existence of time in this world, a time that is open to decision, to hope, to the unforeseen, as the sphere for *that* activity which fashions the possible from the utopian and in consequence time itself.[42]

God's eternity can explain our time in our temporal world. In *Time* (as I shall later quote) Rahner writes: 'God removes time from eternity but not ... eternity from time'.[43] This statement implies that time and eternity are related concepts. Can we convert this relationship and say: not only does time imply eternity, but vice versa, that eternity, in a way unknown to us, implies time. Rahner's approach to time and eternity can be characterized as one of a simultaneous correlationship. Can we therefore truly attribute time to God's eternity? It is mainly this question with which I shall be concerned in my comments and questions.

⁂

I shall start my reflections with a quotation from the father of process philosophy, Alfred North Whitehead, which contrasts with and is, I believe, at the same time is similar to Rahner's contribution to the concept of time and eternity:

> Ideals fashion themselves round these two notions, permanence and flux. In the inescapable flux, there is something that abides; in the overwhelming permanence, there is an element that escapes into flux ... The perfect moment is fadeless in the lapse of time. Time has then lost its character of 'perpetual perishing'; it becomes the 'moving image of eternity'.[44]

Whitehead wrote these words in the concluding the section of his lectures summing up his idea of a 'bipolar' God. Like Rahner, he assumes that time and eternity are not contradictions: they belong, in a way, to the same category. Furthermore, both start with our everyday experience of time as an 'inescapable flux' within which they discover 'something that abides', something that is 'permanent and fadeless [say: eternity]'.[45]

Time therefore is not a 'perpetual perishing'. Whereas it is 'the perfect moment' that saves the past for Whitehead, for Rahner it is the decision made in freedom. Like Whitehead, Rahner starts by assuming a certain simultaneity between time and eternity. (The concept was not unknown to traditional thinking through the influence of Augustine and Boethius.) Rahner's method of analysing the nature of this relationship is, however, different from that of Whitehead, who has no difficulty in demonstrating this simultaneity since he assumes that time and eternity are already present in the Godhead. The question is, would Rahner also agree with Whitehead's final phrase: time is the 'moving image of eternity'? This phrase implies that time is compatible with God's eternity: 'in permanence [interpreted as eternity] there is an element that escapes into flux [i.e. time]'. For Whitehead the concept of time can hardly be denied to the concept of eternity in God.

Rahner, in spite of his different approach, is tempted by a similar solution. A throw away sentence in the last brief section of *Time,* asks about 'the sort of time which belongs to God himself'.[46] He connects, however, this question with God's essential attribute of *immutability*, a dogma of the Church.[47] Although Rahner accepts the attribute of immutability by identifying it with God's non-temporal nature (*Unzeitlichkeit*, that is, timelessness[48]) he straightaway refers to the incarnation: how is it possible that a God, 'timeless' and unchangeable by nature, can enter into the time of history by becoming man? Does this mean that God's eternity is also temporal? Rahner's answer is perforce a very dialectical one:

> Christian theology must hold firm to the 'immutability' and 'eternal' timelessness of God. At the same time, however, it will have to say that God *himself*, in the otherness of the world, undergoes history, change, and so too time; the time of the world is his own history.[49]

If it is therefore correct to affirm both timelessness and an own history to God's eternity, then time must somehow be attributed to God. It is evident: for Rahner eternity is not just timelessness, but something communicable, something in which the created world and humankind within it can share. This statement is consistent with his basic principle of creation: God 'posits' the creature as different from himself and at the same time, by maintaining this difference, communicates himself to what he has made. Further to understand this dialectical statement we should recall another sentence of Rahner: 'God removes time from eternity [meaning that God 'creates' time or rather a temporal creation] ... but not eternity from time [since creation itself is already the communication of God's eternity].[50] To put the same thought in other terms:

> [God] ... establishes his own eternity to be the true content of time, *he makes his own proper time* in order to impart his own eternity as the radical effectiveness (*Gültigkeit*) of his own love.[51]

This statement of Rahner's already anticipates the self-communication of the God of grace in the very creation of a time-bound universe: though our time is the creation of God who is beyond the flux of time, the very meaning of time, 'its true content' is eternity. In this sense 'timelessness' in God can coexist with a certain aspect of time for eternity is the time of God. If, however, the 'true content' of our time is eternity, then eternity can be the 'measure' of time: something outside time's inexorable flux, an eternity within time, a permanence in time which is in Whitehead's words 'a moving image of eternity'.

The apparent similarity of Rahner's and Whitehead's approach to time and eternity ceases however in the divergence between their respective concepts of God. While Rahner maintains the timeless, immutable and unchangeable quality of God, he must labour to smuggle some form of time into God's eternity. Whitehead, on the other hand, inserts time into the very concept of his 'bipolar' God who in the abstract core of his primordial nature is timeless and unchangeable, but whose consequent nature is exposed to the temporality of this contingent world.[52] Timelessness cannot be attributed to the consequent nature of God for this aspect of God is in correlationship with a constantly changing world in 'flux': not only is the world related to God through its dependence, but God, too, relates himself to the history of his contingent creation.

To deny timelessness to God's eternity, therefore, leads us back, to the concept of God. Elsewhere I have tried to elaborate a 'bipolar' image of God by assuming and affirming that in his personal 'pole' God is not immutable: despite his omnipotent power God can change.[53] We can then affirm that God, through awareness of human decisions now and of their execution then, is subject to time, that is, can change in accordance with events in our free history. Thus, provided the two 'poles' or aspects of God's selfhood are one and the same, God is in time. God is not immutable, is not timeless in his personal relationship to the world. This, however, is not true if we consider God in his substantial 'pole', namely, as he 'posits' himself to be. If God *is*, he exists in a special way: he is always the same 'omnipotent, omniscient' being, accessible only by analogical reasoning. His essential attributes are postulates of rational reflection. In his 'overwhelming permanence' God is beyond time, he is indeed immutable.

This analysis can be strengthened by the concept of the Trinitarian dynamism. If God has revealed himself as triune, existing in the relationship of the three divine Persons, he is not static, but his very being is dynamic in the 'movements' of begetting, being begotten and proceeding in the Holy Spirit. This 'happening' in God cannot exclude time.[54] Time exists in God, at least as a potential for the history of the world and is thus a prototype of our time. If indeed the triune God creates freely, this dynamism is implied in the time proper to creation.

In his painstakingly argued book, *God and Timelessness* Nelson Pike[55] tries to show that God's eternity cannot be identified with timelessness. Neither, according to Pike, do God's necessary attributes of immutability, omnipotence and omniscience logically entail timelessness. Through the logical analysis of these notions Pike most convincingly argues against the identification of timelessness with eternity, an argument based on the belief in God as a person. The concept of person, according to him, seems to be located in the idea of mental ability, of reflecting, remembering anticipating, deliberating deciding, that is, acting with intention. I would want to add that these activities through which an individual becomes and is a person in relationship with other persons and thereby with their common environment.

Pike's reasoning therefore can be summed up in a syllogism with a radical conclusion: a timeless individual cannot be a person, but God is believed in as a person, hence God is not timeless. Therefore:

> A timeless being could not deliberate, anticipate, or remember ... it could not be affected or prompted by another. It could not respond to needs, overtures delights or antagonisms of human beings. ... I doubt if one could become emotionally involved with such a [timeless] person [just as] ... I don't think that a timeless person could be emotionally involved with another ... a timeless individual could not *respond* in some way to the actions of others (and so on).[56]

Pike does not, in fact, reject timelessness as something irrelevant to our knowledge of God. Rather he regards it as logically compatible with God's essential attributes and among them with that of God's immutability. As a theologian, however, he asks, what do we exactly believe in attributing immutability to God? It is certain that faith does not tell us that an immutable God cannot change in any way whatsoever. Nor can we say that the term 'cannot' in 'cannot change' is to be understood as expressing logical impossibility. He distinguishes between first level and secondary attributes:

> when the Christian says that God is immutable, what he means is that God cannot change as regards his power, benevolence etc. ... The force of 'cannot' in 'cannot change' must be understood differently depending on the specific first-level [i.e. essential] attributes under consideration.[57]

Pike means by this that changelessness is necessary in relation to God in himself and not in relation to a contingent world created by him. Thus the 'cannot' in 'cannot change' means the same as (using my own terminology): God in the substantial pole of his selfhood defines ('posits') himself as unchangeable, omnipotent, omniscient and immortal. Furthermore, God (in the personal pole of his reality) is unchangeable as regards his attitudes to creation: adversities of human history do not change his faithfulness and love, his justice remains the same even if the execution of his unchanging plans may alter.[58]

Hence the general view of faith is:

> On this account, God not only has *temporal location* (. . .) but also has *temporal extension* [and here Pike refers to John Damascene's *Exposition of Orthodox Faith*]. His life is indefinitely extended both forward and backward in time.[59]

There is, however, a recurrent difficulty about this image of God, and this concerns the two essential (or 'first level' according to Pike) attributes of God's omnipotent and omniscient being. Both were once central to a metaphysical image of God and an inevitable ingredient of common religious discourse. A concept of God, whose eternity does not exclude time and whose history images our own history, cannot be perfect: his power is conditioned by potentialities and his knowledge is limited by an uncertain future yet to be experienced. It is this objection that has alienated most people from the image of God as proposed by process theology, including my own version of the same.[60] One could argue: one whose perfection is infinite cannot become more powerful or more knowledgeable as his time runs alongside our time. He, who *becomes* more perfect, could not have been God before, and a less perfect being cannot be eternal. Such a God cannot mould the history of his creation and cannot foresee events which are actualised by his free creatures. He is impotent and to a certain extent ignorant: captive of his own work, he can neither create freely (as Whitehead himself admits) nor can he provide for his own creatures. All-powerfulness and omniscience therefore are essential to God even as regards his personal aspect.

Charles Hartshorne tackles this objection by his theory of 'relative perfection': God can be conceived as 'perfect', that is, perfectly related to each stage of creation and history, yet he still has a completion that lies ahead.[61] His power is 'perfect' in sustaining the creative action of his free creation, yet in foreseeing the whole scale of possibilities, which the creature may freely choose, he prompts (or as Whitehead says, 'lures') their action according to his own designs.

Obviously, Hartshorne will maintain the free creativity of creation, for if everything is pre-determined this freedom is questionable.

Basically I agree with Hartshorne's theory, however, transposed into my own concept of God's 'bipolarity: God is omnipotent in so far as he, in his 'substantial pole', can create ever new possibilities for the action of his free creatures and insofar as he maintains their human actualization according to his purpose. God is omniscient (again in his 'substantial pole') in so far as he sees the totality of all available possibilities and actualities in the history of humankind. P. S. Fiddes in his eschatology[62] formulates the matter thus: 'God knows all that there is to be known', that is, the actual event arising from the given possibilities. This view may be found offensive by a traditional theist, but it sums up the thought of some contemporary theologians.[63] What is worth knowing in detail is the actual event, even if the non-actual is known in the indefiniteness of a real possibility. In this 'omniscience' God is ahead of us: by accompanying our free history he lets his own history be framed; in the long run he can turn to good whatever has gone amiss in our own time and history. He can 'heal' our time, for he is the 'God of the ages'.

If we accept this latter statement as characteristic of God's 'personal pole' we should not be afraid of attributing to him the 'wrong eternity', against which Rahner has warned us in his *Eternity* article. Indeed, this is the eternity that created man is destined to share. Pike writes quoting the Damascene again:

> A man survives (...) through the measurable ages and after his death into the time when time cannot be measured. God's eternity differs from this in that it includes *all* measurable ages as well as the time *before* the measurable ages.[64]

Pike uses this quotation to intimate how an eternal, but not timeless, God enters into time. His interpretation of the phrase '*all* measurable ages', would, I believe, include modern scientific and philosophical ideas about time, an interest lacking in Rahner's writings about time. Although Rahner's own reasoning in *Eternity* starts with time as experienced, it does not seem to advance beyond the three basic moments of past present and future. And when he concludes to a timeless God who is nonetheless related to time, he has already assumed the notion of eternity. The other approach in *Time* presupposes that God and eternity are already known through a transcendental experience and material time is but a 'remainder' concept. It is exactly the lack of any similar presuppositions that characterizes more modern treatments of the question.

Without going into great detail about the analysis of time according to various branches of modern science (for which I am not competent), there are two main insights which we need to accept. First, time is not homogeneous, but diverse; on each level of the universe, from geology up to anthropology there is a plurality of timescales. The quality of time differs to the extent that even humans themselves have slightly varying perceptions of it. This barely perceptible difference enables the Newtonian idea of absolute time, as a neutral receptacle, a generalisation that time can be affirmed of all creation. This idea is supplanted; the notion of time in a constantly evolving universe demands an exposition proper to each stage. It follows, therefore, that time is not a univocal, but an analogous concept that imposes very different kinds of time on the observer of natural phenomena.

Secondly, at each stage there is an irreversible move ahead (Fiddes correctly speaks about the 'arrow of time') which can be measured by the reversibility of the constituents of time. We could not perceive this arrow of time without discovering constantly recurring changes in its course. Although its flow is irreversible, nonetheless it can be measured. A constant flux in itself does not yield an experience of time, unless its stages can be perceived. An animal (as far as we know) is subject to this irreversible flow, without being able to measure its stages.

> That the flow of time is measurable must not lead us to a Kantian view of time as a subjective category of the mind. According to a modern world-view we live in a four dimensional universe, where time is essentially related to space. Space and time (as Torrance states in his 'Space, Time and Incarnation'[65]) must be conceived as the structural functioning of contingent events that are inseparably and objectively rooted in them. This implies, first, that material

things conceived of as agents (active principles) are thereby making room for themselves and create time for their movements independent of human observation: both space and time are real in this functional sense. God could not create time and space as such, but he created a spatio-temporally structured universe. This explains, secondly, that the flow of time of material bodies 'depends on the velocity at which these bodies move, so that space and time change according to the accumulation of mass and the field of gravitation caused by it'.[66] In this sense, too, we are confronted with the basic property of time in general: with the irreversibility of its flow, and with the measurability of its changes.

It is Einstein's insight that, though the flow of time is real, its measurability depends on the observer who lives in his or her own time and space. The notion of time therefore is not only divergent on different timescales, but always relative to the observer. His theory of relativity, at least, as applied to subatomic matter, should be harmonized with the indeterminacy of quantum mechanics – both theories are valid, although as yet there is no comprehensive scientific explanation of their coherence.

Both insights, that of Einstein and the indeterminacy of quantum mechanics (Heisenberg), are important for a theological approach to time and eternity. To state that God, created a temporally structured universe, should be extended by the clause that God in his self-communication relates himself freely to created things in a mode appropriate to their own temporality'.[67] This means that God is related to and communicates with his creatures of the universe existing in a multiplicity of their own times not, however, as static units, but as moving instances in their own sequential time-scales. Would it not follow

> that God can relate to all timescales, because God can participate in them concurrently, moving along with them along their individual time paths, while we are limited to our own?[68]

In this sense God is an integrating factor in the multiplicity of time systems, and as such he cannot be outside of time: his is an 'eminent temporality'. Can we now identify God's 'eminent temporality' with his eternity?

T. Horvath's fine analysis of time in the phenomenon of language (which he calls the 'home of time') interprets the experience of time, and tries to show that this experience also entails another one, namely, that of eternity. We cannot speak without vocal signals, words, ordered in a grammatical structure that can convey meaning, because

> the abstract repeatable symbols make possible the indefinite varieties of sentences, which are not just the combination or summary of the meaning of the various terms, since they involve reference to something irrevocable experienced by the speaker'.[69]

Sounds words and sentences are in irreversible flow yet we could not convey meaning if there were no repeatable units of words, idioms, customary expressions in our speech. It is indeed the 'home of time' and its measure. Horvath (though I believe, with a logical jump) identifies this measure of time with eternity:

> The word 'eternity' is the hermeneutical significance of time in its basic structure where the balance of the multiplicity of sub-times is rooted (ibid.).

Thus for Horvath the basic, underlying structure of language reveals the fullness and meaning of time, which is, as he puts it, the 'inalienable' eternity of a person in whom time and eternity exist in an eschatological unity. He means, of course, the incarnate Christ in the splendour of his risen life.

Horvath seems to identify God with his eternity and eternity, whatever it is, is simultaneous with the word's temporality. Considering, however, with quantum mechanics the indeterminacy in God's moving universe, God's eminent temporality cannot be characterized by a timeless immobility: in his relation to creation God's own time, that is, eternity, must have a future which is basically indeterminate. In this sense God is in or with time, however, in an unfathomable manner open to his own future.

In summary: Both my expository part of Rahner's notion of time and eternity and my reflections on the same have wavered between two possible interpretations of this relationship: the first was the simultaneity of time and eternity; the other, following our everyday experience, the futurity of the eternal over and above time. Though we live in and experience our own time, the thought and desire of eternity will be an experience after death: we are waiting for the unknown. Rahner's throwaway sentences, while retaining the simultaneity of an eternity coextensive with time, seem to opt also for the other horn of the dilemma: he writes about the history of God by qualifying his timeless unchangeable existence: God's own time is his eternity. With this sentence Rahner seems to join theologians who assume time in God's eternity.

Theologians and philosophers of religion in speaking of time and eternity inevitably presuppose a concept of God. Their views are balanced between the simultaneity of God's eternity within the flow of time, and at the same time they are aware that their statements about eternity remain precarious, unless its full reality can be ascertained in the unknown future. They all know that an eternity that is simultaneous with time does not support a fully coherent eschatology. For the last things, and among them eternity too, can really be experienced only at the end of time. In order to set up a bridge between eternity *now* and eternity at the consummation of history and so generate interest in life after death in the *eschaton*, P. S. Fiddes sums up this relatively new trend in modern theology:

> The reduction of eschatology to the 'timeless moment' does not, I believe, either take history seriously or satisfy the demands of justice for the wrongs of historical actions to be righted ... [Therefore] recent theology and philosophy of religion has in fact been challenging any view of a timeless eternity.[70]

Is not this *hereafter* that at which Rahner's notion of *Absolute Future* aims?

3.3 The Absolute Future

Time and eternity are related concepts. Yet when we employ these ideas in eschatological discourse, we are bound by the passage of time. For anything 'eschatological' always involves the qualification: at once 'already and not yet'. Thus eternity may be felt in time, but it is nevertheless not yet – it is in the future. 'Time and eternity' cannot be thought of without the concept of the future.

During the mid-sixties Rahner's interest seems to have concentrated on the concept of the future. His active participation in dialogue with Marxists provides one explanation, as does the challenge of the then emergent 'political theology'. In the encounter with both, the relationship between a this-worldly, immanent, achievement in time and the fulfilment of a transcendent goal as the gift of eternity, becomes a pressing problem. Marxist dialectic would be meaningless without a projected objective and the means of its future realization. Likewise, the political engagement of the Church and her members could not construct a feasible theology of the world, unless it could relate a this-worldly aim with mankind's ultimate destiny. Briefly, if Christian faith is not just opium for the people, it has to affect the historical process without loosing sight of its consummation in eternity.

> A number of significant works concerned with similar questions were published about this time. The 1960 edition of *Lexikon für Theologie und Kirche* (vol. 5, p. 423f) and the 1968 edition of *Sacramentum Mundi* (vol. 3, p. 65) refer under the key-word 'hope' to names like J. Pieper, J. Moltmann, J-B. Metz, on the Christian side, as well as to the reform-Marxism of Ernest Bloch and an ample literature concerning his 'Principle of Hope'[71] Rahner's name of course is not missing from this list. There are about four important articles with a few others related to the same question[72] by means of which I shall try to sum up his thought. In all these the central statement, to which he always returns is that God is – in a way to be further précised – the *Absolute Future* of man and of his world.

It is most probable that the concept was first introduced in *Utopia*. Some two years before, Rahner had given a paper on

'Ideology and Christianity':[73] an almost identical subject, in which the concept of Absolute Future does not appear. He insists more on the historicity of the Christian religion in which the immediacy of God in grace is mediated by a historical process striving for a final consummation. *Utopia*, on the other hand tries rather to demonstrate the compatibility of 'Christian eschatology and the Marxist view of history'. It intends to open a possible dialogue between Marxism and Christianity concerning the future of mankind. The concept of the 'future' mediates between the two, however, with the difference that the Marxist's future is labelled 'Utopia' while the Christian future is qualified by the adjective 'absolute'. Both 'systems' are working toward the realization of an ultimate end within the one and same history of mankind, but whereas the Marxist stops at an intermediate stage, the Christian extends the process into the 'history of God'.

The five theses of *Utopia* develop this notion in generic terms:

(1) Christianity is the religion of the future, an *Absolute Future* which, although it has no *Utopian* ideas of a future in this world, is nonetheless,
(2) not entirely neutral as regards 'movements towards genuine and meaningful earthly goals'[74];
(3) Christianity, therefore, 'will always remain' the religion of the Absolute Future which can live with and tolerate movements geared to exclusively immanent goals.[75]

The last two theses discuss the divergence and the possible coherence between the Marxist and Christian conception of future fulfilment.

With these premises in the background Rahner uses 'Absolute Future' as shorthand for the experience of God:

> the man who opens himself to his Absolute Future, experiences also what is really meant by the word of God [that is:] God is present for us as the Absolute Future.[76]

This quotation gives me the basis on which I shall be able to present this Rahnerian concept in its full complexity. I shall

156 *The Sacrament of the Future*

ask: first (a), about the relationship between Absolute Future and the idea of God; secondly (b), about the 'consummation' that is to be expected from the Absolute Future; thirdly (c), about the Absolute Future as a present and still outstanding goal of God's creation; then fourthly, (d), consider how that leads us into Rahner's theology of hope.

a) The explanation of each of the theses of *Utopia* enables Rahner to recapitulate his entire system of thought about God and the message of Christianity under the 'shorthand' of *Absolute Future*. In using the word 'future' he has found a word more palatable to his Marxist partners in dialogue who, like Christians, propose to achieve a definite future end. When, however, Christianity qualifies this future as 'absolute', Rahner comes very near to the identification of the Absolute Future with God. Consider statements like: 'an Absolute Future gradually approaching the individual and humanity as a whole'; or man is open 'to the approach of the Absolute Future'; or the proclamation 'of an absolute becoming does not continue into emptiness but really reaches into the Absolute Future which is already moving within it'; indeed, man can be 'defined precisely as the possibility of attaining the Absolute Future', for Christianity is 'understandable only by what is yet to come'.[77] Or, to continue: man in projecting the Absolute Future is not merely seeking an immanent 'categorial' (perceptible) objective, which is finite, but an 'unsurpassable, infinite future' which comes towards him so that 'man's *intramundane* concerns always contain the question about the possible encounter with [an] infinite totality as such; in short, with the Absolute Future'.[78] Hence Rahner can conclude:

> Absolute Future is just another name for what is really meant by 'God' [for] God – understood as the Absolute Future – is basically ... the unspeakable mystery.[79]

In these sentences the tendency to identify God with the Absolute Future seems to be obvious. The very same article, however, presents a concept of God under the aspect of God's self-communication and of the event of grace 'sent to us' by God. This event is the 'definitive immediacy of this Absolute

Future within the world' leading to the vision of God. In Jesus Christ this self-communication of God is made perceptible ('categorial'). In the grace of God the 'world has an Absolute Future' and its evolutionary nature attains its goal:

> If the Absolute Future of the world and of humankind is properly called God in Christian terminology, the God-given event by which this happens, is a kind of definitive and instantaneous presence of the world to the self-communicating God ... [i.e.] the vision of God.[80]

Is then the Absolute Future God himself and/or is the Absolute Future the event in which the world attains its goal? If both, God himself and the event of the world's consummation are identical, then Rahner can draw the conclusions of the last three theses (3-5) of *Utopia:* on the one hand, any absolute pursuance of 'intramundane' i.e. purely temporal goals is a mere utopian ideology whereas, on the other, a 'rational and actively planned construction of an intramundane future' that is open to the hope of an Absolute Future is an obligation (see point c. below). Christianity, therefore, since it is a religion that takes God as the Absolute Future is significant for any secular society.[81] This significance establishes also the permanence of Christianity as an institutional religion. If it is indeed 'the religion of the future' then it will always be a 'social quantity', namely, a church.[82].

We can conclude that *Utopia* supports at least a qualified identification between God and the Absolute Future, one that also defines Christian existence; the Christian lives for a divine objective in the anticipation of a future destiny. In this sense Christianity is the religion of the future.

b) This 'anticipated' future, however, is also qualified as an *Absolute Future*, which means an unconditional end, and there comes with it a desired state of 'fulfilment', of 'consummation'. (There are no more objectives to be aimed at; human endeavour has reached its desired end.) The Absolute Future, therefore, is the sum total, the ultimate expression of the eschatological event. Rahner's *Consummation* enumerates the possible events that this concept can include. The word consummation may signify single material events in the

158 *The Sacrament of the Future*

history of the material world. Further, consummation can refer to the history of an individual, or to *all* personal histories regarded as a unity. It is obvious that consummation is inapplicable to the fulfilment of particular instances either material or historical; it should rather be applied to the totality of temporal creation i.e. to the 'world' in its widest sense, to the whole of creation.[83]

> All temporal events have an end by necessity; they have to perish or somehow to cease to be. Thus modern cosmology and biology speak of *entropy*, of a possible consummation of the universe, whether by return to its original stage of infinite density or by disappearing into the mysterious 'black holes' where it simply 'runs out '. A similar disintegration of living organisms is a matter of everyday experience. Such terminal events, however, do not yield a definitive result, they cannot truly be called a 'consummation'; that concept means something more than just 'ceasing to exist'. Consummation in its strictest sense should be the final and definitive stage of a process, one that, nonetheless, is qualitatively greater than what went before its resolution. This 'greater' recognizes the fact that a consummation is not only an end, but at the same time an ultimate objective (*finis*). Rahner therefore restricts the concept of 'consummation' to those events whose origin lies in acts of personal freedom performed in time. He alludes to the individual histories of those beings endowed with spiritual faculties (knowing and willing) in this present creation; they alone can look forward to a final state of consummation - to which Rahner adds - in another sphere of time.[84]

This kind of consummation alone raises the question: is it immanent *or* transcendent; does the one exclude the other; *or* is it, in a certain sense, *both?* Immanent consummation arises from the essential constitution of a free agent tending to its future goal. If however a consummation comes *ab externo*, one conferred independently upon an agent's free action, the agent has no awareness of it, knows nothing that can be discerned purely from the process of freedom itself. It is simply 'impelled' towards it. If the first case of consummation is immanent and the second transcendent, the two seem to be mutually exclusive.

This is certainly not Rahner's own conclusion. He maintains

that neither immanent nor transcendent consummation can abandon its material and historical substratum:

> Consummation is (if the word is to have any meaning at all) applied to a *temporal* event regardless of whether the temporality entailed is simply within our own experience, or belongs to some other conceivable factor.[85]

Relying on this position Rahner can state: *'immanence is, precisely, transcendence'*.[86] To understand this seemingly paradoxical position we should simply recall Rahner's transcendental reasoning[87] and apply it to the question of immanent and/or transcendent consummation. Transcendence implants an orientation to the 'Absolute Future' that opens up in each human action an infinite horizon, and thus is also a relationship of the free agent with God, the absolute mystery. There is no genuine contrast therefore between immanent and transcendent for there is a mutual unity between the two. For a personal being with the freedom to know and will, the expected immanent consummation coincides with the transcendent one: both are brought about by freedom (immanent) and endowed by God, the Absolute Future (transcendent).

> The transcendent consummation of personal freedom is the only true immanent consummation. If spirit really does *constitute* ... a transcendence open to the mystery, to the absolute being, to the incalculable and uncontrollable future, and if it is precisely this that constitutes its very essence, then the terms 'immanent' and 'transcendent' consummation are deprived of any unambiguously definable distinction.[88]

This statement, of course, is all the more valid if we accept Rahner's theology of grace as a self-communication of God, in endowing the free creature with God's proximity in such a way that the absolutely transcendent becomes the most immanent factor.[89] Briefly, to use Rahner's own terminology, if uncreated grace (God) is the constituent of created grace then:

> in the concrete order of reality, not only the consummation, the goal (*beatitudo objectiva*) of the spiritual creature, but the principle constituting the progression which is most proper and

necessary to it, is the sole truly connatural principle by which it is impelled towards the consummation of this goal.[90]

This kind of reasoning can be found in the rest of Rahner's theology: 'striving towards a goal is to be at the goal', as he affirms repeatedly. The earthly process in time is 'sustained by the future itself'. This statement also implies that man has no merely natural goal, which has to be superseded by another, transcendent, consummation *ab externo*. We are created for the immediate *visio Dei* in which our destiny achieves its eternal fulfilment.

If we now reason further in genuine Rahnerian fashion, the above statements are equally valid for the whole of mankind and, too, for the whole of material creation. Rahner's transcendental theology has already insisted on the unity of mankind and on the unity of spirit and matter. The concept of 'hominization'[91] according to which the material development of non-human organisms 'produces' a qualitatively new species images the process by which mankind's (immanent) history in this world reaches its consummation at an essentially higher (transcendent) level. The proviso is, of course, that this self-movement of the creature is, 'right from the outset sustained by divine power, which consists in Love bestowing itself absolutely in freedom'. The innermost principle of this movement is the incomprehensibility of God as the Absolute Future.[92] Mankind and the world reach the Absolute Future that is God at the consummation of their temporal progress through life. Absolute Future, therefore, is not only identified with the God of grace, but also with the consummation of temporal existence on earth.

c) If we are ready to accept Rahner's transcendental reasoning, we can work out *a priori* what he means by 'future'. Two essays from 1966/67 spell out this view: one in *Future,* and the other in a rather meditative consideration about the meaning of future.[93] Rahner calls the future a mysterious element in our lives, something that we cannot attain but which comes to us 'unprompted' – and he adds: 'when it decides to' come. What we mean by future is something that does not evolve out of our present; it cannot be planned; it is not under our control. Briefly,

The future is that which silently lies in wait, and [when it comes it] rips up the nets of all our plans and the false 'future' which we ourselves have constructed, so as to create that which we have not planned or foreseen.[94]

In this quotation, however, 'future' is not yet provided with the qualification of 'absolute': it is neither to be identified with God nor with the notion of the consummation.

One could continue to illustrate this characteristic Rahnerian image of the future and discover thereby his trend of thought. The apparent 'personification' of future is not just a metaphor: it already implies a reality beyond, an event. It implies furthermore a future in which temporal planning and foreseeable achievements will be supplanted: it is the hidden 'mystery' of the Absolute Future. This Absolute Future 'actualizes', guides the agent to its fulfilment and consummation in the reality of present time.

Rahner does not intend this to devalue all human plans and projects. An immanent future is not rejected, but relativized, because the Absolute Future 'gives the future which we construct for ourselves its place in the real and effective openness of true human history'.[95] With this proviso man's correct attitude is twofold: on the one hand he takes fully seriously the future that he has planned and has worked for on earth and, on the other, considers it as the *medium* through which the Absolute Future makes the former relative and conditional.

In this meditation we have the message of Rahner's more theological essay, *Future*, in a nutshell. Its thesis too is foreseeable:

> Christian faith, the subject of theological speculation, holds that the Absolute Future of man, *which is God*, ... is not simply offered as a mere open possibility, but is definitively promised in Jesus Christ.[96]

That is, if the promises of God are once for all realized in Jesus the Christ, then our 'expectation' of the Absolute Future is not only a possibility, but is at the very least an indication of an objective reality. Unlike the promise and expectation of an immanent future, one that is merely planned, Absolute Future 'is a reality which is imbued with the power to influence the present itself and in that sense has become itself real'.[97] By contrast, the scientific appreciation of future possibility deals only with the generalities of life within the this-worldly sphere and remains incomplete and outside 'that which constitutes the goal of Christian eschatology and hope' (ibid.).

The rest of *Future* tries to be more explicit about the connection between an immanent and transcendent future. Human history, though orientated to the Absolute Future, does not eliminate but rather demands responsibility for a 'this-worldly' future. The two mutually condition one another. Just as man's openness to the transcendent entails a relationship to the immanent future, so do our earthly projects relate to the Absolute Future. The future of our temporal planning

> is always unknown, a future which, when it arrives, takes us by surprise. And *precisely for this reason* it can also be the *medium* leading to the Absolute Future ... which is God himself in his inconceivability.[98]

What is sometimes known as modern futurology deals precisely with these this-worldly projects. It was bound to emerge as a kind of science concerned with the almost limitless increase in the possibilities of our age. The greater the human possibilities, the more freedom gained for individuals and communities. We have to reckon with those possibilities in order to live even if we cannot prognosticate their final shape, or foresee all the consequences implied in them. At the same time, all single and collective projects depend always on the free and unpredictable decisions of individuals. All these factors make any possibility 'unresolved and obscure' both in its planning and in its future reality.[99] Futurologists, just as any human person planning the future, have to live with a certain *docta ignorantia futuri*. Rahner regards it as a modality of each and every human free action.

There is a special role for Christian theology in this new situation of the freedom arising from the increased possibilities for human action. According to Rahner: the Christian should be the *guardian of this 'learned unknowing* [or ignorance]' *of* the future.[100] This formulation – at first sight – seems to be wholly negative, as if the theologian should always wag a warning finger at his contemporaries busy at their earthly projects: remember you must in the end surrender to the unplanned occurrence; or whatever you do is merely provisional and remains so – a Utopian dream in the light of the Absolute Future. For Rahner, however, such negativity is only one aspect of the Christian attitude. There is an obligation, precisely in view of the Absolute Future, to exercise one's creative powers in order to construct a this-worldly future. There is a certain Utopian factor in human life that 'constitutes the point of reference for, and [will be] the sign of the presence of the Absolute Future'. In as much as transcendence to the Absolute Future leads human planning beyond rationally determinable objectives, the 'Utopian factor' in this infinite process opens immanent possibilities capable of realization as an enterprise within a this-worldly future. This enterprise can then become the vehicle of the Absolute Future. It follows from this that

> Christianity ... should involve a genuine commitment to the world and an assent to the Absolute Future as one single commitment, and in such a way that each attitude mutually conditions the other.[101]

Rahner thinks that the mutual relationship, the reciprocity, of our immanent and transcendent future can be thus demonstrated.

This implicit 'pleading' for a theology of earthly realities, for a political theology, or simply, for this-worldly objectives and their fulfilment has become, following the Pastoral Constitution of Vatican II, *Gaudium et Spes,* a new topic for theological reflection. It belongs to the vocation of all Christians with their fellows 'to build up the world', to serve its progress and to acknowledge its autonomy. Rahner's essay on the idea of the 'New Earth' insists again on the intimate connection between these twofold objectives, the immanent and the transcendent.[102] In our present situation we do not encounter this world of ours as something undeveloped just as it came out of its Creator's hands. It is a world to the present shape of which mankind has creatively contributed and in which mankind is still at work toward its *'categorial'* (i.e. objectively palpable) goals. Is this 'second' humanized world just passing away, or will it be transformed at the consummation in the hoped for *eschaton*? Is the 'new earth' a return to the shape of God's original creation, or does it mean an entirely new beginning? Are we allowed to say that man's handy-work *too* is going to be saved and transformed in the 'new earth and new heaven' by the power of the Absolute Future which is both goal (*telos*) and *eschaton*?

There is no answer to these questions unless in the dialectical assertion of both horns of the dilemma, namely: 'human history will finally endure, [yet] ... it will be radically transformed'.[103] Whereas the second half of this statement maintains man's orientation open to the Absolute Future, the first stresses, at least, the moral significance of historical earthly achievements. We are responsible for our present history in its progress towards temporal *goals* and their realization.

Beyond this (merely) moral significance Rahner seeks some *real* connection between a future radical transformation and the events constituent of history.[104] He argues first that 'history itself constructs its own final and definitive state'.[105] This means that history in as much as it is the product of human freedom tries, as it were, to *save* itself and therewith some of its values into the new life to come. The work of love endures in individual history. Therefore there must be something permanent in the harvest which history will have produced.

> Consummation is not something that is located 'beyond' history ... it is in history that *that* takes place for which we are responsible (ibid).

One could add: the *that* which endures, saved and elevated into the eternal consummation (Rahner's Absolute Future, indeed).

His second line of argument appeals to the incarnation of the Logos: Christ, in his body, accepted human history as his own and remains the God-Man even after the consummation of his earthly life; his body remains the same body now transformed into a glorified one. It is not glorified just as a reward, one to which Christ's own bodily presence made no contribution. The case of that human history which the Incarnate took upon himself is somewhat similar. Transcendent consummation does not just 'reward' human history and abandon it forever, but shares with it the *eschaton* bestowed on our universe by the Absolute Future. To offer more about what and how the achievements constituent of history endure in the world to come, and what shape the result of final transformation will take, would be to stray into the field of apocalypsis. The future always remains obscure and mysterious, yet it is safely anticipated by hope. Indeed the virtue of hope is the real link between immanent and transcendent consummation, between an earthly future and the Absolute Future.

d) In discussing the topic of of hope Rahner cannot entirely detach himself from his scholastic background; he starts within that theological tradition. Hope is one of the three divine ('theological') virtues and, according to traditional understanding, its direct object is God. Consequently, one cannot discern in principle the difference between hope and faith, between hope and love. The special quality of hope, the property that determines its character, seems simply to be 'God for us': that is the God whose promises guide our history into the Absolute Future. Is this answer sufficient? Are not the other two divine virtues also geared to this Absolute Future that is indeed 'God for us'? Since these three divine virtues are all unmerited gifts of God's self-bestowal, Rahner' article, *Hope,* has the laborious task of working out how the meaning and function of hope differ in essence from that of faith and love.

Trinitarian speculation provides the starting point in *Hope.* Rahner tried to explain the processions of the divine persons precisely from this one self-bestowal of God the Father in two 'manners of subsistence'; first, in the 'inner' life of the Trinity the *Logos* and the *Pneuma* proceed from the Father. The second stage of this self-bestowal 'engraces' mankind in Faith (corresponding to the transcendental *verum* – truth) and Love (corresponding to *bonum* – good).[106]

The origin of hope is God's self bestowal, certainly the explanation of two of the three theological virtues: faith and love. As Scripture in fact places *elpis* (hope) between faith and love as man's attitude to the grace-giving God, hope is often thought as an intermediary only between these two since it has no proper function of its own. Its significance is found in *statu viatoris*, for in our progress towards consummation we believe in the truth of God and we try to love him as the highest good of our lives. In our pilgrim state, however, neither faith nor love can clearly discern its own character and our defective intellects and wills need the virtue of hope to hold fast to them. Such an assumption implies that hope would give way to direct vision and unitive love in the state of consummation. 1 Cor. 13:13, however, contradicts this; Paul ascribes a definitive permanence to all three divine virtues. They will shape our eternal future even as they saved us during our time on earth.[107] The question, therefore, remains:

> Can we interpret this basic act [that of hope] as a mere provisional attitude which will be dissolved once we have attained that state of 'possession' which in turn is itself constituted by 'vision' and unifying love? In that case, hope will be abolished as something that belongs to the past ... But is this line of thought correct?[108]

This question guides Rahner's next step in the interpretation of hope as a divine virtue. One should not understand these divine virtues as 'comprehending', or 'taking possession of' what they know or what they lovingly desire. If vision 'possesses' God's very being and love 'comes into possession' of the highest divine goodness, then hope is indeed only provisional: it would fade away at the moment of consummation.

Rahner rejects these conventional concepts of everyday theology. No, final consummation has a basic modality: the *eschaton* is at once patent *and* concealed. Thus the act of attaining God as *'truth* in vision' acknowledges, in fact, not only the transcendence of God but also his incomprehensibility. The unfathomable mystery always remains something to be experienced with no attempt to comprehend and to control it. Something similar can be said of love at the stage of consummation. 'The act of attaining love is the response to,

The Eternal Future 167

and acceptance of a love' which is totally incalculable and hence incomprehensible, since, apart from his grace there is nothing in us that makes us 'loveable' by God. In the state of consummation, too, this engraced love remains a surrender of the self to the mystery,

> which cannot charm love from the beloved through any act of self-surrender on its part, but lives totally by the love of the beloved whose love has no other basis than itself.[109]

If this is the 'modality' of faith and love at the consummation, their common source is a disposition luring us 'out of ourselves' into something utterly beyond our control. This 'outward orientation from the self', as Rahner puts it, into the absolute unchangeability God finds a proper expression in the virtue of hope:

> Hope is the name of a disposition in which we dare to commit ourselves to that which is radically beyond all human control ... which is attained precisely at that point at which the controllable is definitively transcended, i.e. in the ultimate consummation of eternal life.[110]

The conclusion is that hope has its own independent status and function. It is a continuous process constantly overcoming the provisional in time in order to make room for the exploration of the incomprehensibility of God in eternity. This process is the common factor characteristic of the interplay of truth and love which endow these virtues with an orientation outside oneself into the 'uncontrollability' of God.[111]

The task of a theology of hope is to explain how hope functions in relation to faith and love. Rahner holds that it is not faith that is the launching pad of hope, but the reverse. Faith can only give us a 'theoretical' acquaintance with God's promises, but cannot reveal that God has meant his promises for us and for me. Faith can only express and convey a universal desire for final salvation to us, but not a personal salvation for each one of us. This is exactly the contribution of the virtue of hope. It is

> an act by which we really establish ourselves in a relationship inexpressible ... at the theoretical level ... namely with God

> who, ... is apprehended as the God of grace and under no other aspect.

This other aspect, of which faith is ignorant comprises: God's anger over against his mercy, his condemnation over against his forgiving love. It is an aspect that faith alone cannot provide 'but rather something which is grasped solely by hope as such'.[112] Future salvation is not manipulated or controlled thereby; indeed it is maintained by the act and process of that hope directed to God who in his act of 'self-bestowal' makes himself the Absolute Future of man. Hope is the 'carrier', the condition of our progress towards our God as the Absolute Future of mankind and of the whole created world.

The function of hope as regards our this-worldly task becomes obvious. It is hope that inspires the critical, even revolutionary attitude of the Christian to immanent ends and their realization. Rahner expresses the matter thus: we are empowered through hope to undertake anew an exodus out of the present into the future (even within the dimension of this world).[113] It is the factor that puts every man-made structure under the scrutiny of the uncontrollable and incomprehensible to which the Christian has definitively surrendered him or herself – now and for all eternity. This is the power of a 'greater hope' in which the Christian possesses a 'lesser hope', 'namely, the courage to transform the 'framework of secular life', and in this lesser hope the greater one is made real'.[114] In other words, hope is present when desire for immanent fulfilment transforms our yearning for the definitive consummation of all. And this consummation is the God of grace, the Absolute Future.

Absolute Future is, without doubt, a key-concept by means of which we may gain a general understanding of the whole of Rahner's eschatology. The cautious nature of this sentence signals, however, that before gathering together some detailed remarks concerning its use in the essays which I have just analysed, I intend to question the notion itself. Not that I mean to discard it. On the contrary, Absolute Future is a necessary concept for steering our eschatological thought. In my opinion, however, Rahner's version of it is ambiguous and requires qualification. In reading and re-reading his texts I still cannot not determine whether or not he identifies Absolute Future with God, or with Christ's work; and whether this future (transcendent or immanent, or both together) is truly the 'apotheosis' of a definitely fulfilled human life ('consummation' in Rahner's terminology). To avoid this ambiguity I shall regard the notion, Absolute Future, as a reminder of the unconditional fact of *death*. It is up to the reader to decide whether this suggestion is correct or not: whether my reinterpretation turns out to be a true modification or just a disguised version of Rahner's own insight.

In using the term, Rahner obviously employs his own methodological principle, as laid down in his 'Reflections on Methodology in Theology'.[115] In this he has offered three approaches to the truths of faith: the central one is 'transcendental theology' which relies heavily on the 'metaphysics of knowing and willing' as propounded in his philosophical works, the *Spirit in the World* and *Hearers of the Word*. After presenting the first ('indirect methods') and second ('transcendental method') he concludes with the third and calls it *reductio ad mysterium*:

> Every theological statement is only truly and authentically such at the point at which one willingly allows it to extend beyond his comprehension into the silent mystery of God.[116]

Within Rahner's purview the three 'methods' are inseparably connected: the first leads to the second and the second to the *reductio ad mysterium*. As I understand him, he explains the concept of the Absolute Future by means of these three methodological aspects. The first, the 'indirect' method, is not to our purpose. Absolute Future relates rather to the transcendental horizon of human knowledge and will and consequently to the mystery of hope, the special character of which is different from that of faith and love.

The source of my uneasiness concerning Rahner's interpretation of Absolute Future is that 'transcendentalism' which I have repeatedly criticized in my five previous books. I believe that its use within Rahner's method renders the notion, Absolute Future, paradoxical, for it has to be accepted as an existent reality, one which is both invisible by nature and inept for objective conceptualisation (not 'categorial' in Rahner's terminology), and at the same time something which directs and shapes human desire. Absolute Future is like the reality of God in Rahner's thought in that its existence is affirmed by necessity, and nevertheless it empowers the dynamism of knowledge and will (by way of *quasi-formality*, as he puts it). If Rahner really identifies Absolute Future with God, he must also regard it as the objective[117] (*telos*) of every human being, one which is present and active in every moment of life. Its mysterious character (*reductio ad mysterium!*), however, seems to consist only in the fact that we cannot grasp its essential nature, that we cannot form an adequate concept of it.

Furthermore, the very connection of 'future' with the qualification 'absolute' seems to be a contradiction in terms. While future is and must be an event which rounds off the past and the fleeting present, the qualification, 'absolute', is an attribute of an unconditional reality, which, as an objective of human striving, makes this event a definitive and irreversible state of future human life, in which our desires and designs are transformed into their divine destiny. This final event that Rahner tries to qualify as 'absolute', is an event within the relativity of time: it is not yet. Regarded, however, as an 'absolute' event, it must be beyond time (or in another timescale that we do not know). This interpretation of Absolute Future puts the temporal and eternal into questionable synthesis. In other terms: man's horizontal anticipation (in time) coincides with his vertical pre-apprehension (of the eternal); 'transcendence is immanence and *vice versa*', as he himself emphasises. If he then equates the idea of Absolute Future with *Voll-endung*, this consummation ('apotheosis') of history, too, should be understood as a temporal event.[118] This consummation is, however, is not only the last and definitive event (in time), but also an ever present objective operative in human life: it is a future event (*eschaton*) and, at the same time, an event that functions here and now (*telos*). Can a concrete event (the consummation or apotheosis of history) be at once an ever present and motivating objective? If human life is a process, that is, a series of consecutive events, can we regard the last event of the series as its objective? Whereas I can *only anticipate* an event, I can be aware of the objective at which I am aiming.[119] Anticipation of an event and striving for an objective cannot belong to the same category. Yet this is exactly what Rahner's transcendental approach to Absolute Future would entail. To these questions, however, we shall have to return in another context.

Rahner does not of course entirely forget the third aspect of his methodology: the *reductio ad mysterium*. If the objective and the consummation of human life as summed up by the Absolute Future are still hidden, then it is a mystery. It is a future, as we quoted above, which 'silently lies in wait, and rips up the nets of all our plans'.[120] This transcendent/immanent consummation, however, enters into the very nature of human spirit: a 'transcendence opening to the mystery'.[121] It may be, therefore, a hint of the 'uncontrollable and incalculable', as known and willed by the human spirit, similar to the incomprehensibility of God. In this sense, according to Rahner, Absolute Future is, not a 'mere open possibility', but a promise in Jesus Christ;[122] a 'reality which has achieved [the] power to influence the present itself and in that sense has become real'.[123] The character of the Absolute Future as a mystery, therefore, can be understood as the still undisclosed quality of an immediately present and effective reality: both the objective and the human fulfilment of our transcendental experience. Is this indeed a *reductio ad mysterium?* Can an inscrutable mystery, even when thought of as an objective, guide the designs of human life on earth; can we hope that it will be our definitive state in the future?

Rahner's remarkable analysis of hope, as something different from faith and love, buttresses his argument. Hope has the ability to embrace both this-worldly temporal projects, which are *de se* available and also those objectives in the future that are neither available nor 'achievable' (*machbar*) by human activity. Furthermore, hope is, for Rahner, the divine virtue that has the capacity to direct and to empower the commitment of faith and love, indeed it is the dynamic force that holds onto the truth of faith and renders love's desire for God effective in the life of each individual. And if hope experienced during our earthly pilgrimage does not cease in the state of final fulfilment, can it reveal a future in heaven in face of the mystery of God that remains forever inscrutable? If this be so, in what sense is the Absolute Future the consummation, the true *eschaton* of human life?

These remarks concerning Rahner's interpretation of Absolute Future are not meant to criticize, or even refute his theory. They are meant to express an uneasiness that has emerged inevitably in my attempt to understand his various approaches to the concept. I am convinced that Rahner's Absolute Future provides an insight without which our normal approach to eschatological belief would be restricted to the repetition of traditional teaching on the four last things. Nonetheless, the source of my perplexity remains: Rahner's apparent identification of the Absolute Future with the idea of God and with the ultimate fulfilment of human life, its apotheosis. I believe therefore that a sketchy attempt at an alternative interpretation is in place. It is left to the discretion of the reader to accept or reject it.

I have already indicated the first step of my own approach: instead of explaining Absolute Future by a transcendental experience of God I shall identify the same concept with the inevitable fact of death. In my view the tag 'absolute' of Rahner's Absolute Future denotes nothing more than an occurrence beyond our control; this event simply ends our earthly history. Now death is only an experience of the living if it is the death of others,[124] it is not an objective, a *finis*: in death the human possibilities available to freedom cease and the time of life 'runs out'. Suicide apart, which is not an option for death but for premature dying, death is something that happens; we do not actively embrace it. In this sense our future death is not only a possible, but in fact an absolute unconditional ending. From my own perspective, death is the Absolute Future, the prospect not only of the individual, but also of all creation whose days 'are numbered'.

Rahner's philosophy and theology of death, and those of many other authors are, indeed, very meaningful human undertakings: to interpret this phenomenon is, however, an agonizing task. The interpretation of death involves confrontation with an absolutely final ending, and it must raise the question: does anything follow when time is over? Our immanent time has come to an end: is that ending the threshold of something beyond?

Knowledge of death needs no transcendental self-reflection. The death of others is an empirical experience, but our own death is not; we must leave the realm of present reality and face unknown and unknowable nothingness. This is the point at which a theory of immortal soul, or even an appeal to the reality of the 'living' God could not render the brutal fact of death acceptable. This not withstanding, there exists, as well, a human capacity for thinking beyond the grave. I call it, a mythmaking imagination addressing the possibilities of an unrevealed future. An empirical position can be replaced by an imaginative or theoretical construct based on philosophical or theological principles. We have no innate capacity for knowledge of a time beyond our time, unless it be by use of the imagination.[125] In anticipating the unknowable the interpreter of death seeks, often mistakenly, an intimation of immortality within the flow of time. One finds therein a possibility which is both unavailable and, as Rahner puts it, 'unachievable' (*nicht machbar*). One way of approaching life after death (this unavailable possibility) is through religion. Religion indeed could be defined as a life that lives with and reckons with such a possibility. To be more precise, religion lives with the conviction that what we call God, the Transcendent, can make this unachievable possibility an acceptable one. This, therefore, is the point at which I locate Rahner's attempted identification of the 'Absolute Future' with the idea of God.

My question remains, however: does Rahner really think that a transcendental experience of God's reality justifies us in identifying God as our life's fulfilment experienced in the last concluding event of life? Is the other side of death, the Absolute Future, an opening onto eternity? Such a position is, in my opinion, impossible on rational grounds. It is, however, possible to *believe* that beyond all available possibilities there is a Possibility of all other possibilities or the 'ultimate Possibility'.[126] This is as far as we can get with our time-restricted rational interpretation. Whether this ultimate

'Possibility of all other possibilities' is neutral or personal, menacing or benevolent, uncaring or caring, silent or self-revealing, condemning or saving is a matter for the teaching of religion. For religion is the home of faith hope and charity; it lives with and relies on possibilities beyond human experience, and hence, with the 'Possibility of all other possibilities'. Religion, however, on its own provides insufficient grounds for the belief that this ultimate Possibility is the Absolute Future of human history, unless it is buttressed by the divine virtue of hope. Only hope can give us the conviction that the last event of human life is not death, but another kind of life, another possibility of our future,

Rahner's article, *Hope*, provides us a hint on how to bridge the gap between death, our Absolute Future, and the possibility of survival beyond. Although hope is basically a human act, it can, nevertheless, advert to God, the ultimate Possibility. While faith is the search for the truth of God and love is the commitment to this divine exploration, hope is the capacity to choose and to awaken those hitherto unknown possibilities which still lie in the 'mysterious' future. The hope which desires the definitive fulfilment of life's enterprise can also decide to make God, the Possibility of possibilities its proper objective, since such a God encapsulates our possible future beyond death. In stressing this quality of hope, I am following the main lines of Rahner's own analysis and I am prepared to assert with him that hope is capable of making real (actualizing) this ultimate Possibility. I do not assert, however, that God, even when so explained, is the ultimate aim of human nature, unless through the free choice of religious hope; neither do I believe that such a God is and remains the mystery, just because we cannot grasp his nature in clear cut concepts. God is the mystery, precisely because he is and ever remains for us the ultimate Possibility. Rahner's *reductio ad mysterium* should consist in God's possible being, even though that it is affirmed as really existent by the lure of hope itself supported by faith in God's promises.

Now if we suppose that religious men and women can have the conviction of *faith* that this 'Possibility of possibilities' is indeed God, the proper choice of hope is to trust that this God must be a personal, benevolent, caring, self-revealing and saving possibility in contradistinction to attributes contrary to these. Thus the dynamism of hope terminates not in death, which we called Absolute Future, but beyond it, in the Possibility of possibilities. If religious hope is freely able to identify God through its commitment to Jesus, this God, indeed is 'God-for-us', the God of hope.

Rahner's own idea of an Absolute Future seems to have been motivated by a similar consideration: in comparing the Utopia of time-bound projects with *his* Absolute Future, he insists that the promise that is God is not a mere possibility (that is not one invented by human whim) 'but is infallibly and victoriously promised' in Jesus Christ;[127] or one that is 'definitively promised as coming in Jesus Christ';[128] 'It is a reality which has acquired the power to influence the here and now itself and in that sense has become real' (ibid.). Christian faith in God, the ultimate Possibility, has acquired an explicit expression in Jesus Christ: God's promise therefore is 'more than a mere possibility'. But does it, therefore, follow that it is an existent reality? If this 'promise' refers to our possible future it cannot be an already present reality. If, however, it is identified with God, can we affirm that God is an existent reality that can influence our present life and be real' indeed? Rahner's transcendental reasoning implies such a conclusion. He himself, however, qualifies this 'reality' or 'real influence' with the words 'in this sense'; in what sense therefore? Would it not be enough to say that faith demands the reality of God, and hope trusts that it can bring about the desired consummation of human life? Through the commitment of the Christian to Jesus and to his triumph this happy fulfilment is indeed no 'mere' promise, but an authentic one through which we can trust that it 'is coming' and will be 'infallibly' honoured. There are a myriad possibilities open to us, and there are some which we choose and allow to influence and shape our life. I can truly call them *real* possibilities without attributing actual existence to them. In this sense, too, both God and his promises of a future life do not yet exist except as real possibilities: an 'offer' (*Angebot*) as Rahner himself puts it. An 'offer', however, is not yet an existent reality.

Rahner's essays concerning the future try to argue the continuity between the definitive fulfilment of merely human hope with the 'beatific vision' traditionally interpreted as the sight of God. By 'merely human hope' I understand the legitimate desire of all human persons to achieve their objectives in life, including the values they have adopted. To people threatened by death and despair at the end of their lives, religion offers belief and trust in possibilities beyond immediate experience. We hope to attain our own *eschaton*, the state in which all our values reach definitive fulfilment, and we hope, too, never to loose them. Rahner's argument correctly points out the moral obligation and responsibility which everyone must have for the realization of mankind's secular objectives. In my view, however, no real connection can be proved between those secular possibilities on earth and any future ones. The present dispensation allows free and autonomous choice, but life after death is still an unknown quantity. Can it be shown that earthly projects are indeed media through which ultimate fulfilment is brought about? If we regard God as the Possibility of possibilities, there can hardly be a real connection between these 'two' possible futures. Yet Rahner's theology of worldly values relies on their capacity to mediate an Absolute Future. This is why, I believe, Rahner's theology of earthly realities needs a certain adjustment.

The realization of our time-bound projects is in the unknown future: they are just as much a possibility as is their divine fulfilment. The acceptance of a relationship between human projects and their divine fulfilment as two diverse possibilities is a free and conscious choice of religious commitment: they need not be one and the same objective, since neither implies the other. If a king's earthly project here on earth might well include the welfare of his realm, but its success or failure is independent of its *eschaton*, that is, of the actual shape of its realization. Religious belief can, nevertheless, motivate earthly achievements or compensate for their failure.

Of course merely human projects, too, are related to what I called the absolute future, namely, to death, which relativizes them all. In face of this absolute future we either despair in a world-despising scepticism or we trust that God, the ultimate possibility is the infinite source of further, unfathomable possibilities within the unknown time of his own eternity. One of these possibilities may well be the fulfilment of those values which we have tried to create or maintain in our earthly life.

We Christians who approach God, the possibility of all possibilities, through commitment to Jesus Christ need not abandon our worldly ambitions. Not, however, because our earthly human projects are implied within their ultimate fulfilment, but because we are followers of a human being whose earthly ambitions apparently failed, yet found his own *eschaton* in his resurrection. He who died our death (yes the absolute future of humankind) is raised by God: his *consummatum est* might become the beginning of our own 'consummation': an apotheosis of all that we valued in earthly life.

In this last sentence, however, I anticipated our next topic, for one of the last things is this 'apotheosis' in heaven.

3.4. The Last Things

(A) Individual and Collective Eschatology

Some twenty years ago I introduced my dialogue with Rahner's works by means of an analysis of his short creeds.[129] After offering a 'theological' and an 'anthropological' 'creed' he sums up the essentials of Christian belief in terms of eschatology. This third creed employs concepts we have already examined and presupposes Rahner's general approach to the human capacity for self-transcendence. It seems, however, that this self-transcendence has been transposed into a kind of historical future, one that surpasses all the particular and finite futures in the course of our time on earth. In speaking of the Absolute Future, our previous topic, Rahner identifies it with God's definitive self-bestowal on mankind through Jesus Christ. The word 'definitive' includes the notion of 'irreversible' and that of 'eternal'. I shall now quote this short creed in the translation of W. V. Ditch, reprinted at the end of Rahner's *Foundations*:[130]

> Christianity is the religion which keeps open the question about the Absolute Future which wills to give itself in its own reality by self-communication, and which has established this will as eschatologically irreversible in Jesus Christ, and this future is called God.

178 *The Sacrament of the Future*

This concise text is fully intelligible, neither in the original nor, certainly, in English translation and, I believe, hardly accessible without further explanation. The first line repeats Rahner's earlier statement: 'Christianity is the religion of the Absolute Future'. That same sentence, however, then transposes the abstract German word '*Offenhaltung*' (a disposition of openness), into the active mode: Christianity 'keeps open the question'; what is kept open is not the reality of the Absolute Future, but the *question* of hope concerning the same. It implies some uncertainty about the reality of any future destiny in the religious quest of the Christian. (Though a question may anticipate its answer, it is in itself not yet a positive statement.) The next sentence, however, will resolve this uncertainty: its grammatical subject is the Absolute Future which, or rather a personified 'who', intends to give himself (or rather itself) to humankind by means of self-bestowal in as much as he (or it) in fact exists. This, I believe, denotes God's universal salvific will and implies therewith the offer of grace. This offer to mankind, as yet unrealized, however, realizes itself in Jesus Christ's eschatological victory that is *irreversibly established;* and therefore the Absolute Future can now be equated with God: this future is called *God*.

The English text (when compared with the German original) of this eschatological creed implies an encounter between two 'objectives': human and divine. It is about the fulfilment of both the human quest and God's condescending gift. The same English translation correctly repeats the word 'future' at the end of the short creed. It regards this consummation as something to be realized in the future and not just present at every moment of the course of history: an 'historical' actuality, that is, an event. Rahner, of course, considers two aspects of the end of time: the existential concomitant of our awareness: a goal that sustains 'history in motion'; and the event of the *eschaton,* the realization of which is anticipated by faith in Christ's death and resurrection. The main point is that neither the goal nor its realized *eschaton* are mere possibilities (technically 'asymptotic notions'), but something to be experienced both transcendentally 'in time', and in the future through the mystery of God's gift of grace, insofar as this future is and remains an absolute mystery even when this self-communication reaches fulfilment, Christianity is the religion which keeps open the *question* about the Absolute Future.[131]

Rahner's alternative 'creeds' present Christian religion in terms of 'three theologies'. The first starts with God's self-communication and ends with the definitive fulfilment of mankind, its 'apotheosis' as manifest in Jesus Christ (the theological creed). The second starts with the 'transcendence' of human love of neighbour and ends with the Church in which this love becomes equivalent to love of God (the anthropological creed). The third 'creed' originates in a 'futuristic' approach to the expression of the essentials of Christian belief, the pre-apprehension (*Vorgriff*) or anticipation of an event dependent of the mystery God'. We can leave aside the way in which these credal statements already entail Christological and Trintarian doctrines, or whether these three 'creeds' are valid only by reason of their mutual coherence. What is, however, common to all three creeds is the transcendent mystery that is God and his self-communication definitively made present to mankind in Jesus Christ.

A creed, however, which sums up the essentials of Christian religion, is not yet theology. The profession of faith is a liturgical act of a community in response to the word of God, or to the word of the Church. It is not the conclusion of theological reasoning, but rather the beginning of reflection on the coherence of concepts used in credal proclamation and on their meaning. Although in itself an act of worship, Rahner's brief future-oriented creed can be regarded as the basis of his eschatology proper. A creed is, after all a framework within which the last events of the promised future can be encapsulated and discussed in the light of developing ecclesial tradition.

If we choose to take Rahner's third brief creed as a self-contained expression of the whole of Christian belief, we are confronted with a methodological question: how to reach a consistent presentation of the last things? In itself a creed is an act of community, and its theological explanation imparts primarily its collective significance; only subsequently does it refer to the individual. Rahner is very much aware of this when he, in his own fashion, states:

> There is necessarily an *individual* and a *collective* eschatology, [however] not as statements about two disparate realities, but rather as statements about each concrete person. But the fulfilment of this concrete person cannot be expressed in any other way except by his being regarded *both* as an element in a human collectivity in the world *and also* as an ever unique and incalculable person who cannot be reduced to the world and to society.[132]

Hence, though the treatments of collective and individual eschatology are distinct, they are interchangeable. They are two sides of one coin. Rahner himself starts with an individual eschatology at the end of *Foundations*. It contains accordingly the traditional topics of the 'Last Things': individual judgement after death, the eternal fate of the dead in heaven or hell, and the possibility of a quasi-temporal process of cleansing past sins in purgatory. The reason for this choice is not quite clear. It could be ascribed to Rahner's usual anthropological approach to theological truths (what happens to me after death?'), or to the dogmatic decision of Pope Benedict XII, decreeing in 1334 that the souls of the just enter immediately to the vision of God,[133] a decree of course belonging to individual eschatology.

Although Rahner starts with the individual's future fate, he omits any assurance concerning the immortality of the soul. The main reason for this omission is that in itself 'soul' is an abstract notion: it expresses an 'entity' essentially tied to its bodily existence. The soul therefore is not 'independent of the transformation of the world and of the resurrection of the flesh'.[134] In order to avoid the contrary view, which he attributes to the Enlightenment, and of which he finds traces in the general understanding of the faithful,[135] he approaches eschatology from the point of view of the individual within a collectivity. Behind the four last things of the traditional treatises, there is always the *subintelligitur*, that is, the final resurrection of mankind and the new world to come. For each one of us, then, the very last event is in *koinonia*, in communion with the whole creation.

In a 'futurological' summary of Christian faith (such as Rahner's third 'creed') the Last Things are God's future work in granting to human history and to the world its irreversible fulfilment. Although implicit in God's promise in Jesus Christ, God's final deed on our behalf remains an incomprehensible mystery to be worshipped in silence and our idea of perfect fulfilment should be 'moving beyond all images into the ineffable'. This mysterious character of God, the Absolute Future, is now transferred to all eschatological statements including those concerning individual eschatology.

୶

In my presentation of Rahner's eschatology I shall, with some hesitation, follow his own treatment in the *Foundations*. My reflections, however build on a presupposition: Christianity's message is not first and foremost about heaven, purgatory and hell, but about the judgement of God on the whole history of mankind as the introduction to the promised new creation. The individual is but a part of this collective and cosmic event and his share in what is to come will depend on divine justice and mercy, as well as on the unimaginable manner of his existence in a future world.

It is, however, not so easy to reconcile these two approaches (individual and collective) and regard them as two sides of one coin. The consideration of the eschatological salvation of the individual involves the consideration of the perfect fulfilment of the whole of humanity. And if this be so what does the general resurrection of mankind and the new world to come add to the state of the just who are already in heaven; conversely, if individual salvation is gained only at the very end along with the rest of creation, final justification and sanctification must be postponed to the last day. The eschatologist Paul Althaus reminds us of this difficulty.[136] If there is but one final judgement and if we accept the existence of purgatory (as we shall presently discuss), we should have to apply it also to each and every justified individual (including also the so-called canonized saints) for whom eternal salvation is secure, and not only to those who died in a state still lacking final perfection (those dying with, so-called,

182 *The Sacrament of the Future*

venial sins). One might ask too: is the vindication of the suffering of the individual just person only to be expected at the last judgement, as the Bible appears to suggest? W. Pannenberg seeks an answer to this question by distinguishing between the merely anthropological expectation of individual believers, and God's final and sovereign action at the end of our time. Whereas the first is unable to resolve the matter, Christian hope can rely on God's promises for a collective consummation, one which emphasizes less the individual's fulfilment than God's act of social justice in redressing the unbalance of a sinful world.[137] We do not find similar considerations in Rahner's eschatology as proposed in the *Foundations*.

There is another point which should engage our attention: both Rahner and Pannenberg assume that this definitive ending of history, including the future act of God implicit therein, is an event, and that this final event has a retroactive influence on the process of human life in our time. The difficulty therefore which I raised in my previous section recurs: how can an event in the future (an *eschaton*) be active in the present? It is not easy to understand how an event (in biblical terms: the parousia) which has not yet occurred could influence the course of history. It is not yet an existent reality. If we omit the consideration of the immortality of the soul (as Rahner does) as something inherent in human nature, Christian hope can only envisage it as implicit in belief in the resurrection of Jesus. This is, however, only a real possibility the occurrence of which does not coincide with the object of our desires. Were it evident (as Rahner assumes) that Absolute Future is identical with God and not with death (as I have tried to show), then the event of the parousia *as an event* would not have a decisive significance for the life in our world: it would gradually grow up into God's eternity. I shall, however, return to this question at a later stage.

These, however, are only an anticipation of my fuller reflections on eschatology. *Foundations* leaves us with a drastically reduced summary of eschatological topics: the final victory of Christ's resurrection and his expected Parousia, the apocalyptic end of the cosmos, the ultimate judgement on mankind's history, the resurrection of the flesh and the manner of mankind's new existence in the realized Kingdom of God. Are these really connected with our yearning in hope for eternal life after death? We need to discuss how collective eschatology enters into our personal pilgrimage toward the 'day of the Lord'.

Rahner was not silent about these themes. I shall have to expound his answers to these questions within my further presentation of his individual and collective eschatology using articles dispersed throughout his work.

(B) *The 'Definitive Validity'[138] of the Individual*

Rahner's anthropological approach to the Last Things is conditioned by his concept of freedom: human beings are free before God, *the Absolute Future*. During our time on earth, therefore, we are capable of choosing between two alternative possibilities; we can make a decision for or against God. Either choice can determine our ultimate fate; one is called heaven and the other hell. Heaven is the 'final definitive state of happiness and fulfilment for a person who enjoys God's self-communication in grace', and hell the absolute loss of that definitive state. What then are the preconditions for making this fateful option?

Before offering an analysis of the nature of this free option Rahner has good news for us: the two possibilities, heaven or hell, are not on equal footing, they are not complementary statements. The choice of heaven depends on God's 'powerful grace' which engenders in the faithful the unshakeable hope that:

> we are living in the *eschaton* of Jesus Christ, the God-Man who was crucified for us and has risen for us and who remains forever; we know ... that in spite of the drama and the ambiguity of the freedom of the individual person, the history of salvation as a whole will reach a positive conclusion for the human race ... But we neither can nor must say anything about the end of an individual who suffers final loss.[139]

In other words, whereas the hope of heaven is always validated by God's promise in Jesus Christ, hell remains a serious possibility to be reckoned with only within the context of our earthly history. The ultimate motive behind each individual choice is an attitude to the promised salvation of the whole race (hence, collective eschatology), and we know of no one who has been or is going to be damned. Such an optimistic premiss, of course, does not reassert belief in *apokathastasis,* that is outright salvation for all, unless this is interpreted as subject to the uncertainty of hope. Nor does it presuppose the existence of an immortal soul (a spiritual constituent of our human nature) which enjoys the bliss of the vision of God while the body is still in the grave, for 'each individual person is fulfilled by final fulfilment in God as one existent spirit and body'.[140]

Those, however, who hope for final beatitude at the end of their lives on earth must cross the threshold of death. Eschatology has always to confront this obstacle, one which screens the path to our future destiny. Remember that I have called death *pace* Rahner, *the* absolute future of man; for me, indeed, the first of the Last Things – in contemporary eschatology – is the notion of death. It is the common theme between the speculation of philosophical anthropology and of Christian theology: the existence of life after death is disclosed by the virtue of hope.[141] It is clear, Rahner says, that to cross the limit of earthly life, and to enter into another manner of living must imply, according to sound theology, that our present time does not last indefinitely. The concept of time as 'lasting for ever' is a conceptual model that may help some, but would, in fact, generate more trouble than comfort. In dying into life eternal we do not change horses to ride on for ever: 'death marks the end for the whole person' because

> eternity comes as time's own mature fruit ... subsumes time by being liberated from time ... so that freedom and something of final and *definitive validity* can be achieved ... Eternity is a *mode of the spiritual freedom* which has been exercised in time, and therefore it can be understood only from the correct understanding of freedom.[142]

Rahner offers, then, two key concepts by means of which to conceive of entry into eternal life through death: 'definitive validity' and 'mode of spiritual freedom'. They are also conceptual models for conceiving life after death in the eternity of heaven and hell.

No one acquainted with Rahner's works will be surprised at his constant return to the interpretation of death and immortality.[143] Though I have already dealt with his theology of death elsewhere,[144] it is useful to return here to some imprecision inherent in its central idea, namely: the ultimate free option at the point of death. I shall assign two extremes between which his thought shifts: on the one hand, that of Ladislaus Boros according to whose thesis the timeless moment of death marks a clear choice in the face of the whole reality of God as experienced by the soul in process of separating from the body (*Endentscheidungshypothese*)[145] and, on the other, the force of a lifetime of partial options which together decide definitively a person's destiny. The first (although Boros is often called Rahner's disciple) is unacceptable because (among other reasons) it returns partly to the conceptual model of death as the separation of body and soul; and the second, though more in accordance with traditional Christian ideology, is questionable: one particular option (e.g. a 'mortal' sin) would then imply the definitive rejection of God, while one virtuous act could represent the 'final validity of human existence' required for entry into eternal bliss.

In 'Ideas about the Theology of Death' Rahner seems to distance himself from L. Boros' hypothesis of *Endent-scheidung*, i.e. the decisive decision at the moment of death. He begins by emphasizing that, even in our present temporal state, 'we take absolute responsibility for our lives'; each single act of freedom is an existential decision. Such choices provide us with an experience of decisions that are radical, final and possessed of definitive validity. Thus eternal life is the 'radical interiority, now liberated and brought to full realization, within that history ... through which we are even now living'. Eternal life, our immersion in God is part of the 'here and now'; we opt for or against God in every conscious action of our lives. This idea, however, becomes slightly modified when Rahner insists that these radical decisions are 'fully brought to birth in death'.[146] There is, therefore, something *more* to the 'act of death' than our former decisions, and we seem to be back with a modified *Endentscheidung-hypothese* of Ladislaus Boros.

We must, to be sure, emphasize the adjective 'modified'.

186 *The Sacrament of the Future*

This modification becomes clear, too, in *Ideas* where Rahner analyzes life after death explicitly as the object of hope in face of the 'comfortless absurdity of death'. Death is regarded yet again as the radical conclusion of all former decisions, even if neither we nor those at death's door can conceive it.[147] 'Conclusion' implies here 'a demand that it must constitute the sum total of [our] life as an act of freedom in which the whole of life is gathered up'.[148] Death, therefore, must be the act (of hope, to be sure) in which we experience our freedom eminently. The dying person adopts an attitude toward death and hopes for

> a unity, a reconciliation of the contrary elements [in life]; a meaning to existence; an eternal validity for all love freely accepted; an assent to absolute truth'.[149]

Here again the act of dying is regarded as a unique occasion, as the 'real and comprehensive act of freedom [contained] in the total disposal of [one's] existence for or against God' – even if that is 'taking place throughout the whole of life'.[150] Although Rahner differs from L. Boros ('The free decision ... does not need to happen mysteriously at the very moment of physical death'[151]), he holds that death (the *certa moriendi conditio* or the *prolixitas mortis* of Gregory the Great) involves something more than a definitive conclusion of all decisions in life. Rahner's short *excursus* in *Dying* on the teaching of Scripture and dogmatic tradition about death and the particular judgement indicates a clearly modified approach: a true

> theology of Scripture sets death as an essential internal limit, as a *consummation of freedom* from within, and not merely an end to the history of moral freedom, an end assigned arbitrarily by God 'on the occasion' of biological death.[152]

Nonetheless what happens at the point of death is absolutely decisive for it constitutes the *'finality of man's basic option*, which permeates his history and in which he disposes himself in confrontation with God'.[153]

This imprecision (if not ambiguity) in Rahner's theology of death, a position between strict *Endentscheidungshypothese* and the teaching of tradition, can only be justified if we assume with him that death is an a priori transcendental idea occurring throughout life's history. In this sense death is present, whether recognized or not, in every act of freedom, indeed, death is the 'elevation of the history of freedom into its finality'.[154] Recall how he views freedom and its history: since a free act that occurs in time is not subject to the variations of time, an act of true freedom is not just an irrelevant choice to be revised at any time, but always a 'once for all disposal by the subject of itself' and thus 'spread over space and time'.[155] It is 'once for all' and its result is the 'inalienable *responsibility*' of the subject. The freedom of a moral act is a radical decision the authenticity of which functions beyond time and is no longer temporal:

> Wherever a free and 'lonely' (i.e. personally responsible) act of decision has taken place in absolute obedience to a higher law, or in a radical affirmation of love for another person, something *eternal* has taken place, and man is experienced immediately as transcending the indifference (i.e. contingency) of time in its merely temporal duration.[156]

Death should be such a free act of the person. If death is not a free act, is it not a fatal event originating from outside the spiritual self, perhaps: the 'Fates cutting the lifeline of the living at random', or of the inscrutable decree of a divine power? Rahner would certainly reject both these beliefs. Instead, he introduces a subtle dialectic into the act of death: it is both an act of free decision and at the same time an act which sums up the whole history of personal freedom. It results in the absolute and eternal status (in Rahner's term: 'definitive validity') of the person and at the same time represents the totality of those decisions taken throughout life that make a person 'disposable'[157] for eternal life. This ultimate disposition (*disposability*) finds its radical manifestation in death.[158] This ultimate disposition (an idea receiving no emphasis in his *Theology of Death*) presupposes the transcendental affirmation of God in that freedom which usually reaches its full maturity in the personal response to revelation. It is the experience of powerlessness before God, the awareness that the actual realization of transient decisions, though 'eternal' in character, is subject also to mundane (technically, 'categorial') objectives. In other words, the 'eternal' is still controlled by the finitude of time; it is, in spite of its infinite horizon:a *finite* freedom. This dialectic between the infinite and finite as regards man's ultimate disposition is manifested in death.

By means of this dialectic Rahner, following his own transcendental reasoning, associates the anthropological with the theological elements: the free act of death unifies ultimate self-fulfilment with a disposition of soul acknowledging absolute powerlessness in facing God's judgement. Both elements remain intrinsic to the personal history of freedom, even though each single fundamental option is diffused throughout time. The free disposition of oneself and the open acceptance of God's judgement of it are unified in death. There is, therefore, something threatening in the 'hiddenness'[159] of human death; we can never be certain whether or not a person's ultimate fundamental option can be associated in death with an absolute powerlessness of ultimate disposition. Within the flux of time we cannot assess our final standing in our encounter with God; we can do no more than hope to the very end. The proximity of the incomprehensible mystery of God (both God's selfhood and his freedom of relationship with each person) makes 'the incomprehensibility of death definitive in its hiddenness'.[160]

This fine dialectical statement of Rahner tries, in my opinion, to clarify a position between the characterization of death as an exclusive act (the tenor of the Boros hypothesis) and the traditional conception of death according to which the final outcome can depend on one single act. Final salvation or damnation, heaven or hell, are subject to a person's ultimate disposition and to the judgement of God, both of which are inscrutable. Faith teaches that judgement is the destiny of the individual at death and of the whole human race on the last day. The eschatological future of each person, the outcome of a personal history of free action, is ultimately dependent on God's merciful judgement. Individual and collective eschatology are two sides of one coin.

We are, however, still engaged in the consideration of the manner in which human beings enter into eternal life. We have seen that 'definitive validity' and the 'new mode of spiritual freedom' have been coined as characteristics of eternal life, and that they depend heavily on human dispositions both during life, and at the moment of death. Rahner is aware, of course, that the great majority of human beings seem to be incapable of true existential decisions throughout the history of their personal freedom. It is not just that we are all too weak to live with such a high degree of existential awareness, but countless members of our species never attain full consciousness during their short lifetime. Rahner has to explain this phenomenon, unless, indeed, he accepts L. Boros' quaint hypothesis that the 'act of death' so supplies for immaturity that the spiritually retarded die with the same capacity for ultimate decision as the spiritually gifted.

In *Dying* Rahner puts himself a similar question acknowledging that his approach to ultimate self-determination 'imposes an enormous burden on the problem of this unique history of freedom':

> How can a subject of this kind, with the creaturely finiteness of his freedom and in the poverty of his spatio-temporal history', really and definitively and once for all decide for or against this infinity of his real life, which is purely and simply God himself?[161]

In spite of admitting this difficulty Rahner insists that such a decision is not only possible, but essential to Christian belief, because human transcendence implies the self-revelation of God. He assumes that God can make any person capable of such a final decision. A similar possibility is affirmed in *Foundations,* though in another context. Human contact with God and his self- revelation instructs us in the discernment of eternity, experienced in time and interpreted with the eyes of faith. For, Rahner argues, if our awareness was only of time, we could escape 'into the radical emptiness of what merely has been', and the subject of definitive decisions 'would be unintelligible, even as an illusion or a fantasy'. No, a fully decisive act is not 'something which is set over against [and restricted to] a mere passing moment', but a decision in which the will, 'risking itself in freedom, is very far from activating a particular moment within a series of non-events, but in fact accessing the eternal'. Briefly, according to Rahner: though we can doubt the possibility of such access by others, we cannot doubt our own experience of our own free activity that there are, indeed, fundamental decisions which determine our eternal fate. Scripture knows of no human life closed to the experience of the eternal, because:

> Revelation presupposes that God's power enables everyone, without regard to ordinary circumstance [i.e. without regard to outward appearances], to have such an adequate experience of spiritual and personal eternity throughout life so that the possibility of eternity ... is in fact realized in actual eternal life.[162]

This Rahnerian optimism has taught us only that eternity is somehow contained in time; the question remains: how to conceive of eternal life after death? The central, traditional answer is, of course, the vision of *God* in heaven or its loss in hell. We have noted already that the customary tag, beatific, is not always added to vision, and that the vision of God is, more often than not, allocated to God's mysterious incomprehensibility:

> God is absolute mystery. And therefore fulfilment and absolute [elsewhere immediate] closeness to God himself is also an ineffable mystery which we go to meet and which the dead who died in the Lord find ... It is the mystery of ineffable happiness.[163]

The language of the New Testament is, of course, almost entirely pictorial in describing life after death. It is, however, noticeable that metaphors introducing the idea of heavenly life are set primarily within the context of a collective end of time, such as: the eternal banquet, being at home in the Father's house, the victorious kingdom of God etc; such images suggest peace and glory shared with God. Rahner reduces all these images of heaven to sober theological terminology: it is eternity which 'brings the temporality of the single, total person to a final, definitive validity'. He adds that this ultimate worth of the person 'can also be called the resurrection of the flesh' (ibid.). There are in Scripture similar, imaginative metaphors about the opposite state: loss of salvation in hell. These, too, like the ones about heaven are to be understood as all eschatological statements are, not in terms of their literary content, but of their intention; they are 'conceptual models'. Eternal fire in Gehenna, the outer darkness where there is 'gnashing of the teeth', etc. are pictorial expressions used by Jesus to teach a serious possibility about which one 'does not need to know ... more than' that the possibility of hell is not on equal footing with the promise of heaven. To ignore the possibility of hell would be to diminish the seriousness of the free power of decision. Indeed hell is possible, because we are free; heaven is possible because we are saved in Jesus Christ.

What is then the characteristic content of the state of eternity as opposed to that of an eternity already experienced in time? Rahner's answer lies in the quotation cited above: the relationship of the blessed to the mystery that is God. He expresses this relationship in many ways in an attempt to develop the Christian tradition in which the blanket term *vision* is so static an image that it may suggest to a modern mind the horror of eternal boredom. Peace (as Augustine said at the very end of *De civitate Dei*); there shall we holiday (*ibi vacabimus*) and contemplate (*videbimus*) in constant praise of the divine majesty: passive attitudes, therefore, compared with the free and active memory of a past lifetime. The spread of Christianity within a Greek world interpreted the scriptural 'vision' as *theorein,* as wisdom: the quietude of the philosopher in face of theory that has been made concrete. Augustine, however, extends the same word with the concept of love (*ubi amabimus*).

The emphasis placed by Rahner on relationship to God through the 'immediacy' of grace, and eminently through the experience of the blessed in heaven, echoes this attitude. This immediacy, of course, as we shall presently see, is mediated through the risen Christ.[164] In his later writing, however, this immediate intimacy with the incomprehensible mystery of God is expressed by the concept of disinterested love for God. The stress is on the 'disinterested' nature of love for God's sake alone: 'true love is self-abandoning, never returning to itself'; the miracle of forsaking self 'without any prospect of returning'; salvation consists in a lover's entrusting himself to another person 'without any safeguards'. Now, the argument continues, Christianity 'stubbornly' insists that only love of God for his own sake will save us in life, but clearly holds, too, that human love for God is only possible through the initiative of God's love for us: it is a reciprocity between unequals. If this is the only way to salvation on earth, all the more will the blessed in heaven allow themselves

> to fall, to regard [God's] mystery as the true light illuminating everything, to know that death is the gate to life, and that the love which seeks, not itself, but the God who is loved as such, means true life in eternity.[165]

Beatitude, the ultimate authentic expression of the fulfilment of freedom, is perfect happiness in heaven. It is, at once, a state attained in death, and the gratuitous gift of God for all eternity, a gift anticipated throughout life. Thus, the transformation of the ideal of perfect love of neighbour into the vision of the incomprehensibility of God means that interpersonal love is the true content of beatitude.

How, one wonders, can the love existing between persons on earth become a more eminent, a higher, love at the point of death? Traditional Roman Catholic theology, indeed, postulates a process of maturation after death in which this ultimate perfection can develop: *purgatory,* a place of 'purification', a doctrine not shared by Evangelical Christians and never really accepted by the Orthodox. Rahner cautiously introduces this doctrine in *Foundations* with the verb 'it seems' that there is such a place where this process can take place. Now a process presupposes a development with disparate phases, here: an evolution of personal integration and, above all, an intermediary state between salvation already gained and immutable heavenly bliss. It seems therefore to introduce the temporal into the eternal. We need, therefore, to reintroduce some kind of time after death if we are to take this concept seriously.

I am not going to revise here the historical origins of this doctrine (which many Catholics take for a dogma of the Church[166]). In view, however, of its apparent plausibility, it is worthwhile considering its possible meaning. This is what

Rahner does in *Foundations* and in other short references to the same. Purgatory is indeed plausible in view of our incapacity for reaching the state of ultimate perfection, that of unselfish love in this life; and of our obviously imperfect dispositions ('disposability' to use Rahner's own expression) at the point of death; together with, of course, the tragic occurrence of (early) death allowing the person involved no possibility of full maturity. Other cultures, indeed, take continuing maturation after death for granted, and millions believe in the transmigration of souls or in reincarnation. Surprisingly, although Rahner maintains the view that eternal destiny is decided by each person's history, he considers such ideas possible provided that they are not 'understood as a fate for man that never ends and will continue [i.e. lasts] for ever'.[167] The common concept of purgatory is not unlike, and, in the context of Roman Catholic theology, connected with the doctrine of indulgences.

In a small critical article, however, Rahner distances himself from the idea of an intermediary state.[168] In 1336 Pope Benedict XII published a decree (*Benedictus Deus*) in which he asserted that souls after death and before the resurrection of their bodies are immediately *(mox)* admitted to the beatific vision or damned in hell. The medieval interpretation of this statement presupposes the existence of disembodied human souls until history ends with the universal resurrection. Rahner does not take this as a dogma of the Church, but rather as an 'intellectual framework' associating statements about collective and individual eschatology. This intermediate state would represent a 'time' between two moments of ultimate fulfilment. Can we imagine a lapse of time after death, however differently conceived from the time attached to material things or from time experienced in human freedom? How can we postulate both that the separated soul has already reached perfection before God, and that it is still awaiting the re-assumption of its own body? A soul existing in separation from the body would certainly militate against the essential unity of the human being. And what about the dogma defined by Pius XII, that of Mary's bodily assumption into heaven? Is this an exceptional privilege, or is it a true possibility for all human beings whose exercise of free decision enables them to reach their final status in heaven as a member of the collective resurrection of the body? Although Rahner takes the matter no further, he does suggests the possibility of bodily resurrection immediately after death:[169]

> Why then should we not assign the resurrection to the moment of death, the moment at which personal history is finally complete?[170]

Any anthropological and theological treatment of death in fact excludes the notion of some intermediate state as one binding as Catholic doctrine. Rahner indeed calls it: a 'little harmless mythology, which is not dangerous as long as we do not take the idea too seriously'.[171] On the other hand, he takes the concept of purgatory more seriously. It is part and parcel of Roman Catholic teaching and deserving of further speculative attention. Indeed, his essay, 'Purgatory',[172] is a dialogue between two imaginary theologians who exchange ideas about a state after death conceived of as something short of definitive human fulfilment through the vision of God.

The very dialogue form of this essay betrays the embarrassment of the two imaginary theologians. This embarrassment first concerns the historical origin of the idea, inasmuch as one of the reasons for which it was introduced was ancient penitentiary practice that involved a long process of penance before absolution, something which not all penitents were able to complete before death. Purgatory, then, became the possibility of doing this after death, an explanation which the Church 'shamefacedly almost completely avoids'.[173] Until the time of the Council of Trent, when the existence of purgatory was defined,[174] medieval thought defended this doctrine as a place of purification of the faithful before they could enter the definitive state of heavenly bliss; in principle they were already saved, but as yet 'excluded' from heaven and, in the popular imagination, tormented for (or even by) the memory of their sins. It envisaged a process of purification to satisfy the distributive justice of God: a period of reparation for past sins measurable by a special kind of time. This, of course, was Trent's doctrinal basis for indulgences: the 'poor souls' suffering in purgatory could be helped by the prayers and 'merits' of the faithful – an idea which later led Luther to the rejection of purgatory itself. This concept, however, was not imposed on the faithful by higher authority; it was consonant with a long-standing *sensus fidelium,* one even reasserted in our century by Pope Paul VI.[175] The scriptural base, however, is sparse and the patristic evidence by no means overwhelming. Hence the misgivings of theologians are understandable: is it indeed 'part of revealed doctrine and binding as such, or merely an ideal type [i.e. imaginative construct] which in the last resort remains without binding force'?[176] Whatever the proper answer to this question, the traditional idea of purgatory has to be made 'intelligible, credible and compatible with the rest of [Christian] anthropology'.

Rahner, though gingerly, attempts so to do. Hiding behind the two imaginary theologians he first appeals to the inner 'plurality (diversity)' of human nature:

> I assume that a human being, despite the unity of his origin and goal, is an inwardly plural being, about whom ... diverse statements can rightly be made ... and determine [define] him in different ways and refer to different realities in him'.[177]

Rahner here postulates the necessity of some kind of integration of the whole person, in as much as an existential decision for God does not completely alter the diverse elements constituting human personality. It is an everyday experience that conversion is never comprehensive. 'We cannot assume that these unintegrated realities ... simply cease with death ... and thus become irrelevant to the permanent existence of the personal subject'.[178] Death then opens up a process with several possibilities. This process, of course is not identical with the living experience of time. Yet it participates, though analogously, 'in the fundamental temporality and historicity of the world' (ibid.). It is important to interpret this 'time' after death as by nature analogous. It can be, for instance, thought of as a 'process' in the instant of death itself. According to this image 'purgatory is an aspect of death'. However death in prospect is viewed by the living, purgatory itself is an anthropological 'thanatology' (doctrine of death) after earthly time ceases.

One of the imaginary theologians even tries to use this image to justify the ideas commonly connected with purgatory. He sees the possibility of defending the offering of suffrages for the dead by the living. Such suffrages now refer to 'the event of purification identified with the ... depth and intensity of the pain man experiences in death itself' or, maybe, the purifying event of death itself *is* what could be meant by purgatory. At this point, however, the identity between death and purgatory, even as an apt image, becomes precarious, for the idea of some kind of 'process' can hardly be eliminated. Those who try to consider purgatory without excluding any kind of time must needs accept some adumbration of the previously rejected idea of an 'intermediary state'. Nor can they account for the aspect of punishment due to God's retributive justice, an ancient idea still ingrained in the minds of some of the faithful. Hence at the end of all this theorizing a valid question arises:

> are we simply to remain silent from the very outset in face of the majestic darkness of death, content with the assumption that the Christian sustained by hope falls through death into the incomprehensibility of God, to regard this as 'beatifying' and thus to refrain from all further differentiation in regard to life 'after' death?[179]

This silence, however, is not observed by the other imaginary theologian, for he too tries to tackle the same question, but from a different aspect: its historical root 'in human thought and speculation which can be traced back long before the time of Christian revelation properly so-called'.[180] In other words, he appeals to ancient traditions maintaining the possibility of further development in the dead. According to him the doctrine of purgatory, in some way, creates scope for these traditions of mankind. This indirect approach is introduced by a question (one deeply suspect surely for all rigorous dogmatic theologians!): whether in Christian eschatology full personal integration is a requirement for every human being without exception, or whether exemption is possible for a class of people who cannot achieve their maturity in life-time? He thinks of human beings who never came to an existential decision for or against God and points to unbaptized children who are incapable of such a definitive act, to persons innocent in their permanent immaturity, and asks whether 'an opportunity of free personal decision' offers itself 'within the confines of purgatory'? In fact he postulates a *'postmortal* history of freedom for anyone denied the same in history of his earthly life'.[181]

This way of explaining the possibility of the existence of purgatory, leads once more to the idea of the 'migration of souls', as Rahner had already hinted in *Foundations*. There might be some truth in this, as representing the heritage of oriental thought now infiltrating the West. He even believes that a modified belief in this doctrine may be compatible with Christian dogma, and he adds: for those who 'did not reach a final personal decision in this earthly (or, first) life and, of course not for others'. The doctrine of metempsychosis can be tolerable, provided

> that the eternal cycle of a person's birth and death can be brought to a halt: [and that] .. there is [a final] decision which Christianity assumes as normally happening in every life.[182]

The life of the same person remains but can go forward to its own consummation.

These highly speculative approaches to the doctrine of purgatory and life after death bring us to to Rahner's last sentence:

> surrendering myself unreservedly but in hope to the eternal mystery which is called God and say yes to myself.[183]

We have to acknowledge the obscurities, the uncertainties, and possible contradictions that surround our thought about our future destiny. Keeping in mind the truth of Rahner's last statement, I shall now introduce some of my own observations.

୶

It is unsurprising that modern eschatology continually returns to the hurdle that is death. In many ways, death is the origin of human religious sensibility, the evidence for which can be documented from archaeological finds. It has become, too, a matter of great importance to contemporary secular philosophy, especially in the writings of Heidegger, Sartre and others.[184] W. Pannenberg characterizes these philosophies, in which religious belief in immortality is no longer considered, as a natural phenomenon arising out of the organic constitution of human life: death as an absolute end belongs to the very nature of humankind.[185] Accordingly, death is not an arbitrary chance that afflicts human life from outside, rather a consequence of being human. Death must be, therefore, in some way the goal of life (*Sein zum Tode*) in which the whole of our existence is epitomized (Heidegger), or a contingent event that marks the end (Heidegger's 'thrownness': *Geworfenheit*) of human existence and renders life ultimately meaningless (Sartre).

Karl Rahner adopts two seminal ideas from Heidegger: he speaks of death, on the one hand, as a natural fact at the end of existence and, on the other, regards it as the (active) consummation of life, a consummation which has the additional quality (not of course, recognized by Heidegger) of being a choice for or against God. Whereas the first corresponds to contemporary secular thought, the second provides a religious perspective within which revelation can be accommodated, including life after death in the eternity of God. Death is a human act in which both the natural and supernatural qualities of human existence are finally fulfilled.

To resume the drift of my earlier remarks on Rahner's eschatology: death, I repeat emphatically, is not a human act. If death is indeed the 'absolute future' of human existence, it cannot be a human achievement; it just happens or occurs. We have no experience of it, nor can we consciously imagine ourselves dead, unless as a spectator of events taking place in another and imaginary world. Death in itself it has no content that we can envisage, a view nearer to that of Sartre than to that of Heidegger. Not so Rahner, however, whose whole *thanatology* searches for some positive content to death, and elucidates it in terms of eternity, expounding it as the 'definitive validity of the person' or as a 'mode of spiritual freedom', both of which are achieved by the act of dying. My presentation above, therefore, noted Rahner's vacillation between two, rather arbitrarily chosen, views: that of Ladislaus Boros; and that of the more traditional stance which holds that single or partial choices throughout life are decisive for our eternal fate. Since both suppose that death has the character of a human act (which I deny), Rahner's wavering between the two is understandable, but irrelevant.

Is it true, then, that the course of life on earth is irrelevant to life after death, a life in which we Christians have to believe? Is it true that eternal life does not depend on the exercise of freedom during our time on earth? Rahner's affirmative answer to these questions was challenged in fact by E. Jüngel in his book on death.[186] If we hold, however, with contemporary Protestant theology, that death annihilates our past life in order to be re-created by God into a life after death, it becomes difficult to maintain any continuity between the self before and after death. My dilemma lies precisely between these two positions: death as an act fulfilling human existence, or death as an utter passivity dependent on God's judgement: *in mortis examine*. I shall leave this dilemma unresolved at the moment and try to find a way out of it later.

Since death cannot be a human act to be assessed by its purpose, it is hard to use transcendental reasoning in explanation of it. The objective of any act does indeed persist throughout the whole series of subsequent actions. The free choice of a particular vocation, for instance, is, in a way, always present and should determine other decisions, too. Since death is not an act, it cannot have an objective goal. Hence the all-presence of death throughout life can only be regarded as a threat, not as something implicit in human life. Of course, our myth making or 'mythifying fantasy' (a term that I, for lack of a better coined elsewhere[187]) can imagine the circumstances of our own death, but such reveries are illusory.[188] Their value, like that of the apocalyptic imagery describing the end of the world, lies only in their capacity to motivate present subjective behaviour. Any human anticipation of a state after death is and remains problematic.

This is why, in my opinion, Rahner introduces the notion of ultimate disposition ('disposability') in his later essay, *Dying*. This notion, if I understand him correctly, refers to some hardly foreseeable state of mind that may occur at the point of death.

The God we encounter in the same moment most probably differs from the image of him projected by hope during our lifetime; by necessity a change will take place, the effect of which cannot be expressed. This is *our* part in that encounter. We have to believe, however, that God's free judgement assesses our personal holiness on our entrance into a new mode of life. Does this divine assessment coincide with our ultimate disposition (Rahner's 'disposability')? Are we then free to accept or reject this divine judgement? Remember, Rahner's dialectic presupposed a free human act in the moment of death as well as that ultimate disposition ('disposability'): can then this free option determine our ultimate disposition *and* God's judgement? Whatever the option implies, it is one of passive acceptance against which there is no appeal. For if I opt for God's verdict on my final disposition, I have to assume with Ladislaus Boros an act of human decision peculiar to the situation of death, a situation, too, in which man reaches final fulfilment before, but not by, God's free judgement. Rahner wants it both ways: in the moment of death the dying is free and powerless at the same time.

> The parable of the last judgement in Matthew 25 teaches something very similar: the saved or damned are not aware that their practice or neglect of love of neighbour *de facto* corresponds to the criterion of God's definitive judgement ('Lord, when have we done it to you?'); the same dynamic rules our encounter with God and entry into our eternal destiny. The ultimate disposition (Rahner's 'disposability') may be the effect of our free options throughout life, but we shall be powerless in face of its divine assessment. If this is Rahner's position I readily agree with him.

Eternity is as a vital topic as that of death. If Rahner, as I pointed out previously, ultimately identifies the absolute future with God, God is not only the goal of human life, but also the content of its realization, its *eschaton*. Christian tradition from the New Testament onwards identifies this content as the beatific vision of God in which the *beati* share God's eternity. Hence eternal life for Rahner is the obverse of death. 'To see God', of course, is not the resolution of a lifetime of enigmas and tensions, but rather a confrontation with the Mystery 'which the dead who die in the Lord' will encounter, and in which their ineffable happiness will be achieved. Yet he never tries to explain what this happiness will be like. The mere assurance of a future happiness without any imaginable content (even if that proves to be false or inexact) is doomed to be meaningless.

Rahner's image of eternity seems, therefore, to lie between death regarded as the absolute end of time, and an eternity involving some different dimension of time in which theologians located *Purgatory* as the necessary purifying process after death. Though absolutely rejecting terrestrial time after death, in assuming the idea of purgatory Rahner had to accept some kind of duration in eternal life. Can he then characterize this indefinable state in terms of the 'definitive validity of the person' and of the 'new mode of spiritual freedom'? Both expressions presuppose some total fulfilment of the person, achieved, apparently, without development.

Suppose, however, that the absolute future of man is death, and not man's final destiny (the *eschaton*), our concepts of eternity and the ultimate fate of man will need revision. First of all: the position should be questioned which holds that eternity is already present within the unfolding history of human persons. Rahner's sayings that freedom is the 'faculty of the eternal' through which decisions taken 'now' are taken for 'ever more', and that the 'now' of the present moment, is the presence of eternity within time, ('the other side of death is eternity', as Rahner states), are often repeated. It is, however, an empirical fact of past and, more particularly, of present experience that no one is or, at most, few are capable of irrevocable decisions. We may *intend* that some of these should be of an eternal value, but very frequently unforeseen circumstances can force us to review or modify our most cherished decisions. To argue that a decision taken at death, an event which has no future in our time, has to be 'eternal' presupposes something that we have just denied: death in itself is the absolute end of our earthly possibilities, a separation from all experience to which we were related in life, including the possibility of our belief in God. There is a truth in the psalmist's desperate cry:[189]

> I am reckoned among those who go down to the pit; I am a man who has no strength, like one forsaken among the dead, like the slain that lie in the grave, like those whom thou dost remember no more, for they are cut off from thy hand. (Ps. 88: 4–5)

Death for the psalmist is separation from God and from all earthly relationships ('thou hast caused lover and friend to shun me' – Ps. 88:18); he faces nothingness, unless he can interpret *sheol* in terms of trusting in the promise of a blessed eternity. Within the flux of time the 'now' of eternity can be an apt metaphor for this promise. It is an inkling only of eternity, but not the real thing.

In the second place, in assuming that death is *the* absolute future, we have to acknowledge another separation: the farewell to one's self. To avoid any misunderstanding, I need to re-assert some anthropological facts, ones which I have tried to promote throughout this work. Human beings are not, in my judgement, static substantial natures created by God, but 'processes' constituting themselves through interaction with the world, society and other selves: human beings become '*subjects*' in relationship with inanimate objects, individuals within society, and true persons through interpersonal relationships. By 'separation from self', therefore, I mean exactly what the psalmist may well have meant by 'entering the darkness of death'. The dead become totally unrelated to society and to other individuals. Death, therefore, can be regarded as the loss of selfhood. Does this mean, however, that the fate of the dead is termination: irremediable nothingness; and not eternal life? The sheer fact that the psalmist addresses God in his despair shows that he has still one relationship to draw upon: the mysterious and unknown God who defies all earthly images. We can speak of the loss of selfhood, but *not* of the loss of a personal relationship with this unknown and unknowable Possibility, believed in as God. Briefly, then, the loss of selfhood does not mean the loss of personhood. It follows that eternity cannot be evaluated except by the permanence of the person. 'Behold the eye of the Lord is on those who fear him ...that he may deliver their soul from death' – is man's desire of eternity (Ps 33:18). Another psalm says: 'my flesh and my heart may fail, but God is my strength and my heart and my portion *for ever*' (Ps 73,26). The heart that perishes, then, is not the heart that eternally trusts in God's deliverance: the psalmist sings symbolically of a self that perishes and of a person who survives in the love of the unknown God.

To further develop this account of the characterisitics of human life, and to show how the concept of eternity fits within individual eschatology, we need to abandon Sartre's interpretation of human existence: the *pour soi*, the autocracy of self-centred freedom. Though human freedom is autonomous in generating the self, it is at the same time 'centrifugal' in the sense that it finds fulfilment in others; it is also *pour les autres*. As I have formerly pointed out: freedom is not identical with responsibility.[190] While freedom is creative of self, responsibility, by presupposing freedom, transforms the individual 'I' through relationship with another. My individual self is what I have become by my free actions, and my personhood is what I have become *en rapport* with others. The person is the one destined for eternity.

> The approach to eternity from the point of view of individual eschatology seems to confirm Rahner's interpretation of the meaning of the 'eternal mystery' of the vision of God, and at the same time, to be more in accord with the Church's traditional teaching about the Last Things. Among them is belief in a particular judgement (the *mox* of Benedict XII), a divine judgement at the moment of death, different from the universal judgement at the end of history. This teaching does not in itself necessarily involve belief in souls separated from the body. We cannot, however, postulate 'two' judgements without assuming the existence of some kind of time after death. Rahner may implicitly reject any intermediary state as mythology, yet his worries about existence of purgatory betray, at least verbally, his assent to the teaching of the Roman Church about an intermediary state after death. If my distinction between self and person is right, it is unnecessary to suppose some fulfilment of the self in an imaginary 'intermediary state', but rather to consider the gradual acceptance of personal development within God's eternity. And if this 'gradual acceptance' means growth in love, similar to that of the spouses of a happy marriage, then we can have some inkling of what time within eternity could mean. A more detailed expla-

nation would be a work of 'mythification' postulating migration of souls or, more acceptably, a process of purification in which the self that was abandoned at death, is re-integrated with the person already accepted in God's eternity.[191]

Against this approach to death and eternity, which I tried to sketch above, the objection already mentioned still stands: how can a human being entering into eternity preserve his previous identity, if his or her selfhood developed in life is lost? Shall we find ourselves awakening into life eternal changed beyond recognition? The answer to this objection can only lie in the basic unity of and difference between individual and collective eschatology.

(C) *Church and Parousia: a Collective Eschatology*

The basic distinction between individual and collective eschatology is, for Rahner, consequent upon the social nature of humankind, for the 'definitive validity' of the individual (i.e. that final, irreversible status in the sight of God) reaches perfection in the Final Consummation of the whole cosmos: the resurrection of the body and the enjoyment of eternal bliss in the vision of God. That this final stage is inaugurated by some final and definitive event to take place *in the future* must challenge any notion of eternity that is somehow implied within the flow of time. This event we call the *parousia*. Does, however, this event, the parousia, which brings about our future and final status, exclude that eternity is, indeed, in some sense, always present?[192] There is rather a dialectical tension between an eternity considered as already present and eternity as introduced by the future event of the parousia, the universal and collective end of everything. Collective eschatology has to face this tension and then address the future state which follows upon the last and definitive event of history.

> I can illustrate this dialectical tension as implied in the notion of parousia by the acclamation made at the central moment of the Eucharist: '*Christ has died. Christ is risen. Christ will come again*'. It does not applaud three separate events, the Cross, the resurrection and second coming, but their inseparable unity in the glorified Christ, a unity anticipated here and now in our celebra-

tion of his presence in the Mass. The acclamation as proffered in the *present* recalls the *past* ('Christ has died, Christ is risen') and refers to something 'not yet', something that is still outstanding in the *future* ('Christ will come again') Past, present and future are summed up in one and the same acclamation. When, therefore, Rahner's articles in various Lexica[193] define the meaning of the word *parousia,* as 'the coming of the Lord', a tension is inevitable: the *parousia* is already the definitive presence of the whole work of salvation history completely fulfilled in Jesus Christ, the glorified Saviour. Parousia, therefore means for us both a presence 'already' and 'not yet', since it involves future time, the duration of which is so entirely dependent on the freedom of God, that no one can know its length (Mark 13:32). What we do know, however, by faith is that Christ's return finalizes salvation or its opposite for each individual person. The parousia is also the judgement on all history, a judgement of which the resurrection of Christ is both the origin and central meaning (*Sinnmitte*) as well as the driving force (*tragender Grund*). In one sentence: parousia is (Rahner's coinage) 'the end to be ended' (*das beendende Ende*).[194] The central acclamation of the Mass not only anticipates the promised end, but also 'makes it present', it 'realizes' the future in a sacramental sense. It is already an end, yet not *the* end, that ends the time of our history on earth.

Collective eschatology in the above sense, receives but brief treatment in Rahner's *Foundations*. It is presented rather as the 'definitive validity' of the individual who thereby becomes participant in the fulfilment of the whole of history.[195] Rahner is more preoccupied with the significance of Christ's resurrection seen as the driving force of salvation history. As we can gather from his occasional remarks dispersed throughout his works in writing about this key scriptural event, Rahner cannot refrain from connecting Christ's resurrection with the resurrection of each individual: 'We therefore can and must say: because Jesus is risen, I believe in and hope for my own resurrection'.[196] Our resurrection is the 'end to be ended' at the 'not yet' of the parousia. Resurrection means for us, as it did for Jesus 'the unconditional hope that (the) forgiveness and ultimate acceptance of man takes place through this mystery'.[197] Hence, Jesus' death, resurrection and ascension are one and the same historical event[198] in which 'the *peri-*

patheia (literally: the 'circumincession': coincidence of several events in one) in which the drama of world history (as the work of) eternal salvation, has already taken place'.[199] Without the resurrection of Christ, the outcome of history remains indeterminate, but with it the real possibility of universal salvation is already there.

For the rest of Rahner's concept of the parousia we can only collect some occasional remarks dispersed throughout his whole work. As already seen, it is based: (a) on our faith in Christ's resurrection as the ground of our belief in the final and universal resurrection of the dead. Furthermore, this belief implies (b) an idea, imperfect as it is, about the relationship of the individual risen body to the whole society of mankind raised to life, as well as its relationship to the renewal of the whole cosmos in which we shall find our ultimate abode. Last but not least, this final fulfilment of all things raises the question (c) of God's relationship with the definitively saved universe. As a corollary I shall ask (d) whether the difference between the particular and the general judgement (identical with the parousia), still maintained by dogmatic tradition, is an adequate expression of the above mentioned tension that is implied in our belief: between the 'present presence' of eternity in Christ, and the future event of the parousia an event indeed, which 'ends the end' of fully redeemed human persons.

1. *The Resurrection of Jesus*

Rahner starts with the firm conviction that the resurrection of Jesus is not an event touching one individual only.[200] It is obvious, therefore, that our faith in the resurrection of Jesus has its antecedent in human nature: a desire or hope for survival after death, a survival not of one part, the 'soul', but of the whole person. Indeed it is an anthropological fact that we strive, even unwittingly, for our own resurrection. To put it into a typical 'Rahnerese':

> If anyone understands the Resurrection *aright*, if at the centre of his own existence, he yearns for his own 'resurrection' since on any true anthropology, he can only understand himself

as a man who hopes for that which is described in terms of resurrection, then, in my belief, he has also achieved an *a priori* perspective such that, while it certainly does not excuse him from the *free decision* of faith in the Resurrection of Jesus, still at the same time it does justify him in believing in such a thing as the Resurrection of Jesus, i.e. in accepting the Easter experience of the disciples as a matter of his own intellectual honesty.[201]

Rahner establishes then an a priori condition preceding the free decision of faith in Christ's resurrection and removes some element of surprise from the testimony of the apostles about that event. Jesus' destiny reached its fulfilment by his having been raised from the dead; and the acceptance of this statement is in harmony with the existential need implicit in our own quest for salvation. It is important to note that he does not treat the resurrection of Jesus as an objective fact of history (the empty tomb of the Synoptics is no evidence for it), but rather as the experience of witnesses. He supposes that the risen Jesus has shared his own experience with his disciples, and that their testimony 'involves *some reality* which is not identical with itself [i.e. with their subjective experience] as such'.[202] For this to be the case, however, exegesis can and must show that Jesus had conveyed some hint of the resurrection *before* that event. 'According to the findings of contemporary exegesis it can be said ... that the pre-Easter Jesus understood himself as the absolute eschatological event of salvation', as the 'unsurpassable summons of God',[203] truths in terms of which his preaching may have developed into an anticipation of his own resurrection. Hence Rahner can conclude *ad hominem:*

> how in all seriousness could the first disciples have arrived at their Easter faith if they had known nothing beforehand about Jesus from his own understanding of himself.[204]

The 'intellectual honesty' of our faith in the resurrection of Jesus can safely rely on this argument. We know now that the resurrection itself is, indeed, the motivation of faith since 'this saving event of faith finds [in it] the historical ground which makes faith possible and legitimate'.[205]

It is more difficult to assess how the first witnesses of Jesus' resurrection understood his risen life. Their experience must have been *sui generis,* and quite unlike the other resurrection stories in the Bible. Their faith in their experience seems to suggest that they have encountered someone from some other sphere of existence, one located outside our time and space.[206] Or to express their experience with greater precision: the apostles see that Jesus has risen 'in what we can call human nature, human reality', yet one that has been transformed into a new kind of presence. After the resurrection he is no longer part of their everyday experience of transitory phenomena in time. Even if they could touch his body and eat with him, their faith must have perceived more than his corporeal appearance; and this 'more' is the 'fact that this man is he who has been definitively delivered'. Such an insight is not just their own subjective vision, but also one of salvific significance. Rahner puts it thus: the manner in which Jesus has risen 'into the incomprehensibility of God' is not grasped by experience, but by the insight of faith.[207] If the original reaction of the first witnesses to the resurrection includes the fleeting contact with a risen body *together with* its significance, then Jesus has become the one who has reached 'precisely *that* point toward which everything tends as a goal'.[208]

2. *The resurrection of the flesh in a renewed cosmos*

In the early fifties Rahner had published two articles – on the dogma of the Assumption, 1951, and on the resurrection of the body, 1953 – which can illustrate his basic insights about life after death in the state of a risen bodily existence within a renewed world.[209] These articles, too, anticipate his later, explicit, approach to eschatological statements. In order to elucidate the dogmas of faith the systematic theologian had to deal with various images and pictorial descriptions of life after death, some found within Scriptures, and other expressions of traditional piety expounding the meaning of dogmatic faith. The bodily assumption of Mary into a 'place', called heaven, and the existence of a risen human body within a renewed cosmos can only be imagined, since both are inaccessible to our experience. Rahner addresses here a sceptical audience as did Paul on the Areopagos: at the idea of the resurrection some scoffed, others politely dismissed his preaching or said they would hear him later (Acts 17:32).

A modern reaction would not be all that different. Indeed, though the immortality of the soul is frequently central to the beliefs of many orthodox Christians, faith in the resurrection of the body is often regarded as an accessory. Many theologians, too, demythologize traditional images and emphasize their present existential significance without retaining any reference to a future reality. Rahner's task is therefore to ask

> what reality – according to the intention of the Scriptures themselves – these eschatological, popular and poetic illustrations are actually meant to convey.[210]

The attempt to disentangle and to harmonize these images is just as otiose as it is to try to establish some clear distinction between their expression and their content. Christian faith, nevertheless, holds on to belief in a risen bodily life in a renewed world.

The New Testament blends together images of the consummation of the world with those of the resurrection of the body. Together they present us with an objective faith in the fact that the world will have an end; and, on the pattern of the resurrection of Jesus that this end is not a sheer cessation, but the beginning of a transformation into a state of final perfection:

> The end of the world is, therefore, the perfection and total achievement of saving history which had already come into full operation and gained its decisive victory in Jesus Christ and his resurrection.[211]

The parousia is the definitive manifestation of the event in which 'the world as a whole flows into his resurrection and into the transfiguration of his body' (ibid.), for that final consummation ('perfecting of the world'), already present in Jesus, will be shared among all created reality. This is, then, the proper context in which to examine the doctrine of the resurrection of the body.[212]

In his early articles on the Assumption and the 'Risen body' Rahner does not enter into a discussion about the immortality of the soul and/or the resurrection of the body, but takes it for granted that body (*Fleisch*) refers to 'the whole man in his proper embodied reality' and that this body enters into God's eternity. He is more interested in specifying the characteristics of the risen body: what kind of existence has it and where? Ancient pictures of the glorified body based on some special experience, or contemporary ones based on some present perception, are meaningless to a contemporary mind. Rahner, therefore, follows Paul's first Epistle to the Corinthians chapter 15, and asserts some total transformation proper to a glorified body (1 Cor. 15:42ff.). The depiction of heaven or hell demands a like transformation, since it is commonly represented as a more perfect, the definitive, form of the present world. This, however, does not mean that there is no reality corresponding to our belief: one should not spiritualise these eschatological realities out of existence. The glorified body of the risen Christ remains the model.

Assumption is forthright on this issue: 'because He [Christ] descended among the dead and rose again there exists the resurrection of the flesh'.[213] Christ's whole past life is summed up and reaches perfection in his risen body, however elusive that fact seemed to the first witnesses of his Resurrection. Something similar is bound to happen to us. Furthermore, the question as to *where* this newly acquired bodily existence will be 'located' must correspond to some sort of reality. This new 'spatiality' is the final outcome of saving history; it is a 'place' formed within time; 'it comes to be by the fact of Christ's rising from the dead (it is not given in advance) and that creates the possibility and the place of this glorified state'.[214]

Risen body adopts a similar approach: the glorified body of Christ and that of Our Lady (and others Mt 27:52?) *is* the pattern of our future risen condition. It is not just a state of mind, but has a definite, if unknown, special locality.[215] This latter article, too, introduces a new idea: the need to understand the 'perfecting' at the end of time within the context of an evolutionary world-view. The historical process will attain its destiny in as much as it participates in the 'Personal Spirit' (meaning God) and thereby 'the meaning of the whole of history':

> The world remains a reality, one which has transcended earthly history, as the proper environment of the human spirit which has achieved its ultimate purpose in fellowship with God and simultaneously that of its own history and that of the world.[216]

One can feel here the inspiration of Teilhard de Chardin for whom, too, the 'Omega Point' coincides with the perfect fulfilment of the human spirit incarnate in the world. Perhaps, too, another idea lies behind this statement: Rahner's insistence that the whole past history of all human beings should somehow be present in their risen life. He writes some years later in a more meditative vein: when we arrive in heaven 'we find our whole life and all its real possibilities' returned to us:

> There is not only a resurrection of the body but also the *resurrection of time*.. For everything one did in the past was one thing only: (viz.) one tried to attain [fulfil] oneself completely, together with everything one possessed by nature and grace, and to make a complete transfer of this single reality into the incomprehensibility of God through faith that loves.[217]

In writing about the bodily assumption of Our Lady into heaven Rahner seems to take it for granted that she was the selfsame person in the state of resurrection as she was on earth. If we believe that the final consummation for every human being will be similar to that of the *Assumpta*, then the same identity must also be assumed for a resurrected mankind. It is surprising that Rahner does not seem to have any significant difficulty in asserting this identity. The reason, I believe, is that his template for a risen existence is the resurrection of Jesus. Though his resurrected body is entirely transformed ('totally different from the earthly body'), it is still the body of his life on earth.[218] The same seems to apply to us. Resurrection, indeed, does not mean the continuance of one particular part of man in which his perfect selfhood will be established; a 'disembodied soul' for instance, (itself indifferent as regards salvation) can hardly be the recipient of salvation. It must be the whole person including what he or she had lived for in life that is fulfilled in 'permanent validity'. To say that the resurrection of Jesus means only the survival of his work on earth would be mere idealism, whereas to say that the risen person of Jesus leaves his earthly life and task would mean that his redemptive function is finished, with no continuation 'at the right hand of the Father'. If person and work are identical in the risen existence of the risen Jesus, it follows that the earthly achievement of all humans is present in the state of resurrection.[219] Rahner, indeed, uses 'soul' to express this essential unity between the person and work.[220]

3. *Eternal life in God*

The ultimate perfection of 'soul', in Rahner's sense, is not only to be located within a renewed cosmos and interpreted in terms of definitively saved history. A lecture given in 1963 starts with the statement that 'the life lived by man in his unity and as a whole [= the 'soul' in his sense] is the preparatory stage of eternal life'.[221] We have to pass through this life and through the radical transformation of death to attain the perfection of eternal life. At this moment, however, our previous life disappears by transforming itself, body and 'soul', and withdrawing into the unutterable mystery of God. The human body and, in and through it, the whole of the cosmos, together with the whole history of salvation are perfected and find their ultimate abode in this absolute mystery of God.[222] It is through this relationship with God that our eternal life, together with the renewed life and history of the world establishes, for want of a better term, a new environment.

Christian tradition calls this new situation of the definitively redeemed the *beatific vision of God:* to be interpreted both as an ultimate objective and as man's eschatological destiny. Rahner accepts and adapts the same idea: grace for him is the anticipation of this final state. The interpretation of this basically Greek concept is, however, modified. His often quoted essay 'On the concept of "Mystery" in Catholic Theology', maintains that this mystery is the incomprehensibility of God, and one which does not cease in the immediacy of the presence of God: '*God remains incomprehensible in the beatific vision*'.[223] The positive content of this 'Mystery' is the beatific vision: for the redeemed it is 'the bliss of love'. Rahner's transcendental theology engineers the argument of this essay, for the experience of this ultimate bliss depends on the transcendent awareness proper to a supernaturally 'elevated' person: man's supernatural being 'is ontologically orientated to the beatific vision'. In other words: he speaks of the transcendental experience of grace. Though grace is the condition of the possibility of this final bliss, the mystery of God will be self-revelatory, even if never fully attainable in the immediacy of the beatific vision. Although the human endeavour to know and attain this mystery may well be felt as burdensome, as groping in darkness, it is nonetheless the sole source of peace for those who trust themselves to it, love it humbly and surrender themselves to it fearlessly in knowledge and love.[224] The mystery is eternal light and eternal peace.[225] We cannot grasp it, but it will grasp us. The beatific vision, therefore, can only be understood as the possibility and reality of the immediate presence of the holy mystery. Its incomprehensibility is not only an attribute of God, but the characteristic of God's self-communication to all creatures. Rahner can sum up:

> The vision of God is the radical form of the general ontological relationship between that Being whose self communication establishes both the distinctness as well as identity ... (of) ... our finite reality.[226]

This quotation is still subject to the abstractions of a technical language game. Rahner, however, transposes the same into the more meditative text of 'Unity – Love – Mystery' and speaks of the beatitude as the harmony achieved in the acceptance of the vision: in submitting one's 'reasoning powers and effort to achieve ones own salvation and surrendering oneself to the unfathomable love of God', which is, indeed, the very content of the beatific vision.[227]

Rahner's concept of the beatific vision, however, does not tell us how this ultimate fulfilment is going to take place, not only for the individual person, but for his or her society, his or her world and for the whole material Universe. It can, however, be inferred from his thought in so far as he always presupposes the unity between the human spirit and the material world[228] and assumes the essential embodiment of the

214 *The Sacrament of the Future*

individual spirit into the world. At the final consummation all human beings together with the whole world will undergo the ultimate judgement of God so that everything can enter into that relationship with God for which the whole universe is destined, so that, indeed, 'God may be all things to all (1 Cor. 15:28). Rahner identifies the parousia with the last, universal judgement as an entry to the beatific vision.

4. *The double judgement?*

The second Council of Lyons (1274) decreed that the souls of the good and the wicked enter into their eternal destinations, heaven or hell, *before* they resume their own bodies, even if (*nihilominus*) there is another general judgement, which they still have to undergo.[229] At that time, however the terminology concerning 'two' judgements was unclear. Different interpretations of them, therefore, could be advanced, and Pope John XXII did just that. This rather controversial Pope denied the complete perfection of the beatific vision to disembodied souls. Borrowing an image from the book of Revelation (6:9f.) about souls 'under the altar' who still had to be clad by the white robe of the finally redeemed, John XXII affirmed that, although they were able to contemplate the perfect humanity of the risen Lord, the reward of the just and the punishment of the wicked would be postponed until the final judgement at the general resurrection. Within the history of the Church even popes have been censured; a commission of cardinals rejected his view in 1333, and a year later the Pope recanted on his death-bed. His successor, Benedict XII confirmed the Doctrine of Lyons about the fate of humans after death. His bull *Benedictus Deus* emphasizes the immediate (*mox*) endowment of the separated soul with the perfection of beatific vision, for the just have an 'intuitive, facial and immediate' vision and enjoyment of God's very essence already before the general judgement when every human being with their reassumed bodies 'are called to the judgement seat of Christ.'[230]

If we accept the traditional view, still current in Roman Catholic theology, it is be hard to assign any purpose to the general one. The divine Judge, whether he be the Son or the

Father, would preside at a trial in which human beings, already enjoying the beatific vision, or condemned to hell, would have the former definitive verdict confirmed. Does this mean that the first, particular, judgement was only provisional? Or that the first verdict can be revised? Or that a higher court passes the second verdict? Simon Tugwell writes in exposition of the traditional view: 'By the end of the twelfth century, then, it was clear that there was one judgement too many'.[231] Either the last or (eventually) the individual judgement of each and every human soul is superfluous.

Rahner as we have seen, dealt briefly with the problem of a double judgement in 'Intermediary State' without, however, attributing dogmatic value to the *Benedictus Deus* of Benedict XII.[232] He holds that tradition 'places that judgement as an event occurring at the death of the individual, [even though] sometimes, as a communal one at the end of world history'.[233] This, apparently, wavering approach to a traditional tenet arises from the unresolved relationship between individual and collective eschatology. In Rahner's opinion Catholic scholars maintain the 'two' judgments in dialectical unity:

> For the consummation of man as a cosmic being (... the 'resurrection of the flesh') is also an element in the consummation of man's uniqueness (so that even as spirit he is only consummated in the full sense in that event), that is, the consummation of the individual human being as his unique self (through the beatific vision) is an element in cosmic world-history.[234]

This dialectic, however, may reflect the tension between 'eternity now' and in the future, but does not explain the difference between the 'two' judgements. Rahner is, however, certain that *Benedictus Deus* was a decree issued in the context of medieval penitential practice and has the idea of purgatory at the background. Although 'it is not intended as an instrument of ecclesiastical threat' (ibid), it advocates man's serious responsibility in life.

If we now look again at Rahner's treatment of eschatology, we will find hard to single out statements which belong exclusively to the individual or to collective elements of this doctrine. The two, individual and collective, are so entwined that there is a reciprocal relationship between an individual's ultimate destiny and the final consummation of the whole of creation. For Rahner eschatological statements are projections of our present experience either by means of transcendental reasoning or by the anticipations of pious imagination. He deals indeed with the Absolute Future which, as we have seen, is either a short-hand term for God or, at least secondarily, refers to a glorified humankind in the state of a new heaven and new earth. In the Absolute Future the parousia is both here and now as well as open to the future unity of creation within God's incomprehensibility.

Collective eschatology seems to have but marginal importance not only in *Foundations*, but also in the whole of Rahner's work. This is understandable, since whatever we try to state about the future can only be known from our present experience. The truth-value of eschatological statements relies on the coherence between the 'already now' and the 'not yet'.

I shall start my reflections on Rahner's method by examining the nature of the coherence between present and future and I shall then offer some reflections on the main themes of collective eschatology by following roughly the four points under which I have collected Rahner's references from various parts of his writing.

ᘒ

1. *Present and Future*

As already mentioned in the expository part, I see two possible ways of approaching future events from present experience: by means of a 'transcendental disclosure' or by way of anticipation. The first is Rahner's method and the alternative is yet to be discussed. Neither of these results in a clear and distinct knowledge of the future: they are and remain projections claiming, however, intellectual honesty for their affirmation. Eschatological statements are true and reasonable, even if lacking in the certainty of precise knowledge.

Transcendental disclosure allows two a priori presuppositions which can guarantee the truth-value of a statement concerning the future. If we agree with Rahner that we can experience God's grace in our present life and that this experience, in Rahner's own terms, pre-apprehends the future fulfilment of our final salvation at the end, then our eschatological statements are basically true. The experience of *'engracement'* is a foretaste of the beatific vision in heaven. Furthermore, this Rahnerian 'pre-apprehension' must also presuppose that our present experience recognizes future events as objective goals. In other words, the promised end is not only an *eschaton* , but also a *telos,* two terms I have already used earlier. The first indicates the reality we are aiming at, and the second the dynamic driving force, the *finis,* constantly directing our actions. The use of this transcendental method enabled Rahner to ensure some truth-value for his eschatological statements. For instance, if we interpret the parousia of Jesus at the end of history as a goal, as well as the state of consummation, it would mean that the very nature of history requires a veiled presence of the Last Day which will manifest itself as a 'fuller' presence when it occurs: we would already live within Christ's parousia. If we take the resurrection of the flesh as the *telos* of bodily human nature we are, in a sense, already raised. If Christ's risen body is the pattern as well as the goal of our future bodily life, there must be something in our material constitution that already strives towards the same. Likewise, the promised 'new earth and new heaven' taken as an objective of our universe in a 'transcendental disclosure' would be a hidden, but present reality, the outcome of which would not be an altogether surprising event of the future.

As an alternative to 'transcendental disclosure' I shall use another approach which, for lack of another term, can be summed up by the generic word: *anticipation.*[235] Rahner's own method, of course, is also an anticipation, one which, however, relies on the belief in the (existent) reality of a future event to which we are destined. Anticipation, on the contrary, is a *trust* in the occurrence of an event that we can expect as the possible outcome of those desires insinuated by the metaphors and images of our creative imagination. Anticipation, too, involves the attitude of waiting: we need to envisage an unknown and unknowable future that is still hidden in God's promises. Whereas 'transcendental disclosure' depends on the *reality* of the future, a reality that is retroactive on a present experience, anticipation of the promised end is a possibility the outcome of which in our present remains uncertain.

We can distinguish between a 'realized' and of a 'futuristic' eschatology. In many of its statements of John's Gospel, exemplify the first, 'realized eschatology' ('He who believes is already saved and who does not is already judged'). This and similar sentences have, however, to be reconciled with the Book of Revelations (especially if the authors are identical!), in as much as salvation therein is still open to a the future about which we can only use apocalyptic language. Linguistic symbols can only enlighten those who are waiting for the final consummation of all things. Rahner's approach could, I suggest, be characterized as 'realized' and the alternative as a 'futuristic' eschatology. The reality on which his kind of realized eschatology is built up is the resurrection of Jesus interpreted as the pattern of things to come.[236]

2. *The resurrection of Jesus*

We have to admit that the biblical accounts about the resurrection are rather confusing.[237] Rahner himself is somewhat cautious in handling the reality of that event: instead of taking it as the 'cause' of our own resurrection, as did 'Thomas Aquinas,[238] he starts from the faith of the believers in the resurrection of Jesus or from the commitment of the disciples, and emphasizes the rapid spread of the Gospel throughout the then known world. Our access to it cannot be direct, but is mediated by the testimony of a small group of people who, in one way or the other, experienced his presence amongst itself. Whether it was a bodily presence or a vision is less important than the factual existence of that short period up to Pentecost when the significance and meaning of Jesus' resurrection could be grasped as the common faith on which the Christian movement could build. It was, so to speak, an 'overwhelming presence' that made the disciples remember his teaching before and after the Easter event. Indeed, that the twelve and their followers could be united in this conviction is perhaps a miracle on a par with the reality of the event itself.

Rahner insists of course that the surprising miracle of Whit Sunday must have been prepared for by the teaching of the pre-Easter Jesus in forecasting his own resurrection. I doubt, however, that we can affirm that he knew *how* exactly it would happen. Obviously, Jesus had a firm hope in the final coming of the kingdom of God to such an extent that he identified himself with its hidden arrival and had connected with this hope the belief in the resurrection into a new and risen life. He shared this belief through parables and imaginative metaphors: the probable source of his forecasts about his own resurrection, and something never understood by his disciples in Jesus' lifetime. It was *after* the event that they could see what must have been meant by a risen life and what was its significance. It meant that the risen life of Jesus in a totally transformed bodily form was nonetheless identifiable with that of the person they knew; it was a bodily presence which had been in communication with them and through which they could envisage their own belief in a genuine life after death. They shared this belief with their own contemporaries and, first and foremost, with their Master in his pre-Easter life. On this belief they could anticipate the possibility of their own resurrection.

Before the Gospels were written Paul had tried to interpret the significance of Jesus' resurrection. I identify three strands of thought within his genuine writings. The two epistles to the Thessalonians (the first written in belief of an imminent parousia), still have the prophetic images of the 'Day of the Lord' when Christ descending from heaven and as the judge of the world would take the just away 'to be always with God' (1 Thess.: 4:13–18), even if this last triumph would be preceded by the turmoil within human history (2 Thess: 2:1–4). The next strand offers a more detailed testimony to Christ and our bodily resurrection, according to which the living have to die like the corn we sow in the earth in order to be endowed with a body given by God, 'as He chooses'. 'Sown as a physical body, it is raised in a spiritual body' (1 Cor. 15:43 and 46) or in the glory of 'a heavenly body' (Cf., Cor. 15:40) bearing the image 'of the man of the heaven' (2 Cor. 15:49). The third line of thought reappears as Paul's desire to leave his present 'earthly tent' ('away from the body': 2 Cor. 5:8) and not to be left naked (that is to die), but that he 'would be further clothed, so that what is mortal may be swallowed up by life' and 'we will be with the Lord' (2 Cor. 5:4,8). It would be tempting to understand 1 Cor. 15 as a 'spiritualized' resurrection and interpret 2 Cor. 5 as a desire to be clothed with the glorified body of Christ, a 'building from God eternal in heaven' (2 Cor. 5:6).[239] The further exegetical detail of these texts, however, is not the job of the systematic theologian; that is rather to notice Paul's insistence that this faith in the resurrection is maintained by the Holy Spirit who makes us capable of reading the signs of our own life to come. But does this interpretation imply the objective goal of our earthly life, or is it rather a vague desire of the promised end? Will it be indeed, our own life?

3. *The resurrection of the Flesh*

Belief in our future resurrection cannot avoid the question: if we are raised at the end will it be in *our own* body? The testimony of Jesus' belief in the resurrection of the dead makes it obvious that he was thinking of a risen body which is, on the one hand identical with the previous one yet, on the other hand, entirely different in some characteristics: we are going to be judged in it and then we shall live like the 'angels in heaven' (Matt. 22:30 and par.) Jesus affirms a continued bodily identity, yet with a difference. Our future resurrection, therefore, cannot be thought in terms of the raising of Lazarus (John 11:38) or as that of the son of the widow from Nain (Luke 7:11f). On the other hand, Jesus may not have meant that we cease to be human in the resurrection and change into an entirely spiritual mode of existence. Some identity remains between the two states. In his controversy about the resurrection with the Sadducees Jesus skilfully avoids answering their question: belief in the God of the living is enough to prove the fact, even without understanding the *how* of a risen body (Matt. 22:32). Nonetheless in the parable of Dives and Lazarus, for instance, the rich man seems to be the same person after death, now delivered to the torments of Hades (Luke 16: 19ff.). The Gospels do not give us a clearcut answer: it is later theological thought which has to explain this identity in difference.

I shall pass over more recent speculative attempts which appeal either to the surviving memory of the dead, or to a transference of the individual properties of the present body into another space by means of a computer simulation:[240] I do not think that any of these can demonstrate either the premises on which this 'transference' is based or the identity of persons between the two states. Nor would the hypothesis be satisfactory that God, after the total annihilation of the whole person, recreates him or her in a body identical with the previous one.[241] The solution of the early Church had regarded the permanence of the immortal soul as providing the necessary continuity within this transformation. This view has become controversial in our day: it has been challenged first by Protestant and later by Catholic theologians.[242] The main objection against it is its underlying 'dualism' - rightly or wrongly — attributed to Plato.[243] Rahner's protest against this same dualism is correct: in the natural immortality of the soul there exists an element in the human condition which is *heilsneutral* i.e. the soul itself is considered apart from the rest of God's salvation as a substantial entity endowed with immortal power in spite of its relationship with the body. Faith in the resurrection of the flesh, in whatever form it is advanced attributes the event to God's restoring or creative might.

I shall attempt a slightly different approach to the question of identity and difference between the present and the risen body. Its main lines are anthropological and allow for a semi-dualistic conception of the human being. Such an outlook is not entirely alien to the Bible. Paul uses two words for the human body: *swma* and *sarx:* I shall translate them here as body and flesh. They are not two parts of which bodily human life is composed, but two aspects of it in tension. The Pauline body (*swma*) has two other connotations, namely, the corporate body of the Church and the Eucharistic bread; as an aspect of human life it is something holy: the temple of indwelling Spirit of God which will be raised like Christ's resurrected body (1 Cor. 6:13–15). The flesh, on the other hand, is the force inclining to sin and to final perdition.[244] Like the evangelists, Paul hardly mentions the soul or the human spirit, but when used, such words mean the whole person.

I do not now believe that later Church Fathers, when they took over the notion of the soul from their Greek environment identified this with the Pauline body (*swma*), but they did something very similar. In order to explain the survival of the body after death they postulated first the continued existence of the soul as a substantial entity and then, under the influence of Aristotelian thought declared the soul to be essentially belonging to the body, that is, as an ontological principle which one could call the condition of possibility of the basic identity between an earthly and risen body.[245] Following the teaching of Thomas Aquinas it has become the standard teaching in the Church:[246] we speak of the soul as essentially belonging to the body (*anima forma corporis*) yet enjoying its own dimension – even separate from the body. (Remember, too, Fathers and Scholastics had also to explain the possibility of the existence of the soul between the individual's death and the final resurrection into a new world.)

The semi-dualism, that I am about to advocate, does not coincide with this latter explanation. Yet it arises nevertheless from two aspects of human being: the *self* and the *person*. By the 'self' I understand the inborn capacities and the acquired characteristics of an individual human being; by the 'person' his or her relationship to the environment in which each individual lives, communicates, and interacts. This environment constitutes the person as such, already in earthly life.[247] Now at the point of death (death being the absolute future of human being) the former integrity of the earthly self and its qualities are partially lost, and yet survival can be hoped for, owing to man's relationship with his fellows, to the cosmos and to God himself. We remember, in fact, that the early Old Testament idea of *sheol* was not one of irretrievable annihilation, because a person's trust in God left the hope of a certain survival after death. It was not, however, the achievement of the former self, but a new possibility arising from the person's continued relationship to God. On this ground I venture to assert that the identity between the present and risen body consists in the identity of the person and not in that of the self. Our human self is lost in the resurrection of the flesh: it is absorbed by the person that we have become.[248]

The main and hitherto unresolved objection against such a

view is the loss of individuality which, of course, would militate against the identity of a human being before and after death. But does it? If we take the distinction between self and person seriously, the 'loss of self' is only partial. As a person I shall be what I have become, not however by my own achievements in isolation from others, but also as this particular person recognized by others with whom I interact. P. S. Fiddes, whose view of personhood seems to coincide with my own, distinguishes between 'individuality' and 'particularity':[249] individuality is what I mean by the self and particularity is that which identifies the person through the communicative interaction with others and with God. My individual self is the gift with which I am born, the particularity of my person is due to my free encounter with my environment. God's creative love does not intend the absorption of the dead into his divine being or the disappearance of personal particularity within the society of the blessed.[250] No, God's saving love maintains the survival of his creatures in a continuing love-relationship, in a further and unending dialogue in a life of encounter with himself, and with our risen fellows in a new cosmos. Individuality, on the other hand, may mean a self *incurvatum in se* (self-enclosed), a solipsism of the Ego relying on its egoistic inclinations. It is this 'egoity', as John Hick terms it,[251] or self-centredness which is to be shed, just as Paul's concupiscent *sarx*. The person, on the other hand can, by God's free will, regain his or her particular body in the Body of Christ and in the communion of the saints that is the triumphant Church.

4. The Life of the Dead

We can now ask what kind of life is granted to those risen into an eternity within this new society and new cosmos? Since, as I have already argued, eternity does not necessarily involve timelessness, we can presuppose a certain relationship between time and eternity. Following Rahner's conviction that eternity is the fruit and not the abolition of time (or even, that eternity is the measure and condition of the possibility of earthly time) any possible continuity becomes also a discontinuity: an unimaginable time in which the risen life of human persons, their society and the cosmos can be located. Such a 'time' and 'space', however, can only be described in apocalyptic, metaphorical language so that we can anticipate it in religious beliefs and theorise about it in theology. There are many different elements that can establish a more or less adequate picture of a veritable life after death

If life is a continuous growth and development both in its material and moral aspects, then at least human life cannot be without change or advance. Since, however, man's history is definitely closed at death and redeemed human persons will have attained their perfection in the resurrection, the 'time' in which they are going to live cannot be the identical with that on earth. In this new 'time' which is not *the* time we now experience, the saved are established in goodness in both their newly acquired bodily and moral life: they will not age or corporally deteriorate, they cannot undergo religious conversion nor can they acquire new virtues. If, however, it is love that determines their new life (as Paul and John write) there can be advance and growth: their journey is 'from good to good'.[252] They live not in an abolished but in redeemed 'time'.[253]

If personal life is to be embedded in manifold relationships to an environment in which the living are supposed to be in interactive communication, it is hardly imaginable that this can happen outside time and space. Were the definitively saved stabilized in the state in which they died, there would be no possibility of growth within their relationships, in a qualitative sense at least. There must be further possibilities of deepening and enhancing the same, not only as regards other persons (including God), but within the whole material world.[254] The counter-argument that this world would then be 'spiritualized', that is, without a proper resurrection of the body, is to return to the idea of the immortality of the disembodied soul and not of the survival of whole person. We do not know, however, in what kind of 'time' and 'space' human life will be experienced in the hereafter, even though we know that Christ, risen from the dead, as long as he dwelt among his followers, led an intensive corporate and interpersonal life in *his* own 'time' (forty days?) and 'space' (Jerusalem or Galilee) the limitations of which he now no longer suffered.

I shall add here a further explanation one which relies on my concept of the person: personhood is not just one of the perfections of the self, but the quality of the relationships of each particular human being. But there are millions of humans who die without reaching maturity, there are millions who in their lifetime could not develop their inborn capacities and again millions who were never allowed to make use of life's opportunities, yes, the oppressed and outcasts of a cruel history. Should we, therefore, now imagine that God, by a miracle, restores at the moment of death what was missing in a wasted life? Should we, then, affirm that this 'miracle' creates new perfections of the self with no contribution from the person raised to eternal life? The answer should be negative since, I believe, the purpose of human life is not the enhancement of one's self, but personal growth; human life is a 'person-making-process'[255] begun in our earthly existence, and one which can gain a limitless horizon after death in the ultimate encounter with the living God. Neither can it be imagined that in the new earth and heaven where, contrary to the present, justice and undisturbed peace prevail, the saints would not be able to relate themselves to this new social and ecological environment. Their life, if it is to be a life, must happen in a kind of time and space beyond our knowledge.

I believe, therefore, that the ultimate perfection of the definitively saved does not consist in the acquisition of the self's missing embellishments at or after death. They cannot acquire new virtues just as they can no longer sin; they cannot develop new skills that they lacked in life, nor can they abandon the good habits of a lifetime in exchange for others. Nonetheless within their new relationship to other persons, to a now just society, to a renewed cosmos new possibilities can emerge for the quality of personal life.

A true image of a life after death, it seems, can only be understood as a continued discontinuity within the 'time' and 'space' of the hereafter. Our eternal abode is God' life. Paul's spiritualized image of a new life to come in 1 Cor. 15 is insufficient to illustrate it. It has to be developed in terms of Paul's desire in 2 Cor. 5: the shedding of 'our earthly tent', and 'putting on our heavenly dwelling' (*oikétérion*), a reference perhaps to some place wherever this 'place' is. With John we believe that if we see the

Father, we shall have found our dwelling in his Son (1 John 5:20) and thus 'we shall be changed' (1 John 3:2). Of course, as John says, we do not know *how* that shall be, but perhaps his insight of faith could be worked out with apocalyptic imagination as helped by the 3rd Isaiah, Ezekiel and John's book of Revelation?

We are, therefore, in search of a 'time' that is not a time, and for a 'space' that is not a space, indeed, for a presence of God which is already here, but when it really comes to us will be of a different kind. That 'fuller' presence of God in which we shall dwell forever should also be a 'time' in which personal development is possible.

5. *The God of Life Eternal*

A simple statement about the beatific vision of God is unsatisfactory. This idea is not only strange to modern minds, but in itself: does the concept of 'contemplation' (*theorein*) convey a mode of life – even if it implies a never-ending heavenly liturgy? Secondly, how does the concept of a 'beatific vision of the Divine' refer to the life of God? If we accept the concept of the triune God,[256] we will have to change the premises of the discussion. I shall propose that the ultimate dwelling 'place' of our eternal life is the 'life' of the Trinitarian God. This, indeed, should be the ultimate abode of resurrected human beings in the new creation. In order to substantiate this assertion we have to revise some traditional concepts concerning Trinitarian life, that is, of the 'history' of the Father, the Son and the Holy Spirit.

> There are two premises of traditional theology on which one could build. Augustine received from the Cappadocian Fathers the equation between the divine Persons and their relationship to one another. Relying on this insight Medieval theology, *duce* Thomas Aquinas, introduced the notion of 'substantial relationship'. Because, however, Aristotelian logic was then in vogue according to which relationship was regarded as an accidental quality of two or several definite substantial realities, Thomas found it difficult to apply 'relationship' to the three divine Persons.[257] If we conceive the notion of relationship in such a way, we may land in a tritheistic position: it would entail that there are three separate subjects in the one God. If, however,

relationship is but an accidental quality, the Persons would lack their own reality. Instead of three subjects the scholastics proposed one and simple substance or nature in which the relations (i.e the Persons) 'subsisted'. A new concept was introduced, one that neither multiplies the divine substance nor detracts from the reality of the Persons.

Nonetheless, in trying to grasp what these relations (that is, the Persons) were in themselves, Thomas spoke of a 'movement'[258] within the life of the blessed Trinity: the Father begets the Son and the two together spirate the Spirit, yet the three Persons in the freedom of their work outside of the Godhead act as one and the same principle according to their common substratum, the divine nature. This Trinitarian speculation has become standard in western theology with the result that the personal aspects of the Divine have remained in the background, and complicated rules of 'attribution' are needed to explain how God acts. As regards the rest of theology the primary aspect of the Godhead has become the one and simple divine nature. What the Persons in themselves are is the core of God's impenetrable mystery.

When we venture to speak about the 'history' of the Trinity, the personal and communitarian nature of God is primary to the concept of divine life. God's life is profoundly personal,[259] and the three Persons that constitute that communal 'movement' are operative both within the divine life and its outside action; the Persons 'set' or 'posit' the unchangeable nature of the Godhead; whereas without: the Persons in their particularity 'work' together as Persons in their creative and redemptive activity. Contrary to traditional theology, it is not the 'threeness' but the 'oneness' of the divine Persons that is and remains the unfathomable mystery within the mystery of God.

This 'Trinitarian inversion', however, suggests the revision of our whole image of God. This revision indeed cannot be done by starting from the premises of Aquinas who enquired into the existence and nature of an ultimate reality. Our own question is about the personal God who is not understood primarily as the cause and source of all that *is,* but rather about a God who is the 'Possibility of all other possibilities': the Sovereign Freedom which may or may not make room for the emergence of things other than his divine nature. The blanket term, 'Possibility of possibilities', does not relate us creatures to one simple divine nature, but through the free assent of faith to the Person or the Persons in Community: a relationship that gives sense and meaning to all that can be realized outside of the Divine. The 'existence' of God is not imposed on us by necessity. The life of the universe, however, demands that we freely relate ourselves to God, a demand 'that is more than necessary' (Jüngel) for the life of the universe. There is no absolute necessity, indeed, to love another person, but there is an absolute need for a lover to accept and return love offered in freedom. We can know God only through the conversion implicit in loving faith or, God forbid, through the free aversion of neglect, fear or even hatred of life with Him.

It follows, therefore, that the Persons, the 'substantial relations' of tradition cannot be known objectively as three subjects or three 'selves' who are in mutual relationship; they can only be known by entering into, by participating in their life, which finds its communality not in the one and simple divine nature, but in mutual love for one another. This loving communion within the Trinitarian life of God is an imaginative interpretation of faith, a possibility enhanced by the anticipation of our desire for heaven.

6. 'Time and Space' of Final Fulfilment

Faith teaches that the encounter of the dead with such a God will happen at the judgement. The sources of written revelation attribute the role of judge either to the Son or simply to God[260] and the judgement is either that of individuals or of the nations. This apparent ambiguity can suggest a double aspect of final judgement, one that points in the same direction as, but does not correspond entirely to, the 'double' judgement of Benedict XII. The judgement of the Son (if indeed the judge in Matt. 25:31–46 is the Christ) is not a verdict imposed upon the dead from the outside, but a disclosure of the personal self as he or she has developed throughout life in encounter with the ultimate truth which is Jesus in person (John 3:17ff; 12:47f). It is a self-judgement, since Christ 'has come not to reject but to save'. Deeds, the quality of which are now manifest, divide the sheep from the goats and send them to the place reserved for them by the Father. Texts in which the judge is God, on the other hand, refer almost without exception to the eschatological judgement in the finally established kingdom of God that comprises the whole of humankind and the material universe. This last and irreversible judgement introduces the 'new heaven and new earth' together with the preceding travail as depicted in apocalyptic literature culminating in the canonical Book of Revelations. It is a judgement in which the creative power of the divine communion is again at work by assigning an ultimate abode for the nations and for each individual.

What, however, is this ultimate dwelling, this 'place' in which the whole of creation can find an eternal home? Or more precisely: what is the status of the redeemed within the 'space' of God's Trinitarian life? Traditional theology still finds it inappropriate to speak of 'time' and 'space' within the Divine. The reason is the still lingering idea that God is spirit 'living' in a timeless and (consequently) space-less realm: to speak therefore of a 'Trinitarian history' would be metaphor only, since history requires time and time presupposes its own space. If, however, timelessness is not essential to the concept of eternity, some kind of 'time' is inevitable for a life that 'moves' and relates one Person to the another. If it is inevitable to assume such a 'time', it is not unreasonable to speak about a spatiality, inaccessible for our present state.

> Since at this stage nothing but image or metaphor can help us, we must consider those views that project 'space' into the Divine imaginatively. One of these is the Cabalistic *Zimzum* theory[261] which indeed seems to presuppose the Creator as the source of all possibilities. Accordingly, divine creation has been made *possible* by a God who 'withdraws' himself and thus restricts his own 'space' by leaving room for a creation other than God himself. However fanciful this 'spatial' metaphor is, it aptly suggests three unavoidable truths: first, that creation has its own space where its free and autonomous history can develop in time; secondly, this free and autonomous creation is nonetheless surrounded by God's 'space' – it is not alien to God in its growth and development; thirdly, the *'difference'* between Creator and creation is thus

maintained, and it is exactly this difference which enables creation to enter into the relationship of free communion, a covenant with God who freely offers it to the emergent world. The life of the resurrection in an eternity proper to creatures supports the same difference, and can participate in the ineffable communion of the triune God – not by being absorbed in it, but by intercommunication with the divine Persons. The 'time' and 'space' of the blessed becomes that of the interplay between the Father the Son and of the Holy Ghost.

This, for us unfathomable, temporality of the eternal life of those who have risen can now be characterized as the continuing development of personal relationships with neighbour, with society, with a renewed universe and, last but not least, with God. Free creatures are, while on earth, creative in the sense of realizing their own possibilities, and not only those with which they were endowed (or 'programmed') by an all-determining omnipotence. By making God's possibilities their own, human beings can transcend their natural selves and create their own history on earth. Something similar, if qualitatively different, should be present in a new and redeemed situation. Man's risen life is an adventure in love for others: through being a living member of a just society (the kingdom of God and the communion of the saints); through an ('ecological') appreciation of the 'new Jerusalem' descending from heaven (Rev. 21); and eminently, through an ever-new 'discovery' within the riches of God's Trinitarian mystery. Since God is not the all-determining Creator, but a source of new possibilities for human life on earth, so God is that, too, in heaven: the 'place' and the 'time' of the triumphant history of the Church now comprising the whole universe.

The Trinitarian God is the 'space' of our life here on earth (Acts 17:18) and if He deigns to grant us that future, unfathomable eternity in which, as a member of the body of the Son (society) and under the guidance of the *Spiritus recreator,* a blessed humankind can advance indefinitely into the infinite depth of the Father.

At this point some corollaries are necessary. Most of these are scarcely mentioned by Rahner, yet the positions I have put forward need further explanation. My insistence on 'time' and 'space' in eternal life is not only inspired by the present situation of humankind facing a new age, but also by the signs of disintegration of which we are becoming so aware. In fact, some desire for a more perfect world has always been the dream in rapidly changing times, experiencing an advance in human know-how and a pitiful regression of individual morality, socio-political disturbance and natural disasters. There exists the desire to prolong time and find space where present tribulations can be replaced. Religious thought has not been exempt from this dream; indeed, it has accompanied all our imaginings about a life after death, a life in which though past memories survive, they do not suppress the future by an everlasting present. We should not relegate this desire to sheer anthropomorphism, or opt for a 'wrong eternity of changing horses at the point of death and ride on into unending spaces' (Rahner). There is, or there must be, an option between these two extremes.

As far as I know, Rahner never mentions the long survival of *chiliasm,* the thousand-year reign of Christ and his saints before the final curtain is closed definitively on the drama of world-history. The author of the Book of Revelation knows about it: in chapter 20 he reports that Satan is going to be bound for a thousand years and the souls of the martyrs and saints come to life again in the '*first* resurrection' (Rev. 20:1-6). The universal judgement comes only after a further period of tribulation, when all the dead will to be judged 'by what they had done' (Rev. 20:12f). This prepares the final vision of 'a new heaven and new earth', of the holy city of Jerusalem where God 'will dwell and we shall be his people' (21:1ff). After the author has described this sacred place of eternal life in much detail, partly borrowing images from the Old Testament prophets, the visionary is told to not to 'seal up the words of the prophecy of this book' (21:10): whether on this earth or in heaven he must be the one awaiting the coming of the Lord. His last word is 'Come Lord Jesus'. I believe that this looking forward to and yearning for the 'coming of God' actually projects the 'time' and the 'space' of human happiness into the future.

Whether this apocalyptic vision is built upon the ambiguity of final resurrection, as foretold by Jesus (the resurrection of the just alone, and then the rest of humankind[262]) or upon the very human desire for a *utopia*, where evil is revenged and justice reigns (in fact, an *eu-topia*), can never be decided. If, however, something corresponds to this desire, one has to assume a double event of resurrection with a time-in-between. The Church has not accepted this hypothesis: Augustine's *De Civitate Dei* interpreted it as a spiritual anticipation of universal resurrection rewarding the saints in heaven,[263] and Thomas Aquinas rejected it as heretical[264] by relegating this intermediary time to the current historical time in which the Church holds sway.[265] In spite of the repeated revival of milleniarism throughout history, this time-in-between has been relegated by Benedict XII to the 'time' between the two judgements of the individual soul after death and the universal resurrection on the last day.

The idea of *purgatory* has found its place through the acceptance of this hypothesis. It is indeed difficult to envisage the reality of this 'place' (in German 'Reinigungs*ort*') without any notion of 'time' and 'space'. Nor is it possible to dispense with any growth or development of humans beings in this state. As John Hick states in his redoubtable 'eschatology': 'A rehabilitation of the notion [of purgatory] was much to be desired; for the basic concept of purgatory as that of the period between this life and man's ultimate state seems to be inevitable.'[266] Of course Hick has in mind a conclusion different from Catholic orthodoxy, but this 'inevitability' presupposes 'time' and 'space' in eternal life. On the other hand, Joseph Ratzinger in commenting on the classical prooftext of purgatory[267] states: 'Man does not have to strip away *temporality* in order thereby to become "eternal" ... a person's entry into the realm (the *Ort* = place) ... is an entry into his definitive destiny and thus an immersion in eschatological fire. The transforming moment of this encounter cannot be quantified by the measurements of earthly time. It is not eternal but a transition, and yet to qualify it as 'short' or 'long' duration is impossible. The 'temporal measure of this encounter lies in an immeasurable depth, in a passing-over where we are burned ere we are transformed.'[268]

Our future eternity goes through the purifying fire of God's immediate presence and opens up a limitless further process. Our eternity, as Gregory of Nyssa puts it is greater than what we had before; it does not put a limit on our final goal; rather ... the limit of the good, that is attained, becomes the beginning of the discovery of higher goods. Thus they never stop moving from one beginning to the next ... For the desire of those who thus never rest in what they can already understand; but by an ever greater desire, the soul keeps rising constantly to another which lies ahead.[269]

Granted, this is a highly imaginative picture of heaven couched in the language of our earthly existence, but, I believe, it corresponds to the picture that I have tried to outline about the participation of the blessed in the interweaving life of the Trintarian Persons.

Nonetheless one thing needs to be added to the quasi-mystical anticipation of Gregory. The good in which and towards which the blessed advance is not only on the vertical, but also on the horizontal level. This presence of God to the definitively saved is open to the life of a divine communion of love which, I believe, can best be manifested by the communion of all the saved between themselves. The *eu-topos* of heaven is at the same time the main gift of a divine love that elevates the fragmented society of believers into a relationship of free communication between persons. It is a *present* that allows the desire of the Church be fulfilled: namely, to shed the inevitable dominance of her institutions and to leave room for inter-communion of her members that she could never fully achieve on earth. The Church on earth is and remains double-faceted composed of merely sociological as well as 'mystical' elements; she can now become the communion of the saints within the definitive arrival of the Kingdom of God. She, too, is the *topos* of the blessed, because her members are in communion with the triune God. The 'place' on the opposite side of the divide, the idea of which we cannot deny, is *hell*. And if heaven is the *eu-topia*, hell should be the *a-topia* in the sense that the hypothetically damned lose contact with this horizontal communion, that is, they are 'excluded from the kingdom of God',[270] even though they may retain a surviving personal life of hatred against Him.

These considerations are an attempt to extend the eschatology of Karl Rahner. I believe that almost all the elements on which I have laboured were present in his thought. It was perhaps the scarcity of his references to our promised end or, perhaps, the fear of using the language of apocalyptic imagination or even his preference for a transcendental disclosure of the last things that has prevented him from entering into more detail about our unknown and unknowable future. Though unknown, this promised end is the 'sacrament of our future'.

Epilogue: Sacramental and Eternal Presence

The year 2004, in which I am about to conclude this book, is a double anniversary: Karl Rahner was born one hundred years ago, and it is now twenty years since he died and encountered the Absolute Future, the unfathomable Mystery of God. The heritage he left us amounts to more than some 4000 printed publications; his true heritage is rather: the way in which he sized up the state of Christian thought in the declining years of the twentieth century, and tried to adapt authentic Christian doctrine to the mentality of his contemporaries. Although his works, published or even hitherto unpublished, are gradually being re-edited by industrious scholars of the *Karl Rahner Stiftung* (headed by K. Lehmann, J. B. Metz, K. H. Neufeld, A. Raffelt, H. Vorgrimler), and re-published in *Sämtliche Werke* (thirty-two volumes are planned), it is not *what* he wrote, but rather *how* he rethought the whole Christian faith that still inspires his readers. He is not the Church Father of the twentieth century as some of his admirers have suggested, but rather, a guiding light for those concerned to become the architects of a future theology.

Rahner himself tried several times to state this same intention in public lectures and articles. I do not wish to recall here all his various statements concerning the future of theology; they go back to the very beginning of his theological activity and were revised almost to the end of his career. In the first volume of ST he inserted two studies conceived well before its publication in which he outlined the concept of a new Dogmatic Theology; there he wrote:

> For the past can only be preserved in its purity by someone

who accepts responsibility for the future, who preserves in so far as he overcomes [supersedes]¹

I believe that this aspiration is characteristic of all Rahner's writings, including those on the Roman Catholic sacramental system and eschatology.

I, too, have approached those subjects through an analysis of his writings. It is not so much his words, but his way of dealing with traditional teaching that inspired my own work, one which recognizes, extends and, at times, modifies the thought of a great theologian. This method is by no means new. It was used by those medieval theologians who worked out their own opinions by commenting on the writings of their predecessors. The best examples are the numerous commentaries on the Sentences of Peter Lombard. Those commentaries attempted to develop a current and, often, adumbrate a future theology by using past understanding.

This is indeed what Karl Rahner himself did. He commented upon, though not explicitly, that neo-scholastic philosophy and theology with which he grew up and which he had thoroughly assimilated. Although his dissertation attempting an interpretation of Thomas Aquinas' metaphysics of knowledge proved to be unacceptable to the University of Freiburg, its approach through *Spirit in the World* had been inspired by the great medieval master and his conclusions were in continuity with Thomistic teaching. When, instead of deducing the seven sacraments from the verbal institution of Christ, Rahner explained their source as the 'self-realization' of the Church, and proposed an anthropological basis for them, he did not reject past theology, but developed it and provided new insights in furtherance of the definitions of Trent. When confronted by Marxist atheism he did not revert to the traditional proofs of God's existence, but envisaged God's impenetrable mystery as our Absolute Future; he did not betray a long-standing tradition of the Catholic Church, but, inspired by the same, developed a new aspect of it, which made that same truth more accessible. Indeed, Rahner's theological achievement can be still regarded as that of an advance on the neo-scholasticism in which it was originally rooted.

As did my former volumes so this present one attempts to

Epilogue: Sacramental and Eternal Presence 237

establish a coherent systematic within Rahner's dispersed theological writing. After many years of reflection on his theology, however, I still find it hard to produce a straightforward account of his system, that is: to give a coherent account of his conclusions about theological questions, together with the proofs of them. In general, however, one can identify two principles that guide his thought. One relies on his early philosophical insight that human knowledge is not limited to the actual, but transcends it: for Rahner the dynamism of the mind is *transcendental*. The other principle provides an entry into theological thought: we can actually *experience* our existential situation, in as much as we are so made that we can hear the word of God operative in history; we can 'sense' God's work of grace not only in our own lives, but in the life of our world.

These twin principles mould his approach to sacramental theology, too, and lead to many conclusions that go beyond traditional treatment. It is a fact of human experience that religion tries to grasp the ungraspable by means of a variety of symbols. By living in familiarity with them we also experience their source, namely, the Church in her guise as the symbol of symbols. The Church 'sensed' in sacramental praxis *is* a transcendental reality, and she is for that reason something more than anything grasped or defined through objective knowledge: she actually reveals the presence of redemption, a redemption embracing the whole of humankind. Something similar can also be affirmed of his doctrine of the last things, of eschatology. It is our experience that life ends in death. If, then, we assume that death is not only the proper culmination, but also the aim of life, then it also reveals a future that is absolute in which we are in immediate contact with the Mystery of God. The Absolute Future is the transcendental reality implied in our experience or, as he puts it, our *act* of dying. The end of time, therefore, which we recognize from within its flux, implies an eternity that is the transcendence of time.

I believe, nevertheless, that both system-creating principles can and should be questioned in detail as I have done throughout this and my former volumes on Rahner's theology. It is unnecessary to repeat here my uneasiness concerning 'transcendental theology', something which he himself defined again and again; nor was I happy with his reliance on human experience as having the direct capacity to perceive both the word of God in history, and the existence of grace implied in the dynamism of knowing and willing ('transcendental experience'). Nonetheless, Rahner's attempt to employ these principles in reshaping traditional theology establishes concepts by means of which we are able to tackle contemporary difficulties in the understanding of traditional faith. Some of these I have mentioned briefly in the introduction to this volume.

In that introduction I referred to the opposition between two characteristic attitudes of the faithful to the sacramental system of Roman Catholicism. To hold, on the one hand, that the frequentation of the sacraments is the unique and exclusive means of salvation and, at the same time, to regard it as a possible, though authentic, expression of interior, personal devotion, are two extremes hardly to be reconciled, for the one implies absolute necessity, while the other a certain freedom of choice. If, however, we follow the direction indicated by Rahner's two system-creating principles, we are no longer subject to the same constraints: they are but two aspects by means of which the use of the sacraments can be envisaged.

Firstly: if the sacraments are not instituted by God's and Christ's explicit will, but are self realizations (*Sebstvollzug*) of the Church, then it is the Church itself and not the sacraments that is of absolute necessity for salvation. Our acquaintance with the sacramental symbols of Christian praxis conveys more than the sacraments themselves: we recognize the Church through them. Rahner understands the 'Church' as a transcendental notion implied in the immediate experience of her sacramental praxis. Obviously such a notion of the Church does not imply any experimental acquaintance with her full reality, but only with her function as a *Realsymbol* of life eternal.

Secondly, it is a matter of human experience that certain truths and certain feelings can only be expressed by symbols; they are, indeed, the main vehicles of human communication, the sole condition of engendering human togetherness. In order to manifest membership of a group we have to use symbols intelligible to the rest of its members. The experience of love demands frequent expression; so too our membership of the Church is manifested by means of words, symbolic gestures and deeds. The need for some expression of belonging, however, differs: whereas the Church needs to express herself in word and symbols as the very condition of her existence, her members need to avail themselves of the Church's words and symbols in order to find their home within her. Rahner correctly emphasizes the possibility of justification even without the use of the sacraments: God's will to save is not tied to the ritualistic details of sacramental praxis. Were it so, the salvation of the individual would, as I argued above, be nothing more than rigid 'sacramentalism'.

Such a position, however, does not imply that the use of the sacraments is *ad libitum*, a free manifestation of individual devotion. Although sacraments do not determine the salvation of the individual self, the frequentation of them is necessary for the realisation of that personal existence as saved by the mercy of God. I have insisted on the difference between the self and the person repeatedly: the self is created and can be saved as such, but the person has to develop; the self is 'given' by the Creator and Redeemer, but the person is in a process of development in relationship with the human environment. Since, however, the sacramental words and symbolic gestures are a means of social communication within the Church, their use is 'person-forming'. My aversion to any defence of strict sacramentalism involves a plea for sacramental existence, that is another way of expressing the traditional difference between justification and sanctification in Catholic theology. God's mercy can save and justify us, but the sacraments of the Church open the royal road to personal sanctification, the full completion of which takes place in God's eternity.

The foregoing statement is enough to suggest that to approach the sacraments is an anticipation of eternal life. 'Sacramental' and 'eschatological' are not just related adjectives, but under certain conditions interchangeable. In order to substantiate this statement in a systematic theology we should first consider the celebration of the Mass. The

Eucharist has, indeed, been central to the expository part of this book and to my reflections on Rahner's sacramental theology. Of course, if we interpret the Mass as just a ritual in which bread and wine are consecrated and changed to become the body and blood of the Lord, the coherence between sacramental and eschatological presence cannot be established. Rahner held that the Eucharist is not restricted to the moment of consecration (as some people still believe): the words of consecration pronounced by a priest outside the Mass are meaningless.

It is theologically viable to regard the Eucharist as a cluster of symbols that make present, though to a different degree, that symbolized reality to which they point. These symbols are verbal (the service of the word makes present God's self revelation in Christ), material (the bread and wine offered and accepted as Christ's body and blood) and behavioural (the communion of the faithful together with the re-enacted drama of redemption). If we accept these symbols as a unity, as a true expression of the expectation of the parousia (central acclamation), we have overcome the perpetual flux of time and made present its definitive fulfilment – or as Rahner would say: its 'consummation'. The celebration of the Mass 'not only anticipates the promised end, but also 'makes it present', it 'realizes' the future in a sacramental sense', as I tried to characterise the celebration of the Mass. Or to paraphrase Rahner's own words: 'it is already an end, yet not *the* end that ends the time of our history on earth'.

Are the other sacraments also relevant to our eschatological future? The statement previously made implies a positive answer: all the other sacraments are 'geared' to the Eucharistic celebration of the Mass. If, then, systematic theology can establish this, 'sacramental' and 'eschatological' statements are interchangeable. My reflections on Rahner's sacramental theology tried to argue that each sacrament is, in its own specific way, an initiation into the life of the Church. The argument is not only valid for the so-called sacraments of initiation (baptism, confirmation, priesthood), but also for penance, marriage and the anointing of the seriously sick. The word 'initiation' is a time-bound term. It means in itself 'already and not yet', and hence eschatological. It is, however, important to add that not only these six sacraments that are eschatological, but that the Eucharistic celebration also 'initiates' the participants into the Church, a present reality, and one yet to be fulfilled in the 'communion of the saints'. The character of the Church as mystery consists, not only in the present reality worked by its symbolism, but also by its symbolizing of that Church in which the *beati* in heaven celebrate the liturgy of eternal fulfilment. The Church herself is an eschatological reality.

It is obvious that the present Church is also a sociological unit with rules and regulations. (My fifth volume on Rahner's ecclesiology dwelt repeatedly on her two-faceted nature). One of the rules concerning the participation of the faithful in the Eucharist imposes the exclusion of grave sinners and members of other Christian denominations from communion, even though attendance at Mass is a valid act for those excluded from communion. (Similar legal boundaries are imposed by the Church on the use of other sacraments, especially in the case of marriage in which the symbolic element is inextricably interwoven with human legislation.) The prohibition of intercommunion by the Roman Church is understandable as a custom of an institutionally organised society, even if over restrictive from a theological point of view. It is understandable in that the Eucharist is a symbol of the unity of the Church, a unity measured, too, by the detailed dogmatic teaching of the institutional Church. It is restrictive in the sense that the whole symbolism of the Eucharistic celebration is confined thereby to one valid aspect of its significance: it is sacramental but not eschatological. Consequently this prohibition cannot be unconditional: in given circumstances it can or even must be overruled.

This can also be illustrated by the theory of symbolism discussed in section 2.2 A of this book, where I adopted Buckley's distinction between horizontal and vertical symbols. Our sacraments are to be thought of as vertical symbols, and hence versatile in that they can symbolize a whole variety of realities. This is especially true of the Eucharist.

If the concentration on the unity of the Church were measured, for instance, by the strict theological understanding of the real presence, it would be understandable that some participants should be denied access to Holy Communion. The symbolism of the Mass is, however, not restricted to this aspect alone. It is also a 'vertical' symbol, versatile in its significance.

Rahner often argued that sacramental grace is due to Christ's eschatological victory, the presence of the risen Christ within his Church is tantamount to a real entry of eternal life into her present time. This is the difference between the 'sacraments' of the Old Testament and those of the New. Although I have modified Rahner's *whole* approach to the genesis of the sacraments, it was his insistence on Christ's eschatological victory that inspired my reflections on that subject. Rahner's early attempt at explaining the origin of sacraments on an analogy with the incarnation does not harmonise with what seems to be his later insight, namely: assigning the efficacy of the sacraments to Christ's eschatological victory. Obviously, the incarnation is a necessary condition of the possibility of the *eschaton*. Without it we would not be able to speak of Christ's risen body, nor of a 'sacralized' world and history, whose destiny he made his own. I pointed out, however, that 'sacralization' alone does not explain the sacraments as traditionally understood by the Church. The faithful must always be aware of the future, the uncertainty of which, however, is compensated for by faith in Christ's ultimate victory, and lived out in the hope of eternal fulfilment. Christ's victory renders the promise of eternal life a *real* possibility and this real possibility is what we call sacramental grace. *Such a future is indeed the sacrament of eschatological salvation.*

Paul in his epistle to the Philippians reflects on his own life, now fully converted to Jesus the Christ. He believes that he became righteous through faith; that he knows Christ and the power of his resurrection; that, if possible, he may attain the resurrection from the dead, even if he has not yet obtained it and he is not yet perfect. He is on the way of the 'eternal validity' of his eschatalogical fulfilment:

Epilogue: Sacramental and Eternal Presence

Brethren, I do not consider that I have made it my own; but this one thing I do: forgetting what lies behind and straining forward to what lies ahead. I press on toward the goal for the prize of the heavenly call of God in Christ Jesus. (Phil. 3:9–14)

Notes

Introduction

1. The recent Encyclical of Pope John Paul, which excludes intercommunion, is by no means absolute: it reckons with the possibility of administering the Eucharist to non-Catholics in certain circumstances.
2. Cf., G. Vass, *Understanding Karl Rahner*, vols I–V, the last three of which are under the subtitle 'A Pattern of Doctrines' I–III (Referred to as Vass, volume . . .)
3. Consult the list of abbreviations for quotations.

Chapter 1 The Sacramental Life of the Church

1. It is a fair guess that Rahner was inspired by O. Semmelroth (SJ), *Die Kirche als Ursakrament*, Frankfurt a.M., 1953 – and also Semmelroth's essay in *MS* (vol. IV/1, pp. 318–355) as '*Wurzelsakrament*'. However, there were implicit hints of the same idea in the 19th century cf., M. Bernards, 'Zur Lehre der Kirche als Sakrament. Beobachtungen aus der Theologie des 19. und 20. Jahrhundert, in *Münchener Theologische Zeitschrift* 20(1969) 29–54
2. In *Lumen Gentium* (on the Church) there are three explicit mentions of the Church as sacrament: No 1, 9, 48 and implied in No 59. Cf., 'Tanner' viz. 849 (line 20), 856 (line 20), 887 (line 33), 894 (line 29) in *Gaudium et Spes* (on the Church in the World) the same is already quoted as an authority: (numbers 1, 45 and 48). For a detailed analysis (also for implicit quotations) see in van Eijk, 'De Kerk als sakrament en het heil van der wereld', in *Beijdragen* 47(1986) 226ff; see also Cathechism of the Catholic Church, Numbers 774–776.
3. *Kirche55*, p. 435.
4. Ibid., p. 337.
5. See: Vass, volume 2, pp. 88–111; 145–161, viz. volume 3, pp. 1–45
6. '*Kirche55*' p. 432: The same idea was later extended in his *Christology is an Evolutive View of the World*, TIS, pp. 157ff.=STV, pp. 183ff.

7. I shall refer to W.J. O'Hara's translation, *The Church and Sacraments*, London, 1963.
8. I dealt with these two notions in more detail in Vass, volume 2. 'Supernatural existential' means briefly that although grace is not natural gift, it is the actual state in which we live, influenced by Christ's interim presence. 'Divinization' means that grace is (ultimately) the indwelling of God (or of the Spirit) in man's soul. (Cf., Vass, volume 2, pp. 59-85).
9. *Kirche61*, p. 16 = 15.
10. Ibid., [my italics].
11. Ibid., 17=16. It is a position which I have frequently discussed in my previous volumes on Rahner's theology.
12. 'The New Image of the Church' TI 10, pp. 3-29 = ST VIII, pp. 329-375, referred to as 'New Image'. By this time Rahner must have known Vatican II's decrees on the Church (*Lumen Gentium*) and that on the Church in the Modern World (*Gaudium et spes*) See especially the third part of the article.
13. 'New Image', p. 15 = 340; note that the German text is rather tortuous and the quotation from the current translation had to be reshaped.
14. See Vass, volume 3, section 3 (pp. 105ff.) where I discuss Rahner's concept of symbolism in general – I shall refer in more detail to Rahner's theory of the symbol as applied to the incarnation.
15. 'New Image', p. 17 = 341.
16. See: Vass, volume 4, pp. 45-63, 81-93, where I have discussed its origin and reception of Rahner's theory.
17. 'New Image' 17 = 342f see also his 'Dogmatic Notes on Ecclesiological Piety' TI 5, p. 282f = ST V, p. 385f.
18. *Die siebenfältige* (sevenfold) *Gabe*, Munich, 1974; an English translation was published in London in 1975 as a series of booklets. Each booklet contained a single chapter: on baptism, confirmation, Eucharist, penance, sacrament of the sick, marriage and ordination. Later, an English translation of the original 1974 German edition was published with the title *Meditations on the Sacraments*, New York, 1977. For convenience I use the name *Sevenfold* for this latter publication and use the pagination of the German original.
19. *Sevenfold*, p. X(=8).
20. Ibid. (as the translator puts it) 'does not keep on giving it. The translation abbreviates the German original : '*eine punktförmige Qualität, ein punktförmiges Geschehen ...*' that is, 'grace only touches this profane world in a passing encounter in discrete quantities.'
21. For convenience, I use the name *Revolution* for the articles published in *The Tablet,* 6 March 1971, 236-238 and 13 March, 267-268. Next quotation: p. 236
22. '*Consideration of the Active Role of the Person in the Sacramental Event.*' = TI 14, pp.161ff = ST X, 405ff – hereafter referred to as 'Active Role'. (In *Geist und Leben* 43(1970) 282ff.)
23. 'On the Theology of Worship' in TI 19, pp. 141ff = ST XIV, pp. 227ff.; it will be referred to as *Worship*.

24. See, *Revolution*, p. 237, first column. See also 'Active Role', p. 162f.
25. 'But the reception of the sacrament is of its very nature an attempt to commit ourselves to God in a radical decision of freedom and with the love of one's whole heart', *Revolution*, p. 237. See also Rahner's comment in 'Active Role', p. 165.
26. See *Worship*, p. 141(= 227), See also p. 144(= 230) where Rahner says '... without opting absolutely for one another' and 'without rejecting the first ...' And on p. 148(= 235): 'for some people we can eventually explain the meaning of worship even with the first, traditional model.'
27. Ibid., p. 142(= 228).
28. The statements of this last paragraph are taken from *Revolution* (ca. p. 267) and from 'Active Role' (ca. p.171f = 415f). For a detailed treatment of grace see Vass, volume 2, pp. 85–116.
29. See *Revolution* p. 238.
30. *Worship*, p. 267.
31. Teilhard de Chardin, *Hymn of the Universe*, London and Glasgow, 1965.
32. Cf. Vass, volume 2, p. 64ff about the 'theorem' of the supernatural. For Rahner 'human nature' in itself can only be known, if we 'detract' elements already due to supernatural grace. Nature is thus a '*Restbegriff*', a remainder concept.
33. This and the above *Worship* p. 143(= 229f). See also 'Active Role' p. 169 = 413: 'The sacrament constitutes a small sign, necessary, reasonable and indispensable, within the infinitude of the world as permeated by God. It is the sign which reminds us of the limits of the presence of divine grace, and in ... precisely this particular anamnesis, is intended to be an event of grace.'
34. *Worship* p. 146 = 233. The second half of this quotation is a simplified version of Rahner's complex sentence ('in sociological explicitness and thus conveys to man an explicit and reflex enactment of this liturgy of the world, of salvation history').
35. See the discussion of 'Mysticism and the Experience of Grace', in Vass, volume 4, pp. 124–131.
36. *Worship*, pp. 149 (= 236) – The above quotation is a simplified rendering of Rahner's sentence ('that what clearly appears in it and consequently can be more decisively accepted in freedom is what occurs always and everywhere in the ordinary course of life').
37. Cf., *Revolution*, pp. 267f; See also 'Active Role' pp. 171f(= 418) This and the above quotations simplify both Rahner's and his translator's complex style.
38. *Revolution*, p. 268 See also 'Active Role', pp. 174f(= 418f). 'This 'experience' and the 'subject matter' precisely of it are made apprehendable at the cultic and ritual level.
39. Cf., *Revolution*, p. 268 where Rahner translates the same in his philosophical terminology: what is transcendentally hidden must be manifest in its 'categoriality'.
40. Cf., *Sevenfold*, p. XIVff = 15f. Note that my rendering of this state-

ment is an attempt to simplify the translator's more literal one: 'When the Church as the basic sacrament, in situations of human life which are decisive for the individual or for the group, pledges itself to man with an absolute commitment of its being as the basic sacrament of salvation, and does so historically and palpably, that is, in word and deed, and when man in turn accepts the Church's pledge of salvation and acts it out as the manifestation of the acceptance of his interior grace-dynamic, then we have what we mean by the sacraments of the Church.'

41. Cf., *Kirche61*, p. 20 = 19
42. (45) ibid.
43. (46) *Handbook* II/1, p. 55ff.
44. (47) ibid., p. 324 (a very simplified rendering of Rahner's literally untranslatable sentence).
45. (48) Cf., ibid., note 1.
46. (49) ibid., p. 325 (free translation of Rahner's text).
47. See On Revelation No 2-6 and esp. On Sacred Liturgy No 7 Tanner, 822 (line 15) in slightly different translation
48. 'The Word and the Eucharist' (1960) TI 4, pp. 253ff = ST IV, 313ff (hence referred to as *Word*). It was prompted by his growing interest in the power of the word, also expressed beautifully in his *Priest and Poet* (TI 3, 294ff) and in *Poetry and the Christian* (TI 4, 357ff) applied to the devotion to the Sacred Heart (TI 3, 321ff).
49. (52) *Was ist ein Sakrament?* (*Vorstösse zur Verständigung*), Freiburg in Breisgau, 1971, p. 67-85. I shall refer to it as *Jüngel/Rahner*.
50. (53) *Word*, p. 255 = 315.
51. (54) ibid., p. 257 = 318.
52. Rahner's philosophical terminology expresses the idea that 'transcendental' realities require their own 'categorial' (tangible) expression in human terms. See Vass, volume 1, pp. 23-30.
53. In my opinion the case of mystics are an exception: they are unable to express in human terms this 'inner grace', for it is equivalent to the beatific vision – here and now. See Vass, volume 4, pp. 133-138.
54. (55) *Word*, p. 259 = 320 (note that the translation in TI is slightly emended).
55. (56) ibid., 260 = 320.
56. (57) ibid., in ET. p. 321f. to be compared with p. 69 in *Jüngel/Rahner*.
57. Ibid., p. 261 = 322f (own translation).
58. Ibid., p. 262 = 320f.
59. (60) ibid., p. 265 = 327.
60. (62) ibid., p. 266 = 330.
61. Ibid., p. 265 = 329. Note the two decisive factors: 'radical commitment of the Church' and 'decisive situation of the individual'.
62. Cf. *Jüngel/Rahner*, pp. 75-79, n. 33 : a simplified version of a much longer argument.
63. This view, I believe, is partly borrowed from Thomas Aquinas who characterized grace in the New Testament against 'grace' in the Old,

by emphasizing its efficacy. Cf. *Summa Theol.* I/II Quaestions 106 and 107.
64. Cf., *Word* p. 274 = 340; the quotation in text is a paraphrase of Rahner's original and its current translation.
65. See ibid., p. 276f = 343, which seems to be also a borrowing from Thomas Aquinas, cf., *Summa III,* quaest. 65, art 1.
66. Ibid., p. 277 = 344.
67. It conforms to his very early (1947) article: 'Membership of the Church according to the Teaching of Pius XII's Encyclical *Mystici Corporis Christi* in TI 2, pp. 1ff = ST II, pp. 7ff, in which he extends the confines of the Church beyond the limits of practising Christians.
68. Rahner postulates a similar process also in those Christians who were justified *before the grace of the sacrament.*
69. *Word*, p. 279 = 346.
70. Ibid., p. 280 = 347.
71. In Questions on the Theology of the Sacraments, TI 23,189f = ST XVI, 198f; here 191 = 401.
72. Cf., Faith and Sacrament (1981) in TI 23, 181f = ST XVI, 384f, here 184 = 391.
73. In Faith and Sacrament 181 = 387.
74. Ibid., p. 183 = 389.
75. Karen Kilby, Karl Rahner, in *Fount of Christian Thinkers* (ed. P.Vardy), p. 49.
76. See Vass, volume 3, pp. 11–16.
77. See Tanner', 685, lines 4–5 in its negative wording, and for the positive answer contained in Trent's canon 8 of session 7. The usual translation of *'ex opere operato'* in German is similar: 'on the ground of the performed rite' (*kraft des vollzogenen Ritus'* – (Neuner-Roos: *Der Glaube der Kirche in dem Kirkünden der Lehrverkündigung*, Regensburg, 1971[9]. No. 513) or 'on the ground of performed (sacramental) action [*aufgrund der vollzogenen (sakramentalen) Handlung* – Hünermann 1608.]: *Kompendium der Glaübeusbekenntnisse ünd Kirchlichen Lehreutscheidüngen*, Freiburg in Breisgau, 1991[31].
78. *Kirche61*, p. 26 = 24.
79. Ibid., 28 = 26; note that the examples with which he illustrates his position are taken from the sacrament of penance and not that of baptism. I believe, however, that the origin of the tradition leading to *opus operatum* was the case of infant baptism.
80. *Kirche61*, 30f = 29.
81. Ibid. 32 = 29f.
82. Ibid. 32f = 30.
83. Ibid.
84. With this I attempted to paraphrase Rahner's most complicated German: ibid., p. 80.
85. Ibid., (my translation).
86. Cf. 'Questions on the Theology of the Sacraments' TI 23, 189ff = ST XVI, 398ff) here 192 = 401, hence referred to as Questions.
87. 'Faith and Sacrament', p. 188 = 397.

88. 'This victorious, definitive, irrevocable significance of the Church's word in the sacramental signs is also called the effectiveness of the sacraments of and by themselves: in Latin *opus operatum*'. *Questions*, p. 192 = 401.
89. Cf., Aquinas' *Summa, III.* q. 60, art. 1.
90. See the detailed study of G. Bornkamm about the various uses of *mysterion* in cultic, philosophical and profane contexts (In TWNT vol. 4, pp. 810-817). The same in the Septuagint OT and in the NT (ibid., 817-831) as well as its gradual limitation to the sacraments in the early Church (ibid., 831-834).
91. *Causa vero instrumentalis non agit per virtutem suae formae, sed solum per motum quo movetur a principali agente. Unde effectus non assimilatur instrumento, sed pricipali agenti; sicut lectus non assimilatur securi, sed arti quae est in mente artificis* (*Summa*, III, q. 62 art.1 corpus).
92. 'The fundamental defect that leads all these theories into conceptual' difficulties , consists ... in tacitly laying down the pattern of transitive efficient causality, in which one factor adequately distinct from another must produce the latter'. Cf. *Kirche61*, 37 = 34.
93. See Vass volume 3 (Pattern of Doctrines 1) 4.3 pp. 105-111.
94. Here I cannot resist quoting Karen Kilby (as in the previous section n. 75). She likens real symbols to a kiss: 'The kiss symbolises love. But it is not just a signal of the existence of something completely distinct from itself – or if it is, one would have to describe it as not a very successful or meaningful kiss. A kiss makes real, makes concrete, the love it expresses.' Here p. 41. Likewise Rahner in 'Baptism and the Renewal of Baptism' TI 23, 196 = ST XVI, 406f.
95. In 'The Theology of the Symbol', TI 4, p. 242 = ST IV, 300.
96. *Kirche61*, p. 38 = 35.
97. *Kirche61*, 39f = 36.The italics in text are my translation (... *obwaltet im gegenseitigen Sichbedingens* ...)
98. Questions, p. 190 = 399 (as in n. 10).
99. As for baptism see in Questions, 'Mt 28 where Jesus gives the command to baptize [but] ... does this injunction ... really go back to the historical Jesus? The trinitarian formula used in baptism and mentioned in this text cannot so easily be considered as having been used by Jesus.'
100. *Kirche61* here 42 = 38: Rahner's formulation is very careful. In no way does he affirm that Christ did not institute the Eucharist (cf., ibid. 42 = 38), yet he certainly did not lay down the rite of this celebration as a sacrament objectively conferring (*ex opere operato*) grace. His main point in this place is against the deduction of *ordo* from the Last Supper.
101. Cf., Tanner, p. 754, line 9 '*Quod Paulus apostolus innuit, dicens*'...
102. *Kirche61*, 50 = 45.
103. Cf., ibid., 48 = 43f.
104. Cf., ibid. 51f = 47. He calls this difference an 'intrinsic specialisation' (*Stossrichtung*) of the same grace. Therefore not only the

different rites underline these distinctions.
105. Cf., ibid., 61 = 55.
106. Ibid., 66 = 59f.
107. Consider ibid., footnote 4 on page 61f = 55f.
108. Karen Kilby, Karl Rahner. In series Fount ChristianThinkers (ed. P. Vardy, 1997), here p. 40.
109. *Kirche61*, p. 77(= p. 69).
110. Cf., *Kirche55*, pp. 440ff. The same will be reteated almost verbatim in *Kirche61*, pp. 77–83 (pp. 69–73).
111. *Kirche61*, p. 81(= p.73).
112. *Foundations* pp. 424f(= pp.408f): 'it is the sacrament of the Church as such in a very radical sense'. Also in *Kirche55* (p. 441) and *Kirche61*, p. 82(= p. 74) 'It cannot be put on the level with other sacraments and listed among them.'
113. *Kirche61*, p. 83(= 75). Cf., *Kirche55*, p. 441.
114. *Kirche61*, p. 61(= p. 75) '... vollzieht sich selbst in höchster Aktualität'.
115. *Word*, p. 281(= 348).
116. Ibid., p. 282(= p. 349).
117. Ibid., p. 284(= p. 352).
118. See Tanner 697 in the 4th canon of the Council of Trent on the Eucharist, condemning the view according to which the presence of the Lord is restricted to the moment of consuming the species with full faith; that is *tantum in usu*. It would militate against the principle of *opus operatum*.
119. Cf.,*Word*, p. 296(= p. 354).
120. *Active Role*, p. 169(= 413).
121. Ibid., p. 170(= p. 415), also in *Revolution*, p. 267.
122. In writing about the Mass, Rahner takes it for granted that it, as a sacrament, effectively represents Christ's sacrifice on the Cross. With this he connects the self-offering of the Church herself. See in *Celebration*, to which I shall later return.
123. *Active Role*, p. 172 and *Revolution*, p. 267.
124. Ibid., p. 174(= p. 419). My italics.
125. Ibid., p.175(= p. 420).
126. Ibid., p. 176(= p. 421).
127. Cf., *Foundations*, p. 426(= p. 410).
128. *Presence*, p. 288(= p. 358).
129. *Kirche61*, p. 82(= p. 73f), See also *Active Role*, p. 165(= p. 409): 'Modern man ... all too easily has the impression of acting ungenuinely ... precisely in those cases in which this reception of the sacraments is related excessively and exclusively from the outside to the individual's own personal saving history taken in isolation.'
130. Cf., *Presence*, p. 309(= p. 384).
131. It is true that in the post-Tridentine tradition it was not easy to show the sacrificial character of the Mass.
132. *Presence*, p. 310(= p. 385).
133. See Danzinger-Schönmetzer (DS) 3890; Rahner comments: '... as the

Notes 251

text betrays Pius' fears that the rejection of the term would affirm a merely spiritual presence ... the Church would have had to deny its own being, as it understood itself to be, if it gave up this doctrine.' *Presence*, p. 297(= p. 369).
134. 'The Councils never intended to define the scholastic theses of substance and accident.' F.Selvaggi, as quoted by Rahner, ibid., p. 298, n.16(= 370 n.16).
135. Cf., *Presence*, pp. 300ff(= pp. 372ff).
136. Ibid., p. 302(= p. 374).
137. *Sevenfold*. p. 60 (= p. 156).
138. See Vass, volume 5.3.31 pp. 103ff with my own reflections (ibid., 4.3B pp. 199–206). Note, however, that Volume 5 deals with the ministry as an institution (organ) and not explicitly as a sacrament of ordination.
139. See Vass, volume 5, pp. 110, 112; also in 'How the Priest Should View his Official Ministry', TI 14, p. 216 (ST IX, p. 463).
140. *Kirche61*, p. 100 (= p. 89).
141. Ibid., p. 102 (= p. 91).
142. Ibid., p. 103 (= p. 92).
143. In 'The Renewal of Priestly Ordination', TI 3, p. 173 (= ST III. p. 203).
144. *Celebration* (see note 149 below) p. 31 (= p. 42) A simplified translation of 'for *valid* signs of the reality of salvation and of God's saving activity to which absolutely no inner reality signified by them belongs', is impossible.
145. Ibid., p. 30 (= 41).
146. Cf., ibid., p. 684, line 33: the sixth canon about sacraments in general.
147. Cf., *Tanner*, p. 673, line 31f: chapter 6 of the decree on justification.
148. in 'Personal and Sacramental Piety', TI 2, p. 130 (= ST II, p. 138).
149. See *Die vielen Messen und das eine Opfer*, Freiburg in Breisgau (1951) from ZKT 7 (1949) pp. 257ff.; part of it is translated in 'Multiplication of Masses', *Orate Fratres* 24 (1950) pp. 553ff. The same topic was taken up again in a much revised form in *Die vielen Messen als die vielen Opfer Christi?* ZKT 77 (1955) answering the objections (also) by Pope Pius XII in 1954 to the 1951 publication. Finally with the substantial help of A. Häusling, the first title was taken up again in *Quaestiones Disputatae* 31, Freiburg in Breisgau (1966) and was published in English by W.J. O'Hara.
150. In some prophetic way the same booklet mildly advocated the reintroduction of concelebrated Masses – a custom well known to the *Urkirche*, and after Vatican II taken for granted.
151. *Celebration*, p. 17 (= p. 28.) (My italics.)
152. It seems that the order should not be reversed by postulating that Christ is first made present and then offered in the form of consecrated species to the Father for the salvation of the world. This second alternative not only exposes us to the misunderstanding that we are repeating the one and unique sacrifice (for which Catholics are still

reproached by some of their Protestant colleagues), but to relagating the aspect of the sacrifice to secondary importance, for sacrifice could then either be reduced to mere remembrance or be regarded as an additional sacrament or a 'sacramental' superceding the consecration.

153. Though Christ's suffering and death is a visible event in the past, yet its invisible spiritual component is permanent (i.e. Christ 'sacrificial' will). See p. 23, note 16 (= p. 34).
154. *Celebration*. p. 19 (= p. 30).
155. Ibid, p. 24 (= p. 34).
156. 'The grace-giving action of God and man's laying hold of grace in faith and love do not belong to the constitutive elements of the sacramental rite, yet essentially belong to the sacrament'. Ibid. p. 30 (= p. 41).
157. Ibid., p. 57 (= p. 70).
158. Ibid., p. 57f (= p. 71).
159. Ibid., p. 69 (= p. 73).
160. *Kirche61*, p. 88 (= p. 78.)
161. Cf., Canon 9 of sacraments at Trent, *Tanner*, 685, lines 7-9.
162. *Kirche61*, 88=79.
163. In 'Baptism and the Renewal of Baptism' TI 23,195-207 = ST XVI, 406-418. Here 195f = 407; hereafter referred to as Baptism.
164. Cf., Baptism, p. 200 (= p. 413).
165. Ibid., 201 (= p. 413f.).
166. *Sevenfold*, p. 4 (= p. 24).
167. Cf., ibid., p. 7 (= p. 29).
168. For this and the above references see ibid., 8 = 30f and note the repeated 'already'.
169. Ibid., p. 10 (= p. 35).
170. Ibid., p. 11 (= p. 36).
171. Ibid., p. 14 (= p. 39).
172. Cf., *Foundations*, pp. 416 (= p. 401).
173. Cf.,Trent's canon 3 on confirmation, *Tanner*, 686, 33f : only the bishop, with special authorization a priest, but not deacons.
174. *Kirche61*, p. 91 (= p. 81), see also page 91f.
175. *Foundations*, p. 417 (= p. 401).
176. *Sevenfold*, p. 21 (= p. 51).
177. See his early article (1934), about the pious practice of frequent confession (*Andachtsbeichte*), now in TI3, pp. 77 (=ST XI, pp. 21).
178. First published in *Schriften* II, volume 2, 143-184 = TI 2,135-174; hereafter referred to as *Truths*.
179. First published in a Festschrift in honour of Alfredo, Cardinal Ottaviani 1967/68; reprinted in *Schriften* VIII 447-471 = TI 10, 125-149; hereafter referred to as *Reconciliation*.
180. See *Reconciliation*, 125-128 = 447-450 and the two references to *Lumen Gentium* No 11: *Tanner* 857, line 27f. A similar reference to sin's 'offence' against the Church in *Presbyterorum ordinis,* No 5, cf., *Tanner*, 1047, line 21f.
181. *Kirche61*, p. 93 (= p. 83).

Notes 253

182. Ibid., p. 94 (= p. 84).
183. *Truth*, p. 142 (= p. 150).
184. Cf. *Reconciliation* p. 135 (= p. 457 and notes).
185. Ibid. and in note 183 above.
186. He briefly names in *Reconciliation* Pastor Hermas, Tertulian (in both his Catholic and Montanist periods), Cyprian, Origen and, of course Augustine where reconciliation with God is not only connected with peace with the Church but also this latter is a condition, or even cause, of the former. See *Truth*, pp. 137-141 (= pp. 459-163).
187. Cf., to this in more detail *Truth*, pp. 153-157 (= pp. 161-165) and his preference of Thomas against the 'more superficial' view of Scotus 'who transposed the sacramentality of the whole process of penance exclusively to the priestly absolution'.
188. Cf. *Reconciliation*, 143f (= pp. 465f.); see there testimonies quoted.
189. See for this statement his 'Problems concerning Confession' TI 10, 190ff (= ST III, pp. 227ff) where he 'accuses' present day confessional praxis with legalistic and magical tendencies and tries to point out new directions in the development of the same: 'The theory and praxis of this sacrament will in future tend towards a *theologically fuller* and so *more personal accomplishment* of this sacrament.' Ibid., p. 193 (= p. 229).
190. *Reconciliation*, p. 148 (= p. 471).
191. Ibid., p. 147 (= p. 470).
192. TI, 23 translates: 'The Status of the Sacrament of Reconciliation' p. 205ff = ST XVI, 418ff.
193. *Truth*, p. 137 (= p. 145).
194. Cf. Vass, vol. II, 2.3 and 4, pp. 33ff.
195. 'Guilt and its Remission: the Borderland between Theology and Psychiatry', TI 2, pp. 265ff (= ST II, pp. 279ff).
196. Ibid., p. 279 (= p. 294) – the same sentence, however with a different point, is borrowed from *Truth* (p. 264), 'Even before the *Ego te Absolvo* there has already taken place a miracle of grace in the Church'. By this he means the inner repentance of the sinner which is already a gift of God.
197. See TI 6, pp. 197ff (= ST VI, pp. 238ff).
198. 'Since he cannot in principle attain an adequate objectifying judgement about his own decision of freedom – since he cannot judge himself – he also does not even have the last word about his own guilt, and precisely this constitution gives him ... the last, never surpassable, possibility of doubting or denying the realisation of something like guilt in man'. Ibid., p. 210f.
199. Rahner appeals to this 'cautious scepticism' about spotting real guilt when he gives a Catholic interpretation of the reformers' formula *simul justus et peccator*. See more in detail in 'Justified and Sinner at the Same Time', TI 6 pp. 218ff (= ST VI, pp. 262ff).
200. 'From what we said earlier, no simple answer is possible in relation the quesion as to whether a mortal or a mere venial sin exists in a particular case.' *Sevenfold*, p. 51 (= p. 101).

254 *The Sacrament of the Future*

201. Ibid., p. 54 (= p. 105f); see also *Foundations*, p. 422f (= p. 407).
202. 'Sin as Loss of Grace in Early Church Literature' TI 15, p. 24f (= p. ST XI, p. 48f).
203. *Foundations*, p. 423 (= p. 407).
204. '... because this holy community which is called the Church always lives from out of the death of his Lord, the dying who always die alone are not abandoned by their brothers and sisters.' Ibid.
205. Cf., *Kirche61*, p. 113f (= *p*. 101f).
206. Cf. *Tanner*, 710, line 2f : it 'was regarded by the fathers as the final complement not only of penance, but also of the whole Christian life, which ought to be an ever continuing penance.'
207. ... which is the title of his section about the sacrament of the sick in *Sevenfold*.
208. This second half of my statement is not explicitly present in *Sevenfold*. However, if we apply all of Rahner's insights to the anointing, we are coming near to this conclusion.
209. '... he is totally present in these senses and through them communicates with the world and encounters its perils...' Ibid. p. 90f (= p. 136).
210. See recent dcuments : Paul VI *Indulgentiarum doctrina* (1967); John Paul II 1980 (Catholic Truth Society Do524; and again John Paul II in *Acta Apostolicae Sedis* (1999).
211. See his review of Poschmann 'Remarks on the Theology of Indulgences'; now extended in TI 2, 175ff = ST II, 185ff; and Poschmann's *Der Ablass im Licht der Bussgeschichte*, Bonn, 1948.
212. See under 'Indulgences', SM III, 123a. This definition is taken from a decree of Leo X (just before the Reformation) and taken over by the old canon law.
213. The Council of Trent Session XXV, *Tanner* 796, line 30f. The text was prepared under pressure of the Reformation. It affirms their origin from Christ giving authority to the Church to dispense them to the benefit of the faithful. At the same the decree tries to abolish misuses of the same which may have been one of the reasons of Luther's revolt.
214. Published first in *Stimmen der Zeit* (1955) and later reprinted with some additional remarks in *Schriften*, TI 10, pp. 150-165 (= ST VIII; pp. 472-487); hereafter referred to as *Indulgence*.
215. See under 'Indulgence', SM 3, 127b.
216. *Indulgence*, p. 152 (= p. 474), and the preceding pages.
217. Ibid., p. 156 (= p. 476).
218. Ibid., p. 158 (= p. 480).
219. Ibid., p. 159f (= p. 481f).
220. Ibid., p. 163 (= p. 485).
221. Ibid. p. 162 (= p. 484).
222. For instance Tertullian, Adv. Marcion 5,18; De Monogamia 5.
223. Like Maleachi 2:16 .
224. Luther's *Traubüchlein* BSELK 526,6f and 550,33; Katechism BSELK 612, 13ff as quoted by Pannenberg *Syst. Theol. III* p. 394 n. 800.

225. See W. Pannenberg's short, but fair treatment of marriage in Systematic Theol., 931ff.
226. See 3rd canon on the sacraments in general *Tanner* 684, line 25.
227. *Kirche61* p. 108 (= p. 96).
228. Cf., ibid., p. 109 (= p. 97).
229. Cf., ibid., p. 108 (= p. 97); NB. By monogenetic he does not refer to the technical question concerning the creation of man and woman, whether it was from one couple or several. What he tries to say that all humans are fruit of some kind of heterosexual love.
230. Ibid., p. 110 (= p. 98).
231. Cf., *Sevenfold* pp. 69-78 (= pp. 139-155).
232. *Marriage as a Sacrament*, TI 10,199-221 = *Schriften*VIII 519-540, a lecture first published in *Geist und Leben*1967. Hereafter referred to as *Marriage*.
233. Cf., his remark p. 201 n. 5 where – to my knowledge – the only time he refers to his own 'system' in order 'to give the reader the opportunity to achieve better understanding of unusual lines of thought in the context of the general theological system *which I have worked out*'.
234. Cf., *Marriage*, p. 206 (= p. 525).
235. Cf. Ibid. pp. 207-9 (= pp. 526-8).
236. Ibid., p. 210 (= p. 530).
237. Ibid., p. 211 (= p. 530f) (my italics).
238. 'For this reason there exists not merely an external similarity between the unity in love of two human individuals on the one hand and the unity between Christ and the Church on the other, but also a relationship between the two unities such that they condition one another: the former exist *precisely because* the latter exists'. Ibid., p. 220 (= p. 539).
239. Ibid., p. 221 (= p. 540).
240. Ibid., p. 214 (= p. 533) (my italics).
241. Cf., ibid., 219 = 538 and consult the German original as well as *Foundations*, p. 419f (= pp. 404f) where, as a rule, he *verbatim* repeats the formulations of *Marriage* .
242. *Sevenfold* p. 72f (= p. 145f).
243. His long footnote 33 in *Marriage* pp. 216f (= pp. 536f) is related to this question. It discusses with the canonist Mörsdorf the obligation first imposed by Trent, according to which the marriage of Catholics is only valid if it is celebrated in the Church. (Rahner, of course, holds that the sacrament is administered by the spouses themselves and a priest is present only as witness authorized by the Church.) It is significant that this discussion does not feature in the article itself.

Chapter 2 Comments and Questions: The Ecclesiology of the Sacraments

1. In vol. I: *Die Sakramente als Grundfunktionen der Kirche* pp. 356-366. However, see the already quoted two previous sections about the foundations of the Church (121-156) and the subject of self actu-

alization (157–232) where there are a great number of references to the sacraments.
2. See on this topic, R. Holz, *Sakrament in Wechselspiel zwischen Ost und West, Ökumenische Theologie 2*, Zürich-Cologne-Gütersloh, 1979.
3. Tanner, 849 /32f; see also 856/29; 887/33; 894/29.
4. To mention only some of them: apart from O. Semmelroth who, already before the Council, in almost all of his writings was returning to the same idea, L. Boff greeted this connection with enthusiasm as the achievement of the Council: he found in it a genuine conversion of the Church to the world. Cardinal J. Ratzinger with his usual know-how was more cautious in more or less limiting this concept to Christology and to the doctrine on the Eucharist. And if we are with Germans scholars, W. W. Kasper's succinct study 'Theology and Church' is a very informative and critical introduction to later developments concerning Church and sacraments. In fact, we could go on with other significant names and publications. Scheffzyk, Christus – Ursakrament der Erlösung, in *Christusbegegnung in den Sakramenten*, H. Luthe (ed), Kevelaer, 1982, pp. 9–61; W. Beinert, 'Die Sakramentalität der Kirche', in *Theologische Berichte* 9, (J.Pfamatter – F. Furger eds.) Zürich, 1980. 13–66; idem. Jesus Christus – das Ursakrament Gottes in *Catholica* 38(1984) 340ff.
5. See *Lumen Gentium* No. 2 in which it is affirmed that the Church was implied in God's plan of salvation before the creation of the world. Rahner's thought coincides with this statement, although he does not insist on the 'preexistence' of the universal Church.
6. Cf., O. H. Pesch, 'Das katholische Sakramentsverständnis im Urteil gegenwärtiger evangelischer Theologie', *in Verifikationen, FS G. Ebeling* (ed. E. Jüngel), Tübingen, 1982.
7. 'Die Kirche als Sakrament?' in *Zeitschrift, für Theologie und Kirche* 80(1983) 432ff.
8. For this continuation is indeed what Vatican II insinuates: 'This divine mystery of salvation is revealed to us and continues in the Church, which the Lord constituted as his body... ' According to *Lumen Gentium* No. 52 the Church is called a continuation of this mystery to which Christ points, *Tanner*, 892, line 4f.
9. Jüngel, op. cit., 450: *Dann kann man die Kirche zwar nicht gerade ein (Grund)Sacrament, wohl aber das grosse, Jesus Christus darstellende sakramentale Zeichen nennen.*
10. Cf., idem, *Systematische Theologie III*, p. 54ff.
11. Idem, in Theology and Church, p. 120f.
12. Idem, 'Worthafte und sakramentale Existenz', in *Wort Gottes und Tradition,* Göttingen, 1964.
13. See also O. Semmelroth's *Wirkendes Wort. Zur Theologie der Verkündigung,... ..*1962 which may have influenced Rahner's approach.
14. Idem., *Was bringt das Sakrament? Disputation mit Karl Rahner*, Göttingen, 1970, here p. 122.

15. I shall refer here to his *Einmütig. Gemeinsam entscheidenin Gemeinde und Kirche*, Thaur, Vienna, Munich, 1998.
16. Ibid., 230ff.
17. See Vass, vol. 1 pp. 23-29 and 33-35.
18. Cf. idem., p. 246; Wess quotes C. Schönbronn (now Cardinal Primate of Austria) in reference to Gregory of Nissa with approval who called the priests administering the sacraments 'divinisers'.
19. Cf., idem, p. 239.
20. See also Jüngel, op.cit., p. 444.
21. See Pannenberg, *Systematic Theology* III, p. 367ff. For the two, baptism and Eucharist, Pannenberg even appeals to the authority of Thomas Aquinas (Cf. idem., p. 341 n. 750). Indeed Thomas in *Summa Theologiae* III, q. 64 a 3 insists that sacraments, as instruments in God's hand gain their efficacy from their founder alone, and not from the Church or human society: *'Cum igitur virtus sacramenti sit ab eo qui instituit sacramentum. Cum igitur virtus sacramenti sit solo Deo, consequens est quod solus Deus sit sacramentorum institutor'* (Cf., corpus art. ad 3) ; not even the apostles are capable: *'Unde sicut non licet eis constituere aliam ecclesiam, ita non licet eis tradere aliam fidem, neque instituere alia sacramenta: sed per sacramenta quae de latere Christi pendentis in cruce fluxerunt dicitur eti fabricata ecclesia Christi'*.
22. I have discussed the theme of *supernatural existential* in Vass, vol. 2, chapter 3.
23. See again Vass vol. 2, chapters 3, 4, pp. 67-83.
24. See on baptism, in this book 1.3 C.
25. See on penance, 1.3 D.
26. See on indulgences, 1.3 ibid.
27. See in Karen Kilby, *Karl Rahner*, p. 40: 'What makes him radical is that in trying to cope with difficulties [concerning the interpretation of Trent] he is willing to rearrange radically many of his audience's ordinary ways of thinking. So the fixed points of Catholicism remain fixed, but the overall vision which emerges from Rahner's theology can be anything but familiar.
28. Idem, *The Word of God and Tradition. Historical studies interpreting the Divisions of Christianity*. London, 1968 (Collected essays: especially in 'Considerations to an Evangelical understanding of the Sacrament'.)
29. See his essays 'The Church of Sinners' and 'The Sinful Church' as referred to in Vass vol. 5 (5.1.2) on Rahner's ecclesiology.
30. It was most edifying that in 2000 Pope John Paul II asked pardon for the misdeeds of the historical Church. It was not, however, clear whether this regretted sinfulness referred to the Church herself or to her sinful members in the past.
31. The counter examples, such as the final vow of a religious, an individual reading devotedly the Bible (Ebeling) do not yield a sacrament in its proper sense: they concern the individual in his or her sanctification.
32. This was the conclusion of my volume 5, *On the Church*, a feature that I presupposed in this volume.

258 *The Sacrament of the Future*

33. See Vass vol. 3, 4.3 pp. 105ff, where I have analysed the concept of symbolism more in detail.
34. For Rahner this is indeed a key-concept characterizing the whole of his theology Cf. *Dictionary of Theology*, New York, 1981, p. 469f.
35. Note the difference: whereas, according to Thomas Aquinas, God as known by natural reason is unrelated to the creature, the God of revelation 'relates himself' to the world. Although this statement is not Rahner's own, I believe it is entailed in his concept of creation, which is, according to him is already God's self-bestowal on the world.
36. Idem. 'On Being a Symbol: An Appraisal of Karl Rahner', in *Theological Studies* 40(1978) pp. 453ff.
37. I imply a difference between 'act' and 'function' which is not unusual in ontological theories: think of the *actus purus* of the Aquinas, which is certainly not a 'function', yet it expresses an immanent dynamism.
38. The preface of the saints, indeed, declares: 'You are glorified in your saints, for their glory is the crowning of your gifts'. This prayer presupposes the traditional understanding of *merit* in Catholic theology. It must be, however, a synthesis between God's own deed and the action proper to the saint.
39. J. L. Austin, *How to do Things with Words*, edited by J. O. Urmson, Oxford, 1962 and D. Evans, *The Logic of Self involvement*, SCM, London, 1962.
40. This word is used by Evans in explaining Austin's 'constatives' viz. 'performatives'.
41. 'You are not to know what you are asking. Are you able to drink the cup that I drink, or be *baptized with the baptism with which I am baptized etc* (Mk 10:38-39); 'I have a baptism to be baptised with and how am I constrained until it is accomplished' (Lk 10.50).
42. Parallel to the discussion of this middle stage I could have pointed out another feature in traditional theology. It is about the 'reviviscence' of the sacraments: owing to the *res et scramentum* the reception of grace without due subjective devotion can revive at a later stage. Though I took the same as a 'fleeting moment' it is still within the whole process. It is this process that we can experience and not its fulfilment in grace. See my discussion of Rahner's experience of grace in Vass, vol. 4, 3.2 pp. 63ff.

Chapter 3 **The Eternal Future**

1. *Foundations*, pp. 431-447 (= pp. 414-427).
2. For the first recall especially J. Weiss and A Schweizer's works and for the second C. H. Dodd's realized eschatology and R. Bultmann's programme of demythologizing and existentializing the eschata of ancient Christian faith.
3. See SM volume 2, p. 244.
4. Hemeneutics of Eschatological Assertions, TI 4, pp. 323-346 (= ST IV, pp. 401-428); hereafter referred to as *Hermeneutics*.

5. Ibid., p. 324 (= p. 402).
6. Ibid., 326f and note 4 (= p. 405).
7. Ibid. p. 329 (= p. 408).
8. Cf., ibid. Cf., *Foundations*, p. 434 (= p. 417).
9. Cf., ibid. 330 = 409 Cf., *Foundations* p. 432f (= p. 416).
10. As I tried to explain in vol. 2 p. 64ff; note the influence of Heidegger.
11. *Hemeneutics*, p. 331 (= p. 411).
12. Ibid., p. 332 (= p. 412).
13. Ibid., p. 338 (= p. 420 (my italics).
14. Ibid., p. 337 (= p. 418; compare his later formulation in *Dictionary of Theology* (New York ²1981): 'In present-day theology "eschatological" applies to the present insofar as the last days have begun in Christ ("God's eschatological action"); where it seems to refer to the future alone, it means the future as interpreting the present.'
15. I.e. salvation for all in the final resurrection.
16. *Hermeneutics* p. 346 (= p. 428).
17. *Foundations*, p. 431 (= p. 414).
18. In this chapter I shall print my own remarks and reflections under the sign of ༀ in order to separate them from the expository part of Rahner's thought. We shall see that, as in previous sections, they are not meant as objections or corrections, but rather as possible developments of his insights.
19. Cf., *Hermeneutics*, p. 326ff (= pp. 404ff).
20. By 'goal' I mean in a metaphysical sense the objective we are aiming at, whereas 'purpose' is the conscious striving for the goal. The words 'end,' 'aim' and 'target' are used for both horns of my distinction.
21. I agree with Rahner, when he states eschatology ... constitutes the whole of Christian theology or at least a formal structural principle for all theological statements' In 'The Question of the Future' TI 12, p.182, later to be referred to.
22. Eternity from Time, TI 19, pp. 169-177 (= ST XIV, pp. 422-432, Hereafter referred to as *Eternity*
23. Ibid., p. 171 (= p. 424).
24. Ibid., p. 172 (= p. 426). Note that free decisions are regarded by him as the source of history.
25. Ibid., p. 175 (= p. 429). Cf., 'man .. is a being endowed with freedom to be exercised in time and history which attains to the definitive finality of God in the definitive finality of its own free decision'; Cf., in 'Theological Observation on the Concept of Time' TI 11, pp. 288-308 (= ST IX, pp. 302-322), here p. 298 (= p. 312).
26. As I have pointed out elsewhere in a basically free universe responsibility is specific to the human person. Man without it would have no history, could not have his or her own world, would play a merely passive role in an ant-heap society without being able to shape it.
27. *Eternity*, p. 176 (= p. 430).
28. Cf., 'A Fragmentary Aspect of a Theological Evaluation of the Concept of Future', TI 10, pp. 235ff (= VIII, pp. 555ff), here p. 235ff =(pp. 555ff), including the following references.

29. Ibid., p. 239 (= p. 559).
30. Ibid., p. 240 (= p. 660).
31. Theological observations on the Concept of Time TI11, pp. 228ff (=ST IX, pp. 302ff.): hence referred to as *Time*. Note, however, that *Time* is one of Rahner's most difficult articles: the hermeneutics of a dogma mixed with traditional speculations about time makes it a hard task to read.
32. The Councils of Lateran IV (1215) and Vatican I (1869/70) Tanner 230 (10f) viz. 805 (42f).
33. *Time*, p. 293 (= p. 307).
34. Ibid., p. 294 (= p. 308).
35. Cf., *Time*, p. 298 (= p. 312).
36. Ibid., p. 297 (= p. 311).
37. Ibid., p. 298 (= p. 312).
38. Rahner; most probably Rahner presupposes here the already classical study of O. Culmann, *Christ and Time, Primitive Conception of Time and History*, London, 1951 insisting on linear time as against the 'cyclic time' of platonic thought.
39. *Time*, p. 304 (= p. 317).
40. Ibid., p. 300 (= p. 314).
41. Cf., Vass vol. 2, p. 66.
42. *Time*, p. 306 (= p. 314) (partly emended translation).
43. Ibid., p. 308 (= p. 321).
44. A. N. Whitehead, *Process and Reality* (corrected ed. by D. R. Griffin and D. W. Sherburne, London 1978) here, p. 340.
45. Rahner's approach to time and temporality, unlike Whitehead's, does not seem to presuppose scientific views of these notions. For him the role of time in geology, cosmology, physics, mathematics and biology is only considered peripherally. His way of describing 'temporality' as the positive content of dogmatic truth is more likely parallel to that of M. Heidegger's existential analysis in *Sein und Zeit*, (Cf., idem, *The Concept of Time*, Oxford, 1992) or even of S. Kierkegaard's well known reflections on the 'now'(idem, *The Moment and Later Writings*, Princeton, 1988).
46. *Time*, p. 307 (= p. 321).
47. I.e. part of the early and later creeds: e.g. Lateran I (DS 501), Lateran IV (DS 800) Lyons II (DS 853) Vatican I (DS 3001).
48. Note, however that Rahner uses the word *Unzeitlichkeit* instead of *Zeitlosigkeit* : this latter is strictly 'timelessness', whereas the former can mean the absence of our material time.
49. *Time*, p. 307f (= p. 321).
50. Ibid., p. 308 (= p. 321), as already quoted..
51. Ibid., p. 308 (= p. 321) (partly own translation and italics are mine).
52. See for further detail in Vass, vol. 3, pp. 41ff.
53. Cf., Vass, vol. 3, pp. 53f.
54. Cf., ibid., pp. 60ff.
55. Idem, *God and Timelessness*, London, 1970.
56. Pike, op. cit., p. 128.

57. Ibid., p. 177, where 'first-level attributes' are understood as logical entailments in the notion of God; without them God would not be God.
58. See Vass vol. 3, 3,4.1-3, pp. 72-80 =; there I use the distinction between God's (essential) attributes and God's personal 'attitudes'.
59. *Pike*, p. 182.
60. Cf., Vass vol. 3, pp. 50-57.
61. C. Hartshorne, The *Divine Relativity. A Social Conception of God*, New Haven, 1948, esp. pp. 79-82
62. Idem, *The Promised End. Eschatology in Theology and Literature*, Oxford, 2000.
63. Fiddes, op. cit., p. 128 and p. 177 with note 64.
64. Pike, op. cit. p.184.
65. See T. F. Torrance, *Space Time and Incarnation*, Oxford, New York, 1969) p. 69.
66. Torrance, op. cit. p. 68 with reference to Einstein.
67. This sentence does not necessarily contradict the principle of Thomas Aquinas: whereas creatures are related to God the Creator, God is not likewise related to his creatures. If, however the God of grace communicates himself to the world, then he relates himself freely to mankind and to the whole world.
68. Fiddes, op. cit., p. 130.
69. T. Horvath, *Eternity and Eternal Life, Speculative Theology and Science in Discourse*, Waterloo, Ontario 1993, p. 153.
70. Fiddes op. cit., p. 125.
71. Idem, *The Principle of Hope*, Blackwell Oxford, 1985; J Moltmann, *The Theology of Hope, On the Foundation of Christian Eschatology*, London, SCM, 1967; J.B. Metz, *The Theology of the World*, New York (Herder) 1969; (NB. These works were consulted in German original) ; See also *Erns Block zu ehren*, (S. Unsell ed.) Frankfurt am Main, 1965.
72. 'Marxist Utopia and the Christian Future of Man', TI 6, pp. 59-70 = ST VI, pp.77-88; hereafter referred to as *Utopia;* 'Immanent and Transcendent Consummation of the World', TI 10, pp. 273-289 = ST VIII, pp. 593-609; hereafter referred to as *Consummatio;* 'The Quest of the Future', TI 12, 181-201 = ST IX, 519-540; hereafter referred to as *Future;* 'On the Theology of Hope', TI 10, 242-259 = ST VIII, pp. 561-579; hereafter referred to as *Hope*.
73. In TI 6, 43ff (= ST VI, 59ff); Cf. esp. pp. 52 (= pp. 70ff).
74. *Utopia*, p. 59(= p. 77).
75. See also 'Ideology and Christianity' pp. 55 (= p. 73), p. 57 (p. 75 etc). and compare with *Utopia* p. 65. We should remember that *Utopia* was written in the thawing period of Communism, in the time of Dubcek's 'Spring of Prague'.
76. *Utopia*, p. 59 (= p. 77)
77. See *Utopia* p. 60f (= p. 78f).
78. Ibid. p. 61 (= p. 79).
79. Ibid. p. 62 (= p. 80).
80. Ibid. p. 63 (= p. 81); partly own translation.

81. Cf., p. 65 (= p. 84); my italics.
82. Cf. ibid. p. 67 (= p. 87).
83. Cf. *Consummation*, p. 243f (= p. 593).
84. Cf. ibid. p. 276 (= p. 596).
85. Ibid. p. 274 (= p. 594); partly own translation.
86. Ibid. p. 278 (= 598) and previous pages.
87. See Vass, vol. 1 pp. 23-29.
88. *Consummation*, p. 279 (= p. 598).
89. See Vass, vol. 2, pp. 99ff and Rahner's 'Some Implications of the Scholastic Concept of Uncreated Grace', in TI 1, pp. 319ff.
90. *Consummation*. p. 282 (= p. 602).
91. Cf. Vass, vol. 2, pp. 24ff.
92. *Consummation*, pp. 286ff = pp. 606ff – to the end.
93. 'A Fragmentary Aspect of a Theological Evaluation of the Concept of the Future', TI 10, 235ff = ST 555-560. In my references to this article I translate the German *machbare Zukunft* (:'makeable' future) with 'immanent future'.
94. Ibid. p. 237 (= p. 556).
95. Ibid. p. 240 (= p. 559).
96. *Future*, p. 182 (= p. 520). Italics are mine; see also: 'Christianity is the attitude of abiding openness to the question of the Absolute Future which seeks to bestow itself, which has definitively promised itself as coming in Jesus Christ, and which is called, God.' Ibid., p 190 (= p. 528).
97. Ibid., p. 184 (= p. 521).
98. Ibid., p. 191 (= p. 529), my italics.
99. Cf. ibid., p. 198 (= p. 556) and previous pages.
100. Very close to this reasoning is Metz's *Theology of the World*, esp. in part II, 3: Church and World in an Eschatological Horizon. See also Metz's contribution in *Ernst Bloch zu Ehren*, 227ff.
101. *Future*, p. 199 (= p. 537) for both quotations.
102. 'Theological Problems Entailed in the Idea of the "New Earth"', TI 10, 260ff: = ST VIII, 580ff. See His interpretaion of the Constitution's text, p. 264f = pp. 584ff.
103. Ibid., p. 270 (= p. 590).
104. This particular part of Rahner's reasoning is not only (as usual) complex but also confusing, which manifests itself in its English translation (see esp. idem., Part V, pp. 268ff =558ff).
105. Ibid., p. 270 (= p. 590).
106. Cf., *Hope* and in more detail, Vass vol. 3, 2.2 and esp. 2.3 pp. 31ff.
107. Cf. ibid., p. 247f (= p. 565f).
108. Ibid., p. 248 (= p. 567).
109. Ibid., p. 249f (= p. 568).
110. Ibid., p. 250 (= p. 569).
111. There is a 'perichoresis' between these divine virtues. Just as in the expression *fides caritate formata* so is *fides et caritas spe formata*.
112. *Hope*, p. 254 (= p. 573) – including the above quotation.
113. Cf. ibid., p. 257 (= p. 576).

114. Ibid., p. 259 (= p. 578).
115. 'Reflections on Methodology in Theology' TI 11, 68ff; Cf., Vass, vol. 2, 1.2 pp. 7-15 (expository part) and my reflections ibid., 1.3b, pp. 18-22.
116. 'Methodology' p. 103 (= p. 115) quoted also by Vass, vol. 2, p. 14.
117. In this section I shall use the term 'objective' interchangeable, as I believe, with 'goal' 'aim' and (perhaps) 'end' and corresponding to the Latin *finis* and Greek *telos*.
118. Cf., as quoted above from *Consummation* p. 278 (= p. 598) and some pages before: 'consummation is (if the word is to have any meaning at all) applied to a temporal event' ibid. 274 (= p. 594).
119. See W. Pannenberg on anticipation in *Metaphysik und Gottesgedanke* (Göttingen, 1988) pp. 66-79, concerning Rahner's *Vorgrift*, p.74f. - to which I shall return later.
120. *Consummation*, p. 237 (= p. 556).
121. Ibid., p. 279 (= p. 598).
122. Cf., *Future*, p. 182 (= p. 520).
123. Ibid.p.184 (= p. 521).
124. Refer to Vass, vol. 2, 2.3, *Comments and Questions*, pp. 53ff.
125. And from this apocalyptic reasoning is not excluded but, with caution, can be included. Jesus did the same.
126. See Vass vol. 1 4.3, pp. 62ff and vol. 3, 3.2.6, pp. 55f.
127. *Future*, p. 182 (= p. 520).
128. *Future*, p. 190 and'Reflections on Methodology in Theology' TI 11, 68ff; Cf., Vass, vol. 2, 1.2 pp. 7-15 (expository part) and my reflections ibid., 1.3b, pp. 18-22.
129. Vass, vol. 1 pp. 1-17; Rahner's short creeds were an attempt to sum up the essential message of the Church's beliefs in the terminology accessible for our modern world.
130. *Foundations*, p. 457 (= p. 439) I could perhaps recast W.V. Ditch's translation:
131. *Foundations*, p. 458 (= p. 439f) (*Christentum [ist] die Offenhaltung der Frage nach der absoluten Zukunft*).
132. Ibid., p. 444 (= p. 426).
133. Cf., DS 1000; atopic to which I shall later return.
134. Ibid., p. 434 (= p. 417).
135. 'Consequently, as Christians we do not have to act as though we knew all about ourselves in heaven. Perhaps Christian hope speaks many times in the emphatic way of an initiate ... who knows his way around better in eternity with God, than in the dark dungeon of the present' (ibid.).
136. Idem, *Die letzten Dinge*, [4]1933, pp. 15ff; indeed he regards it as a contradiction.
137. Cf. Pannenberg, *Systematic Theology* III, p. 550.
138. I take over Ditch's translation of the German *Endgültigkeit,* which could also be translated as the final status or definitive destiny of the free individual.
139. *Foundations*, p. 435 (= p. 418) (also for the above quotation) It is to

264 *The Sacrament of the Future*

be noted that most of the eschatology in *Foundations* is borrowed literally from Rahner's 'Life of the Dead'(1959!) in TI 4, pp. 347ff = ST IV, 429ff.
140. Ibid., p. 436 (= p. 419) (own translation).
141. Speaking of the theology of death, Rahner admits that it is a 'combination of revelation and our own human knowledge and experience', ibid., p. 438 (= p. 420).
142. Ibid., p. 437 (= p. 420) (my italics). Compare it with 'Ideas for the Theology of Death' TI 13, pp. 169ff = ST X, pp. 181ff: 'death is the absolute *end* of the temporal dimension', Ibid., p. 174 (= p. 186) and 'Life after death ... is something radically withdrawn from the former temporal dimension and the former spatially conceived time': it is the contradiction of existence' ibid., p. 181 (= p. 192).
143. To name some of these repeated treatments: apart from the Theology of Death, Edinburgh-London, 1961 (First German edition, 1958), see also 'Ideas for the Theology of Death' (1970 as in previous note, hence referred to as *Ideas*; 'Christian Dying' (1975/76 in TI 18, pp. 226ff = ST XIII, pp. 269ff) hence referred to as *Dying; Foundations* pp. 437ff = 419f), and many other remarks on the same subject in dispersed articles, e.g. 'On Christian Dying', TI 7, pp. 285 = ST VII, 273ff.
144. See Vass vol. 2, pp. 33ff and 53ff. Note, however, that neither there nor here do I discuss the peculiarity of Rahner's T*heology of Death* concerning man's all-cosmic transformation in or after death (cf. pp. 27ff), which is challenged by John Hick's *Death and Eternal Life*, New York and London, 1976
145. Ladislaus Boros, *The Moment of Truth*, London and New York, 1965 (first German edition *'Myisterium Mortis'*, Olten and Freiburg in Breisgau, 1962).
146. See in *Ideas*, p. 175 (= p. 187).
147. Cf., Ibid. p. 179 (= p. 192): 'Even as the object of thought, death is, in relation to the individual existence of each person, as inconceivable as absolute nothingness in relationship to the sum total of reality.'
148. Ibid., p. 180 (= p. 192).
149. Ibid., p. 182 (= p. 194).
150. *Dying*, p. 229, viz. 228 (= p. 271f).
151. Ibid., p. 230 (= p. 273).
152. Ibid., p. 240 (= p. 285) (partly own translation).
153. Ibid., p. 236 (= p. 281).
154. bid., p. 241 (= p. 287).
155. bid., p.142f (= p. 288).
156. *Foundation*, p. 439 (= p. 421f) (my italics) see also ibid., 'the immediate presence of the eternal in the absolute value of moral decision' p. 440 (= p. 422) is 'set over the passing moment'. It 'survives time'.
157. Here I took over the translator's word for *Disponibilität:* 'Disposability'. It can mean 'available and open to judgement' or simply 'disposition' which originates through the interplay of several human acts. In what follows I shall rather use 'ultimate disposition'.

158. Cf. for the following, see in *Dying*, pp. 244ff = 290ff.
159. Cf. *Foundation* p. 438f (= *p.* 421): 'It is because we have already become immortal in our lives that death in its threatening and impenetrable appearance of annihilation is so deathly for us.'
160. *Dying*, p. 247 (= p. 293).
161. Ibid., p. 243 (= p. 289). One should note, however, that this question is in the context of Rahner's confrontation with migration of souls and with the continuance of freedom after death.
162. *Foundation*, pp. 441f (= p. 423); (an attempt at own translation).
163. Ibid., p. 441 (= p. 423) (partly own translation).
164. Although I often take exception to the term, 'mediated immediacy', Rahner tries to defend this frequently used, paradoxical, expression in 'Dogmatic Question on Easter' in TI 4, pp.131f (= p. 170f). The 'mediation' is, for him, an ontological presupposition (*Bedingung der Möglichkeit*) of immediacy to God.
165. In 'God's Transcendence and the Concern for the Future' , TI 20, p. 178 (= p. 411).
166. The origin of the idea was introduced as a *post-mortem* completion of penance and was recommended to the prayer of faithful to diminish the temporal punishment of those in purgatory (= purifying fire). Both ideas are definitively decreed at Trent, see *Tanner*, 774, line 5ff.
167. *Foundations*, p. 442 (= p. 425).
168. 'The Intermediary State' TI 17, 114ff = ST XII, 455ff.
169. Cf., also G. Greshake *Auferstehung der Toten*, Essen, 1969.
170. Intermediary State, p. 120 (= p. 462).
171. Ibid., p. 123 (= p. 466).
172. TI 19, pp.181ff = ST XIV, pp. 435ff.
173. Purgatory, p.182 (= p. 435).
174. See Benedict XII edict against the Armenians (to be reunited with Rome) DS 1010 and Trent's final decree in *Tanner*, 774.
175. Published in 1967.
176. Purgatory, p. 182f (= p. 436f).
177. Ibid., p. 184 (= p. 438).
178. Ibid., p. 185 (= p. 439).
179. Ibid., p. 186 (= p. 440).
180. Ibid., p. 188 (= p. 443).
181. Ibid., p. 191 (= p. 447).
182. Ibid., p. 192 (= p. 448).
183. Ibid., p. 193 (= p. 449).
184. To this topic see the instructive summary of J. Hick, *Death and Eternal Life*, New York-San Francisco–London, 1976, pp. 97–109.
185. W. Pannenberg, *Sytematic Theology*, vol. 3, Edinburgh, 1998, pp. 556f (in a context characterizing modern Catholic thought about death and immortality).
186. E. Jüngel, *Tod*, Stuttgart, 1971. ET: Death, *The Riddle and the Mystery*, Edinburgh, 1975. See also Vass, vol. 2, 55f.
187. Cf. Vass, vol. 2, pp. 51, 53, 56 etc.
188. This does not militate against Newman's poetical imagery in the

Dream of Gerontius, accompanied by the unforgettable music of Elgar, or the well known drama of Hugo von Hofmansstahl: *Jedermann*.
189. In what follows I am indebted to W. Pannenberg's work in *Systhematic Theology* and '*Grundfragen systhematischer Theologie*' in 3 volumes. It is to be noted, however, that Pannenberg's 'self' is used roughly the same way as I use the word 'person'.
190. Cf. Vass, vol. 4, pp. 33ff, on soteriology.
191. I do not exclude the view that each and every human being is exposed to this personal development after death, the 'canonized' saint included.
192. Here I would exclude the view of some modern theologians, according to which the parousia takes place *in* or immediately *after* death when we leave time behind with the future expectation of this final state. Among Catholic scholars: G- Greshake, *Auferstehung der Toten*', Essen, 1969; G. Greshake-G. Lohfink, '*Naherwartung – Auferstehung – Unsterblichkeit*. Untersuchungen zur christlichen Eschatologie, Freiburg ²1976. Some of Rahner's writing, indeed, seems to suggest such a position, though it is never explicitly argued.
193. See under Parousia SM, vol. 4, pp. 345aff, LTK vol. 8, pp. 123ff, vol. 4, p. 734; *Dictionary of Theology*, New York 1981, p. 362; under 'Last Things' SM, vol. 3, pp. 274ff; LTK, vol. 6, p. 989.
194. SM, vol. 4, p. 345a corresponding to the German original SM, vol. III, p. 1037a.
195. Cf., *Foundations* pp. 444–447 = pp. 426–429.
196. In 'Jesus' Resurrection' TI 17, p. 19 = ST XII, p. 347.
197. In 'Foundation of Belief', TI 16, p. 17 = ST XII, p. 34.
198. He speaks of his 'death into the resurrection', in 'Following the Crucified' TI 18, p. 168 = ST XIII, p. 201.
199. 'The Position of Christology between Exegesis and Dogmatic', (as in n. 9) p. 169 (= p. 202).
200. 'it is quite impossible for the resurrection to be an individual event ... the Son of Man 'cannot' have risen alone' in 'The Interpretation of the Dogma of Assumption' TI 1, p. 219 = ST I, p.2 45. 'Even if he had undergone a resurrection, his life and his death would not themselves achieve the status of an eschatological event of salvation with significance for all men' in 'The Position of Christology in the Church between Exegesis and Dogmatics', TI 11 p. 187 = ST IX, p. 199.
201. Ibid., p. 213 (= p. 227) (from 'Position' as in note 139 above).
202. Ibid., p. 212 (= p. 224f).
203. Ibid., p. 202 (= p. 215).
204. In 'Remarks on the importance of the History of Jesus for Catholic Dogmatics' TI 13, p. 212 = ST X p .226.
205. SM vol. 5., p. 323ab.
206. Cf., ibid., 324a.
207. Cf. in 'Christology between exegesis and Dogmatics' pp. 210ff (= p. 222f).
208. Ibid., p. 212 (= p. 224).
209. Cf., 'The Interpretation of the Dogma of the Assumption', TI 1, pp.

215ff = ST I, pp. 239ff; 'The Resurrection of the Body', TI 2, pp. 203ff = ST II, pp. 211; hereafter referred to as *Assumption* viz. *Risen body*.
210. *'Risen body'* p. 310 (= p. 219).
211. Ibid., p. 213 (= p. 222).
212. 'His second coming takes place at the moment of the perfecting of the world into the reality which he already possesses now, in such a way that he, the God-man, will be revealed to all reality and within it, to every one of its parts in its own way, as the innermost secret and centre of all the world', ibid., p. 213 (= p. 222).
213. *Assumption*, p. 218 (= p. 243).
214. Ibid., p. 222 (= p. 246).
215. Cf.,*'Risen body'*, p. 215 (= p. 223).
216. Free translation of *Risen body*, p. 213 (= p. 222); see also in 'Christianity and the New Man' TI 5, p. 147f = ST V, 172f; in 'Christology within an Evolutionary View of the World', TI 5, p. 168 = ST V, p. 195: 'the Christian knows that this history of the cosmos as a whole will find its real consummation, in and through the freedom of man, and that its finality as a whole will also be its consummation'.
217. In ' The Comfort of Time', TI 3, p. 156 = ST III, p. 187 (my italics, partly own translation); see also 'Priest and Poet' ibid., p. 300 = 355; esp. in 'Ideas for a Theology of Childhood' TI 8, p. 35 = ST VII, p. 315.: 'He does not bring his temporal mode of existence to an end by quitting it, but compressing it . . . and bringing it with him in its totality into his eternity which is his time as summed up and completed. His future is the making present of his own past as freely lived.'
218. Jesus' 'eternal life is rather the ultimate form of his earthly life itself' . . . a life which is linked with the earlier one' – not only its moral qualities but 'this very earlier life itself is completed and has found eternal validity in and before God', therefore 'the risen Lord is the One who was crucified' in the God-given form of the earthly life belonging to history, in 'On the Spirituality of the Easter Faith': TI 17, p. 13 = ST XII, p. 340f.
219. Cf., 'Jesus' Resurrection' TI 17, p. 21 = ST XII, p. 349 and K. Rahner – W. Thüsing, *Christologie systematisch und exegetisch,* (Freibur in Breisgau, 1972) pp. 36–39 (The ET of the same, A New Christology' does not translate this part.)
220. 'For us, identity consists, now and in the future, of the identity of the free , spiritual subject [i.e. person] 'which we call 'the soul', in 'The Intermediate State', TI 17, p. 120 = ST XII, p. 461f.
221. 'The final transformation of history is the salvation of everything, even matter, even of the bodily life, but it is , of course, salvation into the mystery of God' in 'The Secret of Life' TI 6, p. 146 = ST VI, p. 177.
222. Cf. ibid., p. 152 (= p. 184).
223. In 'The Concept of Mystery in Catholic Theology', TI 4, p. 54 = ST IV, p. 75; Referred to as 'Mystery'.
224. Cf. Rahner's 'Unity – Love – Mystery' , TI 8, pp. 244ff = ST VII, p. 504f.

225. 'Mystery', p. 58 (= p. 80).
226. My own translation of Rahner's sentence: 'The vision of God is the radical form of the general ontological relationship between the Being on the one hand whose self-communication establishes distinction and identity and finite reality on the other'. Cf., in his later essay, 'An Investigation on the Incomprehensibility of God in St Thomas Aquinas' TI 16, p. 250 = ST XII, p. 313. (This more scholarly article should be read with 'Mystery'.)
227. 'Unity – Love – Mystery', pp. 244, 246(= p. 504 and p. 506f):; see also in 'On the Theology of Incarnation' TI 4, pp. 108ff = ST IV, pp. 141ff.
228 See his article on the final perfection of the world in 'The Unity of Spirit and Matter in the Christian Understanding of Faith' TI 6, pp. 153ff = ST VI, pp. 185ff; esp. 'Hence Christian eschatology does not know merely, or even first and foremost, the atomised salvation of each individual for himself in the beatitude of his soul, but rather the kingdom of God, the eternal covenant, the triumphing Church, the new heaven and the new earth', p. 162 (= p. 195).
229. Cf. DS 857f.
230. Cf. DS 1000–1002.
231. As quoted by S. Fiddes (p. 87) Tugwell, *Human Immortality and the Redemption of Death*, London, 1990, p. 131.
232. See my previous section.
233. Partly own translation, see in 'Christian Dying' TI 18, p. 240 = ST XIII, p. 285.
234. In *Dictionary of Theology*, New York, [2]1981, p. 258.
235. See the article of W. Pannenberg, 'Begriff und Anticipation', in *Metaphysik und Gottesgedanke*, Zürich, 1988. P. compares the concept of anticipation with Rahner's pre-apprehension (*Vorgriff*): anticipation is valid for the present expectation of an event which is still outstanding, the occurrence of which is akin to the expected event. Although he agrees with Rahner's *Vorgriff* concerning the metaphysical pre-apprehension of the horizon of being, he denies that this yields an experience of an *event* which is dependent on future circumstances. At the same time he attempts to establish a certain retroactivity of the future on present events that can reveal at least the structure of their occurrence here and now.
236. Can, however, the resurrection of Jesus be the objective goal of our desire for our own resurrection?
237. See here the account of John Hick, *Death and Eternal Life*, New York, London, 1976, pp. 176f, in which he summarizes the discrepancies in the Jerusalem and Galilean version of the resurrection story in the Synoptics, and the rather biased account of the apparition of the risen Lord to Paul whose 1 Cor. was chronologically the first, cf., p. 175.
238. See *Summa, S*upplementum, q. 76a 1.
239. See Josef Schmid in MS vol. 5, pp. 338ff , although in his contribution, he does not point to the divergent connotation of the Pauline texts on resurrection.

240. Cf. Hick, op.cit. pp. 165f for the survival of disembodied mind by quoting and analysing H. H. Price, 'Survival and the Idea of 'Another World', in *Language, Metaphysics and Death*, New York, 1978, and pp. 279ff concerning the 'replica' theory which is discussed in more detail by Fiddes, op.cit., pp. 76ff analyzing Derek Parfit's *Reasons and Persons*, Oxford, 1989^2: the 'encoded' properties of an individual person is transmitted by God to another world!
241. Theologians refusing to admit the immortality of the soul should also admit its new creation after death. See e.g. E. Jüngel, *Death, The Riddle and the Mystery*, Edinburgh, 1975 p: 'With regard to creation and the biblical notion of the Creator , *both* beginning *and* end are involved.'
242. It seems that in Protestant theology the opposition between immortality of the soul and resurrection has become a quasi-dogmatic position; its classical exponents were Carl Stange, O. Cullmann, and P. Althaus (although he later, in his *'retractationes'* softened the edge of his original position). E. Jüngel, op.cit., sums up the Greek origin of the idea esp. pp. 42ff. Publications on Eschatology in English seem to take over the same either/or: see e.g. Hick's summary in op.cit., pp. 178-181 and Fiddes op.cit. pp. 78 and 89; on the other hand, a number of recent Catholic eschatologies which assume the resurrection in or immediately after death imply the denial of the immortality of the soul, against which Joseph Ratzinger (Eschatology in *Dogmati Theology 9* edited by J. Auer) consecrates a whole chapter (see op.cit., pp. 140ff) and in the 6th German edition of the same he adds an *Anhang* in trying to demolish all the opposite arguments (Cf., op cit., pp. 241ff). In these pages I avoid entering into this discussion, nonetheless see my early essay 'The Immortality of the Soul and Life Everlasting' in *Heythrop Journal* 6(1965) 270-288.
243. See a more qualified understanding of Plato in Ratzinger op.cit. pp. 120ff.
244. See J. A. T. Robinson, *The Body*, London ^{8}1974, pp. 11ff.
245. See Vass, 'The Immortality...' (as in note 242), pp. 287f.
246. See *Tanner*, p. 361.
247. See John D. Zizioulas, *Being as Communion*, New York, 1985, the whole first part of the chapter 'Personhood and Being' (pp. 27-49) where he traces the emergence of the Christian notion of Personhood as relationship.
248. Although Hick tries to explain here the convergence of Eastern (Buddhist) and Christian thought (*Death and Eternal Life*, pp. 439ff), by the 'loss of self' I do not mean the annihilation of the self in a kind of nirvana.
249. See, idem e.g. op.cit. pp. 106f. I am indebted to his distinction between individuality and particularity see also ibid., pp. 275f.
250. The 5th Lateran Council is often misinterpreted: it does not define the 'immortality of the soul' (see *Tanner*, p. 605), but rejects its absorption into the anonymity of a universal 'soul of the world', advocated by the philosopher Pomponazzi.

251. Hick, op.cit. His view is influenced mainly by Buddhist sources, however transferred in the last chapter on 'A possible Eschatology', see pp. 450 and passim.
252. Cf. Fiddes, op. cit. p. 135: 'There would be much to discover about the 'manifestations' of goodness and so a journey *within* the good even if not towards the good.'
253. As we have seen above in Rahner's ' The Comfort of Time', TI 3, p. 156 = ST III, p. 187f,; more explicitly in Fiddes, op.cit. p. 139, time is not abolished, but 'healed': 'We might think of God's eternity as a relation to time in which there is indeed succession (a 'before and an after'), but in which God's being is not fragmented by time's passing, as ours is; instead, God would be always integrating past, present and future within a perfect love.'
254. See Rahner's insistence on the cosmic being of man, already in his Theology of Death and passim.
255. In various religious traditions 'Life is a soul-making or *person-making* process We exist in order to grow through our free interactions with a challenging environment towards a human perfection which lies far beyond our present state.' Cf. Hick, op.cit., p. 408 and passim from which one should not conclude, as Hick does, to several lives in different words!
256. See, Vass vol. 3 pp. 40–57 and 72–80.
257. Cf., *Summa* I, q. 28 a 1 speaks of real relationships in which things by their very nature are ordained to another. Thus ibid., q 29 a.4 he identifies the notion of person with relations by stating that these are not accidental qualities, but 'inserted' into the very nature of God, hence 'i. e. *relatio subsistens*'. Speaking, therefore of 'persons' we first think of them as real relationships, but connote their coherence in the divine nature.
258. *Summa* I q. 27 a. 1 c, explains the processions as *actions* by the analysis of movement which terminates in the subject itself.
259. See Vass, vol. 3, pp.74–78.
260. See Ratzinger, op.cit., pp. 204ff for the different assignment of the final Judge, and Pannenberg, op.cit., pp. 614ff, in which he tries to harmonize the twofold attribution (to God and to Christ) by stating that the ultimate judge is God (the Father) but the criterion of the judgement is our encounter with Jesus Christ.
261. G. Scholem, *Schöpfung aus Nichts und Selbsverschränkung Gottes*, Eranos, 1956, 87ff.
262. This ambiguity is conspicuous in the Gospel of John: he speaks of the resurrection of the just in 6; 39f, and v. 50; 11, 21f. On the other hand 5:28f of the resurrection of all. Acts 24:15 of both (just and unjust). The book of Revelation speaks of 'two' resurrections where the first is apparently for the martyrs and saints and the second for the rest of mankind.
263. *De Civitate Dei*, 20, 6/9 and 21, 2–8.
264. Cf. in Summa, Suppl. q. 77 a. 1 and 4. Note, however, that Thomas does not refer to the book of Revelations, but simply quotes Augustine.

265. Ibid., *'Millenarius . . . designat totum tempus quod nunc agitur, in quo sancti cum Christo regnant'* . Incidentally, in writing about purgatory (intermediate time) Thomas presupposes both space and time see e.g. the appendix to the Suppelentum art. 2 and 8.
266. Hick, op.cit., p. 202.
267. (1 Cor:3,1: on that day 'each man's work will become manifest; for the Day will disclose it, because it will be revealed with fire . . . if any man's work is burned up, he will suffer loss, though he himself will be saved, but only as through fire.')
268. Ratzinger, op. cit., p. 230 ; See also p. 182 arguing for time (and space) of the dead in a kind of *aevum* (time of the angels) : 'Someone who has lived during a definite period of time, and died at a definite point in time cannot simply move across from the condition of "time" into the condition "eternity", as timelessness'; and p. 187f 'The guilt which goes on because of me is part of me. Reaching as it does deep into me, it is part of my permanent abandonment to time (purgatory)' . . ., 'as long as history really continues , it remains a reality, even from the vantage point beyond death . . . it is real, and therefore to declare that history is ... cancelled ... into an eternal Last Day after death is impossible.'
269. Sermon 8 quoted by Hick op.cit., p. 422. Note, that Hick quotes it in order to illustrate the convergence of Christian mysticism with oriental beliefs implying the migration of souls or, as he would have it, the repeated after-lives of people in different worlds ('pareschatology', which apparently demands for a final fulfilment.)
270. The existence of hell is not only a question of dogmatic tradition but, as we saw, a real possibility, despite a modern rejection of the very idea (see e.g. Hick, op.cit., pp. 198ff). Jesus' references to damnation, to 'outer darkness', according to Rahner, are of the literary character of threat-discourse (SM, vol. 3, p.7b), nonetheless they presuppose the freedom of man, who can persevere in his aversion from God. It is another question whether the lists of sins, 'which exclude from the kingdom of God' (for instance Gal. 5:19–22; Col. 3:5–9 etc.) refer to eternal damnation or to the exclusion from the communion of the Church. They are sins which Jüngel and Tillich aptly term as loss of relationship (*Beziehungslosigkeit*) with other human beings: Is it of an absolute necessity that their perpetrators lose also their relationship to the merciful God?
271. 'The Prospect for Dogmatic Theology', followed by 'A Scheme of Dogmatic Theology, TI 1, pp.1–37 = ST I, pp. 9–49, here p. 7 = 16 (an example of rather dubious English translation).

www.ingramcontent.com/pod-product-compliance
Lightning Source LLC
Chambersburg PA
CBHW030733250426
43671CB00034B/138